CANADA'S MARITIME PROVINCES

PLUS

NEWFOUNDLAND AND

LABRADOR

FODOR'S TRAVEL GUIDES

are compiled, researched, and edited by an international team of travel writers, field correspondents, and editors. The series, which now almost covers the globe, was founded by Eugene Fodor in 1936.

OFFICES
New York & London

Fodor's Canada's Maritime Provinces, Plus Newfoundland and Labrador:

Editor: Langdon Faust
Area Editor: Colleen Thompson
Contributing Editor: Ralph Surette
Maps: Burmar, Pictograph, Mark Stein Studios

FODOR'S

CANADA'S MARITIME PROVINCES

**Plus
Newfoundland and Labrador
1986**

FODOR'S TRAVEL GUIDES
New York & London

FODOR'S CANADA'S MARITIME PROVINCES, PLUS NEWFOUNDLAND AND
LABRADOR
has been abridged from
FODOR'S CANADA 1986

The following Fodor's Guides are current; most are also available in a British
edition published by Hodder & Stoughton.

Country and Area Guides

Australia, New Zealand
& The South Pacific
Austria
Bahamas
Belgium & Luxembourg
Bermuda
Brazil
Canada
Canada's Maritime
Provinces
Caribbean
Central America
Eastern Europe
Egypt
Europe
France
Germany
Great Britain
Greece
Holland
India, Nepal &
Sri Lanka
Ireland
Israel
Italy
Japan
Jordan & The Holy Land
Kenya
Korea
Mexico
North Africa
People's Republic of
China
Portugal
Scandanavia
Scotland
South America
Southeast Asia

Soviet Union
Spain
Switzerland
Turkey
Yugoslavia

City Guides

Amsterdam
Beijing, Guangzhou,
Shanghai
Boston
Chicago
Dallas–Fort Worth
Greater Miami & The
Gold Coast
Hong Kong
Houston
Lisbon
London
Los Angeles
Madrid
Mexico City &
Acapulco
Munich
New Orleans
New York City
Paris
Philadelphia
Rome
San Diego
San Francisco
Stockholm, Copenhagen,
Oslo, Helsinki &
Reykjavik
Sydney
Tokyo
Toronto
Vienna
Washington, D.C.

U.S.A. Guides

Alaska
Arizona
California
Cape Cod
Colorado
Far West
Florida
Hawaii
New England
New Mexico
Pacific North Coast
South
Texas
U.S.A.

Budget Travel

American Cities (30)
Britain
Canada
Caribbean
Europe
France
Germany
Hawaii
Italy
Japan
London
Mexico
Spain

Fun Guides

Acapulco
Bahamas
London
Montreal
Puerto Rico
San Francisco
St. Martin/Sint Maarten
Waikiki

MANUFACTURED IN THE UNITED STATES OF AMERICA
10 9 8 7 6 5 4 3 2 1

CONTENTS

FOREWORD

New Brunswick, Nova Scotia, and Prince Edward Island, three of eastern Canada's coastal provinces, are known as the Maritimes. When you add the island of Newfoundland and its huge dependence Labrador, the whole area is sometimes called the Atlantic Provinces. None of these provinces bears much resemblance to the rest of Canada, and they are different from each other, unique in character, scenery, and even the disposition of the inhabitants.

In Newfoundland, an isolated and rocky province far out in the Atlantic, spring comes late and fall early, but the months of June through September are distinctively lovely. Whimsical pastel houses in seaport towns, an awesomely rugged coastline, and unspoiled wilderness parks combine with gregarious residents who speak with a thick island accent to make this province an unmatched vacation land.

Labrador, still a vast northern frontier, icy and desolate in winter, austere but oddly beautiful in summer, lures fishermen and dauntless explorers who find its very lack of civilization strangely enticing.

"Nova Scotia" is Latin for "New Scotland," and Scottish-like indeed is the heather that grows naturally on a slope in Halifax, the skirl of bagpipes in Cape Breton, and the occasional Gaelic phrase that sprinkles the natives' speech. In other parts of Cape Breton and on Nova Scotia's northwest shore, from Yarmouth to Digby, you'll hear French, while in settlements like Lunenburg and New Germany on the beachy south shore, the food and the customs often reflect more than a hint of German-Dutch background.

If the ocean calls but woodland trails beckon too, then you can't go wrong in New Brunswick. With three-quarters of its perimeter on the sea, the wide Saint John River cutting through its length, and a mountainous interior, the province covers every kind of terrain—and boasts the warmest beaches this side of the Carolinas as well. Due to the fact that 35 percent of the population is Acadian French and the rest mostly descendants of British Loyalists, there's a unique blend of customs and language.

The terrain of Prince Edward Island is classified as hilly, rolling, and level, but there are no real hills or mountainous regions, just perfect farmland, charming towns, long beaches of fine sand (the Gulf Stream brushes here in August), and lots of seafood. No matter where you make your head-quarters here you won't be far away from country roads and storybook communities. In fact you can tour the island in a day, but you'd miss a lot of its joys . . . one of them, the opportunity to get acquainted with super-friendly islanders.

Although they are all different, the provinces covered in this book have much in common: miles of coastline, spectacular scenery, great camp-grounds situated in areas of natural beauty, and the opportunity for endless outdoor activities. It's a codjigging, sailing, backpacking, and even moun-tain-climbing territory by the sea, where nighttime can nevertheless mean dining and dancing in elegant restaurants, concerts by noted stars, or a moonlight walk on a deserted beach. The provinces are English, Irish, Scottish, and sometimes French, with a good dash of other cultures thrown in, united by location and the hospitable nature of the inhabitants.

In this book we have attempted to provide a broad range of things to see and do, accommodation and restaurant choices. Restaurants, especially, seem prone to close, rearrange hours, or switch chefs; sometimes between researching and publication, things change. In that case, please accept our apologies. We strive to be as up to date as possible. Suggestions from read-ers are always appreciated. Please write:

In the U.S.: Fodor's Travel Guides, 2 Park Ave., New York, NY 10016.

In Europe: Fodor's Travel Guides, 9-10 Market Place, London W1N 7AG, England.

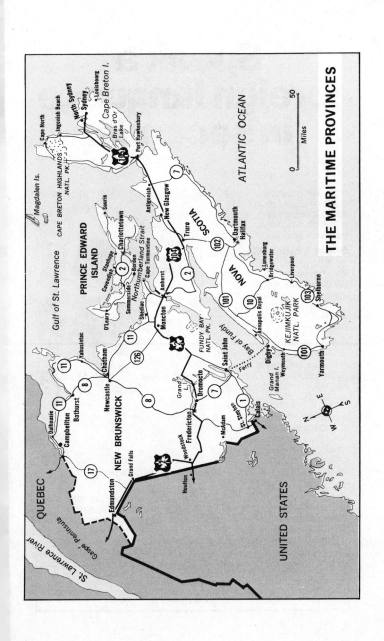

THE MARITIME PROVINCES

Speak a foreign language in seconds.

Now an amazing space age device makes it possible to speak a foreign language *without* having to learn a foreign language.

Speak French, German, or Spanish.

With the incredible Translator 8000—world's first pocket-size electronic translation machines —you're never at a loss for words in France, Germany, or Spain.

8,000-word brain.

Just punch in the foreign word or phrase, and English appears on the LED display. Or punch in English, and read the foreign equivalent instantly.

Only 4¾" x 2¾", it possesses a fluent 8,000-word vocabulary (4,000 English, 4,000 foreign). A memory key stores up to 16 words; a practice key randomly calls up words for study, self-testing, or game use. And it's also a full-function calculator.

150,000 sold in 18 months.

Manufactured for Langenscheidt by Sharp/Japan, the Translator 8000 comes with a 6-month warranty. It's a valuable aid for business and pleasure travelers, and students. It comes in a handsome leatherette case, and makes a super gift.

Order now with the information below.

FACTS AT YOUR FINGERTIPS

 PLANNING YOUR TRIP. Once you have decided where to take your trip, it's time to get down to the details of making hotel and transportation reservations. Do you want to travel on your own or take a package tour? Are you going to fly or drive, or take a bus or train? Consider using a travel agent to help with these details. (See the section "Travel Agents," below.)

If you plan to travel by car and you don't belong to an auto club, now is the time to join one. They can be very helpful in planning routes and providing emergency road service. Write to the American Automobile Association (AAA), 8111 Gatehouse Rd., Falls Church, VA 22047; or the Canadian Automobile Association, 1775 Courtwood Crescent, Ottawa, ON, K2C 3J2; or the Maritime Automobile Association, 869 Main St., Moncton, NB, E1C 1G5 (506–388–1225), which is a branch of the CAA and affiliated with the AAA. All can provide maps and suggest routes in Canada.

If you plan the route yourself, be sure that the map you use is dated for the current year. Maps are available (free) from the provincial tourist offices and (commercially) at bookstores and sometimes at service stations.

 TRAVEL AGENTS. A travel agent can be of great help in making transportation and hotel reservations. He or she will know what discounts are available for flights and what requirements you must meet, as well as be able to suggest suitable accommodations. A good agent should also be able to recommend reliable package-tour operators. Thus, the critical issue when choosing a travel agent is how knowledgeable and reliable he or she is.

Not all North American travel agents are licensed, as laws vary from state to state. To avoid being victimized by fly-by-night operators who seem to be offering bargains, look for an agent who is a member of the American Society of Travel Agents (ASTA); members display the ASTA shield on their offices and all forms. For further information, contact ASTA, 4400 MacArthur Blvd. N.W., Washington, D.C. 20007 (202–965–7520).

 TOURIST INFORMATION. The Canadian Government Office of Tourism is well staffed, efficient, and prepared to handle any kind of travel query. If they don't have the information on hand, they'll refer you to the provincial or local tourism office that does. For specific information on accommodations, provincial events, recommended driving tours, and points of interest, contact the individual provincial tourism offices.

National: Canadian Government Office of Tourism, DRIE (Department of Regional Industrial Expansion), 235 Queen St., Ottawa, ON, K1A 0H6 (613–996–4610).

New Brunswick: Department of Tourism, Recreation and Heritage, Box 12345, Fredericton, NB, E3B 5C3 (506–453–2377, 800–561–0123 from the U.S. and Canada, or 800–442–4442 from New Brunswick).

1

Prince Edward Island: Department of Finance and Tourism, Visitor Services Division, Box 940, Charlottetown, PE, C1A 7M5 (902–892–2457 or 800–565–7421).

Nova Scotia: Visitor Services, 129 Commercial St., Portland, ME 04101 (207–772–6131), or Tourism Bureau, Box 130, Halifax, NS, B3J 2M7 (902–424–4247 or 800–341–6096). For accommodations, call Check In System (800–565–7105).

Newfoundland: Tourism Branch, Department of Development, Box 2016, St. John's, NF, A1C 5R8 (709–576–2830 or 800–563–6353).

 WHERE TO GO. Almost anywhere you put your finger on a map of Canada will provide the raw materials for an interesting tour. Here are some suggestions to help you narrow your choices and map out a tour. For more information, see the individual chapters.

New Brunswick: The northeast section of New Brunswick is primarily Acadian, and French is often spoken. There are lighthearted festivals in each community. Fresh seafood is available right off the boats at the wharf in Caraquet, and there is a re-created Acadian village nearby. The coast south to Moncton is dotted with lighthouses and good beaches. There is a marine museum in Tracadie, seafood restaurants all along the route, and deep-sea fishing opportunities.

South of Moncton, the province becomes mainly English. A good road leads south to Fundy National Park, 270 sq. km of breathtakingly beautiful scenery, with camping and wildlife.

Coming down the west side of the province, you pass along the beautiful Saint John River Valley; Grand Falls, with its 120-foot cataract; the longest covered bridge in the world at Hartland; Kings Landing, a re-created Loyalist settlement of the early 1800s; Mactaquac Provincial Park, with camping and a beach; and arrive at Fredericton, capital of the province. This is a lovely Loyalist town with many attractions, including a cathedral and an art gallery with paintings by Dali and Gainsborough.

If you continue east, you come to the port city of Saint John, the oldest incorporated city in North America, with waterfront cafes, good shopping, and many historical sites. From Saint John, a coastal road leads west, past small fishing villages such as Dipper Harbour, to St. Andrews, a charming seaside resort town with many houses dating back to the 1600s. From several areas near here, ferries can be taken to the Fundy Isles: Campobello, where Franklin D. Roosevelt had his summer home; Deer Island, with the largest lobster pound in the world; and Grand Manan, far out in the Atlantic, with excellent whale-watching.

Prince Edward Island: The island is small enough to be taken in on one tour. The Blue Heron Drive will take you through Charlottetown, where Canada's independence was chartered at the Confederation Conference in 1864, to Prince Edward Island National Park, with its water sports, nature trails, and miles of beaches and bright sand dunes, and the farmhouse that was the setting of *Anne of Green Gables.* Lobster suppers are noted at St. Ann's and New Glasgow. Charlottetown has excellent summer theater at Confederation Centre as well as an important art gallery.

Nova Scotia: The province offers a number of possibilities. West from Truro, a center of Scottish culture, there are the miner's museum of Springhill and the ruins of Fort Lawrence in Amherst. Back to the east again are Pictou and the ferry to Prince Edward Island. To the northeast there are the antique steam engines of New Glasgow, the Gaelic-speaking community in Antigonish, the eighteenth-century Fortress Louisbourg, Sydney, and the historic Cabot Trail. To the southwest are the boat-building community in Lunenburg, the Citadel in Halifax, Captain Kidd's alleged buried treasure at Oak Island, the 40-foot tides of Windsor, and a re-creation of the first Canadian settlement at Port Royal National Historic Park. In addition, there is the famous Lighthouse Route, 227 miles of rugged seacoast from Yarmouth to Halifax, with pirate coves on one side of the road and scenic farms on the other.

Newfoundland: The route from Argentia (where ferries from Nova Scotia land) to St. John's offers bird sanctuaries at Cape St. Mary's and Witless Bay and the headquarters of pirate Peter Easton at Harbour Grace. St. John's, the oldest city founded by Europeans on the North American continent, was the site of Marconi's first wireless message at Signal Hill. It has a spectacular harbor, which is often guarded by icebergs, even in summer, as well as lots of good shopping, restaurants, pubs, art galleries, and theater. Short drives outside St. John's pass snug coves, rugged cliffs, and areas where caplan (tiny fish) throw themselves on shore in June and July.

For the more rugged side of Newfoundland there is the route from Channel Port-aux-Basques (at the end of an alternate ferry route from Nova Scotia) to St. John's. Along the way are Deer Lake and Gros Morne and Terra Nova national parks. The first park is an undeveloped wilderness and the second has interesting wildlife and rugged, forested highlands.

Newfoundland's west coast is the site of L'Anse-aux-Meadows, an early Norse settlement, the first historic site to be put on UNESCO's World Heritage List of sites of outstanding cultural or natural value.

WHEN TO GO. For uncrowded roads and fine, warm but not hot, temperatures, June is the ideal month to travel in the three Maritime Provinces. By the middle of June almost all tourist facilities, including campgrounds, are open and local fresh fiddleheads (a tasty green), as well as the first strawberries, are available.

Newfoundland takes longer to warm up, say by July. Even then, only the hardy swim in its waters and tourist facilities usually have heated pools.

Expect hot weather in the Maritime Provinces in July and August. From the end of June through July and especially in August when the Gulf Stream washes some of the shores, plan on swimming, sunbathing, wind surfing, sailing, water skiing, and almost every other watery sport. Water slides are increasingly popular.

Provincial and national parks have hiking trails for experts or novices, golf courses are part of most populated areas, and every town, village, and city holds a summer festival with a different focus, depending on the local specialty: salmon, lobster, Brussels sprouts, poutine rape . . . you name it.

September is warm and sunny with beautiful foliage toward the end of the month and into mid-October. Roads become uncrowded once again.

SEASONAL EVENTS. In deciding when and where you will travel, you may want to take into account the various seasonal festivals and events. The list below is by no means exhaustive, but it does include some of the more popular events. For exact dates and more information, write to the relevant provincial or local tourist office.

New Brunswick: *May:* Festival of the Arts at Christ Church Cathedral in Fredericton. *June:* Pioneer Days in Oromocto; Potato Festival in Grand Falls; Railroad Days in Moncton; Salmon Festival in Campbellton. *July:* Canada's Irish Cultural Festival in Chatham; Loyalist Days in Saint John; Lobster Festival in Shediac; Annual Antique Show and Sale in St. Andrews; Old Home Week at Woodstock. *August:* International Hydroplane Regatta at Cocagne; Mirami- chi Folk Song Festival at Newcastle; Acadian Festival at Caraquet; Atlantic National Exhibition at Saint John. *September:* Lumberman's Days at Kings Landing.

Prince Edward Island: *June:* Natal Day Regatta in Charlottetown; Welcome to Summer celebrations in Montague; Cape Egmont Yacht Race in Summer- side. *July:* Potato Blossom Festival in O'Leary; Lobster Carnival and Livestock Exhibition in Summerside. *August:* Highland Games and Gathering of the Clans in Elson; Country Days and Old Home Week in Charlottetown; Harvest Festi- val in Kensington; Acadian Festival in Abrams Village; Oyster Festival in Tyne Valley; Prince County Exhibition in Alberton.

Nova Scotia: *June:* Apple Blossom Festival in Annapolis Valley; Gala Kite Weekend at the Bell Museum at Baddeck; Festival of the Strait at Port Hawkes- bury; Nova Scotia Tattoo at Halifax. *July:* Gathering of the Clans in Pugwash; Highland Games in Sydney; Lobster Carnival in Pictou; Annual Jamboree in Bra d'Or; Old Times Fiddling Contest in Dartmouth; Highland Games in Antigonish; Annual Piping Festival in Dartmouth; Acadian Day Festival in L'Ardoise, Cape Breton; Nova Scotia Bluegrass and Oldtime Music Festival at Ardoise, Hants County. *August:* Nova Scotia Annual Gaelic Mod at St. Ann's, Cape Breton; Sam Slick Days at Windsor; International Air Show at Yarmouth; Blueberry Harvest Festival at Amherst. *September:* Joseph Howe Festival at Halifax; International Town Criers' Championship at Halifax; Fisheries Exhibi- tion at Lunenburg.

New Foundland: *January–March:* Winter carnival time in Corner Brook, Labrador City, and other towns and villages. *June:* Opening of rainbow trout and salmon fishing seasons. *July:* Canada Day celebrations in St. John's, Corner Brook, Grand Falls, Paquet, and elsewhere; Summer Arts Festival in St. John's; Newfoundland Amateur Golf Championship at St. John's Bally Hally Golf Club. *August:* St. John's annual regatta; Festival of Traditional French Culture, Music, and Dance at Cape St. George. *September–October:* Regional agricultur- al fairs and exhibitions throughout the province.

WHAT IT WILL COST. On the whole prices in Canada are comparable to those in the United States. If you stay in large hotels, then you can expect to pay high prices. The cost of a room in an average motel or small hotel can be moderate ($50–$60) to downright inexpensive. Campgrounds are numer- ous and provide cheap nightly or weekly rates for campers. Hostels are not plentiful in the Atlantic Provinces and cater mostly to the young. In many cases, small overnight-type cottages can provide housekeeping facilities. Bed-and- breakfast accommodations are expanding rapidly throughout the whole area.

The price of meals is generally higher in New Brunswick than in the other Atlantic provinces, although there are many restaurants where you can get a good meal for a moderate price. Alcoholic beverages are very expensive.

There is a sales tax in each province (11% New Brunswick, 10% Nova Scotia, 10% Prince Edward Island, 12% Newfoundland) that is also levied on lodgings and restaurant meals. U.S. residents will receive 20% or more for their Ameri- can dollars when buying Canadian currency. Residents of Great Britain will find Canadian prices low by their standards.

MONEY. The Canadian dollar, like the U.S. dollar, is divided into 100 cents. Coins and bills exist in the same denominations as in the U.S., i.e., pennies, nickles, dimes, etc., and $1, $5, $10, etc. Actual exchange rates fluctuate from day to day, but the Canadian dollar is usually worth about 80 U.S. cents. You can probably get the most for your money by converting it before you leave home. Most hotels, stores, and restaurants will, however, accept U.S. traveler's checks, make the conversion, and give you change in Canadian money—even if you don't get the *very* best exchange rate. Most banks will exchange U.S. for Canadian dollars. They are generally open Monday–Friday, 10 A.M.–3 P.M.

There are no restrictions on the amount of money you may bring into or take out of Canada. Both Canadians and foreign visitors may convert money from Canadian tender to another currency or from a foreign currency to Canadian dollars as often as desired, in amounts as great as desired, either inside or outside Canada.

CREDIT CARDS. The major credit and bank cards that are widely accepted in the Atlantic Provinces are: American Express, MasterCard, and Visa. Carte Blanche and Diner's Club have more limited acceptance. If you don't already have a credit card inquire locally to see where they are available in your area. Ask about any charges for converting Canadian to foreign currency in the billing process.

TRAVELER'S CHECKS. These are the best way to safeguard travel funds. They are sold in various banks and financial companies in terms of American and Canadian dollars and, with proper identification, are as readily accepted as cash. *American Express* has offices throughout the U.S. and Canada; also widely accepted in Canada are *Thomas Cook* traveler's checks, represented by Canada Permanent Trust Company and Toronto Dominion Bank.

HOW TO GET THERE. By air. Eastern Provincial Airlines and Air Canada provide service to all four provinces. CP Air flies to Nova Scotia, Eastern Provincial Airways and Quebecair fly to Labrador. Most of these flights originate in Toronto, Montreal, or the Atlantic Provinces themselves, so there is a good chance you will have to change planes. You will find more detailed information in the individual chapters.

By train. There is regular VIA Rail passenger service via Montreal to New Brunswick and Nova Scotia. Passengers can reach Prince Edward Island and Newfoundland by connecting ferries and buses. Amtrak connections can be made in Montreal. For further information, contact VIA Rail Canada, Box 8116, 2 Place Ville-Marie, Montreal, PQ, H3C 3N3 (514–286–2311 or 800–361 –7773), or Amtrak (800–USA–RAIL).

By bus. Most major North American bus lines serve the area through interconnecting lines. Local bus service is offered by a number of companies, such as Acadian Lines, 6040 Almon St., Halifax, NS, B3K 5M1 (902–454–9321); St. John's Transportation Commission, 245 Fresh Water Rd., St. John's, NF, A1B 1B3 (709–722–4771); the SMT System, 300 Union St., Saint John, NB, E2L 4S3 (506–693–6500); the Mackenzie Line, 210 York St., Bridgewater, NS, B4V 1R5 (902–543–2491); and Terra Transport, Box 310, 459 Water St., St. John's, NF, A1C 5K1 (709–737–5916).

BUS TOURS. Many bus companies offer package tours of the Atlantic Provinces. For a list of companies that tour the Maritimes, write to Marketing Branch, Tourism New Brunswick, Box 12345, Fredericton, NB, E3B 5C3. Among the companies are the following:

AAA Travel Agency, 2900 AAA Court, Bettendorf, IA 52722.

Acadian Lines, 6040 Almon St., Halifax, NS, B3K 5M1.

All Star Tours, 1560 Victoria St. N., Kitchener, ON, N2B 3E5.

Atlantic Tours, 40 Neck Road, Rothesay, NB, E0G 2W0.

Evergreen Tours Ltd., Suite 305, 1185 West Georgia St., Vancouver, BC, V6E 4E6.

Fidelity Motor Bus Lines, Inc., 1920 Lincoln Way, E., Massillon, OH 44646.

Lincoln Bus Lines Inc., 10 W. Elm Ave., Hanover, PA 17331.

Smith Tours, Box 1460, Henderson, KY 42420.

Trius Tours, Box 1385, Fredericton, NB E3B 5E3.

HINTS TO MOTORISTS. Roads in the Maritime Provinces (New Brunswick, Prince Edward Island, Nova Scotia) are generally excellent, all well paved except for very minor secondary roads. The Trans-Canada Highway, the longest and most scenic highway in the world, runs through most major areas and continues into Newfoundland. More of Newfoundland's side roads, however, are unpaved but usually well kept up. With the exception of some 50 miles of highway from Blanc Sablon to Red Bay in Labrador and local roads in Goose Bay and Wabush/Labrador City, Labrador has no roads. Maps designating road conditions are available from all tourism departments, and up-to-date reports on the conditions of roads can be obtained by telephoning the Department of Highways or Transportation in each province (look under "Government of Canada" listings in the telephone book).

Speed limits vary from province to province, but outside cities they are usually 90–100 kilometers per hour (50–60 mph). Distances as well as speed limits are given in kilometers.

The price of gasoline varies, and figuring out the price can be difficult for visitors. Canada is much further along in adopting the meteric system than is the United States. Liquids, including gasoline, are usually sold in liters (3.78 liters = 1 U.S. gallon).

If you drive your own car into Canada from the United States, you should get a Canadian Non-Resident Inter-Provincial Motor Vehicle Liability Insurance Card. It's available in the United States from your U.S. insurance company. The minimum liability insurance requirements vary from province to province, from $50,000 to $200,000. For additional information about automobile insurance, contact the *Insurance Bureau of Canada,* 181 University Ave., Toronto, ON, M5H 3M7 (416–362–2031).

If you are a member of the American Automobile Association (AAA), then you can dial 800–336–HELP for emergency road service in Canada.

Car rentals. Most cities and towns in the Atlantic Provinces have car rental offices, as do most hotels and airports. A travel agent can arrange a pickup. If you come to Canada by air or rail and want to rent a car, you can make your own reservations before you leave home through Hertz (800–654–3131), Avis (800–331–1212), or Budget Rent-A-Car (800–527–0700). They all have stations at the major airports, and their rates in Canada are comparable to those in the United States. If you are looking for a bargain or a recreational vehicle, however, ask the Canadian Government Travel Bureau for advise or try Tilden Rent-A-Car, 1485 Stanley St., Montreal, PQ, H3A 1P6 (514–842–9445).

FERRIES. You only have to look at a map of the Atlantic Provinces area to realize why ferries are an important communications link. Two of the provinces (Prince Edward Island and Newfoundland) are real islands, accessible only by water or air. Nova Scotia has two long necks on either side of its road connection to New Brunswick, so ferry travel can save miles of driving. In New Brunswick the long Saint John River cuts a wide swath right through the southern section of the province. Free car ferries offer short, enjoyable respites from driving as they crisscross rivers and travel to tiny offshore islands. Others, such as the ferry to Grand Manan, can take two hours and are often accompanied by cavorting porpoises. Still others make the even longer voyages from Portland to Bar Harbour, Maine, to Nova Scotia, (you are apt to spy a spouting whale). From Nova Scotia to Newfoundland can take either 6 hours or 18, depending on the port you choose. One of the most interesting ways to sightsee along the spectacular coast in Newfoundland is by ferry, which carries passengers as well as mail and provisions for outlying communities.

The ferry service of the Atlantic Provinces makes it possible to plan a circle tour of the area.

For information write: CN Marine Service and Reservations, 100 Cameron St., Moncton, NB, E1C 5Y6 (506–858–3600 or 800–565–9470, Canada; 800–432–7344, Maine; 800–341–7981, continental U.S.).

VIA Rail Canada, Box 8116, 2 Place Ville-Marie, Montreal, PQ, H3C 3N3 (800–561–3952). In the United States contact your local Amtrak agent.

Ferry information is also available from each provincial tourist department.

ACCOMMODATIONS. Reserve well in advance for hotels and motels in popular resort areas during peak seasons. Also, remember that during any season a city may be hosting a convention or special event at the time you arrive. Planning your trip early will either provide you with the accommodations you want or give you plenty of time to make alternative arrangements.

If you do not have reservations, then it is wise to begin looking for a suitable place to stay early in the afternoon so you won't have to accept potluck later in the day when most motorists have settled in for the night. When you have made reservations in advance, you should advise the establishment if you expect to arrive late, or they may not hold your reservations.

Most often you will have to pay for parking at city hotels.

Accommodations are listed in the individual chapters according to price categories (in Canadian dollars), and the prices reflected in these categories vary from chapter to chapter. The rates are for two people in a double room. Cribs for children are almost always available—sometimes at no cost, frequently for a minimal charge. Cots to supplement the beds in your room will also involve a minimal expense.

The Maritime Provinces offer reservation services, which you may find helpful:

New Brunswick's Dial a Night Service, a free reservation service available at any of its provincial tourist bureaus, allows you to book rooms ahead as soon as you cross into the province.

Prince Edward Island has a unique radio reservation service that can be utilized at the ferry slips in New Brunswick and Nova Scotia.

Nova Scotia offers a Check In service at their information centres or by a toll-free line (800–565–7105) that can make reservations for you at many listed hotels.

BED AND BREAKFAST. Bed-and-breakfast accommodations (or hospitality homes as they are called in Newfoundland) have become popular in the Atlantic Provinces in the last few years. If you stay at one you can expect a clean, comfortable room in a family home and a Continental or full breakfast with such appetizing treats as home-baked bread and homemade preserves. You'll probably share a bathroom with other guests, but traffic should be light since most homes have only one or two guestrooms. You get to meet residents and make use of their knowledge of local restaurants and attractions. Children are usually accepted, pets often are not. Follow the same rules you would if you were a guest in a friend's home: be quiet after 11 P.M. and show respect for furniture and carpets. Some B&Bs have wheelchair access.

Most B&Bs are not equipped to handle credit cards. Although personal checks may sometimes be accepted, it is best to be prepared with cash. Rates (which can be as low as $15) are usually much better than at hotels or motels.

Each province has a list of bed-and-breakfast homes; write to the department of tourism. In most cases, you must make your own reservations. Some of Nova Scotia's B&Bs are listed in their Check In service (800–565–7105); B&Bs listed in New Brunswick's accommodations booklet can be reserved free within the province from Tourist Information Centres; and Prince Edward Island will try to make B&B reservations with their radio reservation service available at the ferry departure point in New Brunswick.

Reservations are not always necessary. If you want to risk it, you can drive, list in hand, from home to home until you find a vacancy.

FARM VACATIONS. Farm-vacation associations distribute lists of guest farms, inspect facilities, and handle consumer complaints. The following is a list of associations that may be useful for travelers in the Maritime Provinces:

National: Canadian Country Vacations Association, Hopewell Hills, NB, E0A 1Z0.

New Brunswick: New Brunswick Farm Vacations Associations, RR 1, Harcourt, Kent County, NB, E0A 1T0.

Prince Edward Island: Prince Edward Island Visitor Services Division, Box 940, Charlottetown, PE, C1A 7M5.

Nova Scotia: Nova Scotia Farm and Country Vacations Association, Halls Harbour, Kings County, NS, B0P 1J0.

Newfoundland: at this writing has no such program.

HOSTELS. Although there is no surplus of hostels in the Atlantic Provinces, almost every major center in each province does have a hostel of one form or another. Membership in the Canadian Hostelling Association is international and nonmembers are accepted for a slightly higher rate as long as they possess valid identification. You can get free booklets on hostels across Canada from the Canadian Hostelling Association, Place Vanier, Tower A, 333 River Road, Ottawa, ON, K1L 3B9.

The Campus Travel Agency, University of New Brunswick, Fredericton, NB, sells a booklet listing hostels in the Atlantic Provinces. Other low-cost accommodations are offered in the summer by universities throughout the Atlantic Provinces. A list is available from the Food and Lodging Administration, University of New Brunswick, Fredericton, NB (506–453–4891).

RESTAURANTS. Restaurants are listed under price categories in the Practical Information sections. The price ranges vary from chapter to chapter, and are given at the beginning of each list.

Relatively few restaurants in the Atlantic Provinces demand strict dress codes, although some of the more elegant, such as the Keltic Lodge in Nova Scotia, will ask that casual clothing (e.g., jeans) not be worn. Mostly it is casual dining with neat attire (sports shirts accepted in lieu of tie).

Reservations are advisable if a restaurant is highly recommended or popular. Even so, you'll often be able to get a table by showing up at the door prepared to wait.

Shellfish, even here, is the highest priced item on the menu. Occasionally it will be served with fiddleheads (the curled frond of the ostrich fern that grows around the fresh rivers and lakes of New Brunswick and tastes something like artichoke). You'll also be offered Acadian dishes such as poutine rape (grated cooked potato wrapped around pork) or chicken fricot (a delicious chicken stew). Newfoundland has the most unique dishes: seal flipper pie, cod and scruncheons (bits of salt pork fried crisp), or cod tongues.

The more orthodox palate will find familiar dishes and excellent steaks all across the area.

NIGHTLIFE. Pubs are popular in all of the Atlantic Provinces with those of Newfoundland similar to those of Ireland. Often a singsong will spontaneously begin (or possibly a difference of opinion). Taverns are generally large, plain rooms, vibrating to deafening music and catering mostly to the young.

Most cities have favorite after-work hangouts or singles bars, with or without dancing, and some places have nightclubs, where the quality of the performers varies considerably. Halifax, Nova Scotia, is the most cosmopolitan of the area's cities and your best bet for this type of nightlife. Popular singing and recording groups often tour the provinces.

Dinner theater is becoming popular, especially in New Brunswick where Marshall Buttons Comedy Asylum and Peter Pacey's Calithumpians provide a very funny look at the natives. Each province has excellent professional theater. Prince Edward Island presents *Anne of Green Gables* each year, as well as top stage productions.

There are also fine symphony orchestras, chamber music quartets, and other classical pursuits.

TIPPING. There is no law in Canada that says you must leave a tip for service. The unwritten laws of custom, however, make tipping neccessary more often than not. Tipping is an accepted way of expressing appreciation for service that is attentive and efficient. You can make the amount of the tip reflect the quality of the service you receive, and you need not leave any tip for service that is very poor.

In a restaurant, it is common to leave 10–15% of the charge *before* taxes. At counters, many people leave 50 cents, or 10%, whichever is greater. For bell-boys, 50 cents per bag is usual. Taxi drivers in Canadian cities expect 15%; car-rental agencies, nothing. Bus porters are tipped 50 cents per bag; drivers, nothing. On charter and package tours, conductors and drivers usually get $10 per day from the group, but be sure to ask if this has already been figured into the package cost. On short, local sightseeing runs, the driver-guide may get 50 cents–$1 per person, more if he has been especially helpful or informative. At airports and train stations, porters get 50 cents per bag.

SENIOR-CITIZEN AND STUDENT DISCOUNTS. Many hotels, motels, restaurants, and attractions throughout Canada offer discounts to senior citizens— usually defined as 65 or older—and students. For senior citizens, some proof of age, such as a passport or a driver's license, will suffice. Museums, movie theaters, and even some stores often post senior-citizen rates. Some airlines give seniors a 10% discount. Those places offering student discounts are generally more stringent in their proof requirements; a high-school or college ID, international student travel card, or evidence of age may be requested. People under 22 get discounts of up to 25% on stand-by air travel.

HINTS TO HANDICAPPED TRAVELERS. There are millions of people with handicaps who are able to travel and do so enthusiastically when they know they can move about in safety and comfort. A growing number of travel agents specialize in this field. Generally, the tours parallel those of the nonhandicapped traveler but at a more leisurely pace and with all the logistics carefully checked out in advance. One such agency is Acess Tours, Suite 1801, 123–33 83rd Ave., Kew Gardens, NY 11415 (212–828–8334, 800–533–5343). More extensive lists of commercial tour operators who arrange or conduct tours for the handicapped are available from the Society for the Advancement of Travel for the Handicapped, 26 Court St., Brooklyn, NY 11242. A free pamphlet, *Incapacitated Passengers' Air Travel Guide,* is available from the International Air Transport Association, 2000 Teel St., Montreal, PC, H3A 2R4.

A Guide For Travellers With Special Needs is available from Transport Canada, Development Center, 1000 Sherbrook St. W., Box 549, Place de L'Aviation, Montreal, PQ, H3E 2R3 (ask for publication TP 380).

Four important sources of information in this field are: 1) *Access to the World: A Travel Guide for the Handicapped,* by Louise Weiss, available from Facts on File, 460 Park Ave. S., New York, NY 10016.
2) Travel Information Center, Moss Rehabilitation Hospital, 12th St. and Tabor Rd., Philadelphia, PA 19141.
3) Easter Seal Society for Crippled Children and Adults, Director of Information and Education Service, 2023 W. Ogden Ave., Chicago, IL 60612.
4) Rehabilitation International USA, 1123 Broadway, New York, NY 10010.

SPORTS. Canadians are enthusiastic about all kinds of sports. Hockey and curling are national pastimes with baseball rapidly gaining popularity. Swimming, canoeing, and sailing are popular all along the Atlantic coast. Rowing is a championship sport in New Brunswick, and whale-watching from boats is offered on Grand Manan Island. Nova Scotia offers a unique attraction for divers in the nearly 3,000 wrecked ships off the coastline, some of them containing treasure.

Residents of Prince Edward Island and New Brunswick are avid harness-racing fans. Hikers will find a variety of trails in the national and provincial parks. Golf and tennis are also popular, as is cycling. Each province has an active bicycle club, which offers tips and tours. (Write to Canadian Cycling Association, 333 River Rd., Vanier, ON, K1L 8H9, for names of provincial associations.)

There is also a full range of winter sports: ice skating, tobogganing, ice fishing, snowmobiling, downhill and cross-country skiing.

 FISHING. Each of the four provinces offers something for the angler. Salmon, cod, swordfish, bluefin tuna, mackerel, and sea trout are caught in the Atlantic, and there are speckled and rainbow trout and striped and black bass in the freshwater. Limits, seasons, and licensing regulations vary from province to province; inquire in advance at the provincial tourism offices.

A daily license is available for some waters in **New Brunswick,** where fishing is mainly for trout and Atlantic salmon. Many of the streams and rivers, however, are leased to private freeholders—either individuals or clubs. For information, contact the Fish and Wildlife Branch, 349 King St., Box 6000, Fredericton, NB, E3B 5H1 (506–453–2440).

Deep-sea fishing is best off the eastern part of **Prince Edward Island.** The best source of information is the Fish and Wildlife Branch, Box 2000, Charlottetown, PE, C1A 7N8 (902–892–0311).

Nova Scotia has the most stringent freshwater restrictions in Canada, but the availability of Atlantic salmon, speckled trout, and striped bass make the trouble worthwhile. Nonresidents are required to hire a guide for each three fishermen. Saltwater fishing is also popular and almost as restricted. Inquire at Fisheries and Oceans, Box 550, Halifax, NS, B3J 2S7 (902–426–5952).

Newfoundland is 30% water, so there is lots of fresh- as well as saltwater fishing. The booklet *Hunting and Fishing Guide* is available from the Tourism Branch, Department of Development, Box 2016, St. John's, NF, A1C 5R8 (800–563–6353).

 HUNTING. Bag limits and firearms regulations vary widely from province to province. Handguns are not allowed anywhere, but nonresidents may take any other equipment they need into any province. Guides are required in many places and are available almost everywhere. *Good Hunting in Canada,* a booklet offering information about restrictions, game, outfitters, firearms, and licenses, is available from the Canadian Government Office of Tourism, DRIE, 235 Queen St., Ottawa, ON, K1A 0H6 (613–996–4610). The following is a list of some of the variety of game in Atlantic Canada:

New Brunswick: deer, rabbit, ruffed grouse, partridge, migratory game birds, bear, bobcat, fox, raccoon, skunk, porcupine, groundhog, and crow.

Prince Edward Island: small game only.

Nova Scotia: moose, caribou, bear, wildcat, fox, raccoon, rabbit and hare, marten, beaver, mink, otter, weasel, muskrat, ruffed grouse, partridge, pheasant, duck, snipe, and woodcock.

Newfoundland: moose, caribou, bear, rabbit, snipe, wild goose, and duck.

 CAMPING. If you own a tent, trailer, or recreational vehicle, camping may be the cheapest way to travel. Many of the finest campgrounds are in the national and provincial parks, where it is first-come, first-served, with nominal fees. Commercial campgrounds offer the same amenities—such as electricity and water hookups, showers, laundromats, cookhouses, and even game rooms and grocery stores—but usually charge more per night. Nevertheless, camping fees are a bargain compared to the cost of hotel or motel accommodations.

It's a good idea to arrive early because popular campgrounds fill up early. Try to stop in an area that has a number of campgrounds, so that if one is full you can stay at another. Check into how long you can stay as this may affect your travel plans.

If all you need is a clear patch of ground on which to pitch a tent, then you can simply pull off the road on millions of square kilometers of Crown lands and set up camp.

For listings of private and public campgrounds, contact the tourist office of the province you plan to visit. Brochures and other information on national and provincial parks are also available from the National and Provincial Parks Association of Canada, 69 Sherbourne St., Box 313, Toronto, ON, M5A 3X7. Other sources of information are the American Automobile Association and its affiliate the Canadian Automobile Association, 1775 Courtwood Crescent, Ottawa, ON, K2C 3J2, which publish a series of guidebooks to campgrounds in North America.

 NATIONAL PARKS. There are seven national parks in the Maritime Provinces and Newfoundland. For complete information on facilities and accommodations, write to the national office (Parks Canada, Department of the Environment, Ottawa, ON, K1A 1G2), the regional office (Parks Canada —Atlantic Region, Upper Water St., Halifax, NS, B3J 1S9), or the headquarters of the park you wish to visit. A list of the seven parks follows.

Cape Breton Highlands National Park, Ingonish Beach, Cape Breton, NS, B0C 1L0 (902–285–2270). About 945 sq. km, with swimming, salmon fishing, hiking trails, forests, a rocky coastline, and a Scottish atmosphere, as well as cross-country skiing in the winter.

Fundy National Park, Box 40, Alma, NB, E0A 1B0 (506–887–2000). Almost 270 sq. km, with oddly formed sandstone cliffs punctuating lovely beaches and remarkable high and low tides.

Gros Morne National Park, Box 130, Rocky Harbour, NF, A0K 4N0 (709–458–2417). Almost 2,000 sq. km, including the Long Range Mountains, fresh- and saltwater fiords, a rugged coast, and heavy forests.

Kejimkujik National Park, Box 36, Maitland Bridge, Annapolis County, NS, B0T 1N0 (902–242–2770). 380 sq. km featuring rolling woodland and fishing lakes.

Kouchibouguac National Park, Kent County, NB, E0A 2A0 (506–876–2443). 226 sq. km of maritime plain, with beaches, dunes, and barrier islands.

Prince Edward Island National Park, Box 487 Charlottetown, PE, C1A 7L1 (902–566–7050). This park, a strip along the Gulf of St. Lawrence coast sharing with New Brunswick the warmest beaches north of the Carolinas, is now about 20 sq. km, but there are plans to expand to over 30 sq. km.

Terra Nova National Park, Glovertown, NF, A0G 2L0 (709–533–2801). 400 sq. km of park surround Bonavista Bay, with its inlets, boreal forest, and the enormous icebergs that float into the bay to melt.

 FACTS AND FIGURES. The population of New Brunswick is 700,000, that of Prince Edward Island is 125,000, and of Nova Scotia 868,000. Newfoundland has a population of 58,000, and Labrador has an additional 31,000.

Almost 50 million metric tons of lobster come from the waters of the Atlantic Provinces; a good part of this catch is exported.

- Forestry, agriculture, fishing, mining, and tourism make up major industries.
- Dulse, a dried seaweed, is often eaten as a snack by Maritime residents.
- Fiddleheads, the uncurled frond of the ostrich fern, is considered a spring delicacy in New Brunswick.
- The first rays of the sun in North America hit Cape Spear near St. John's, Newfoundland.
- The first chocolate bar was invented in St. Stephen, New Brunswick, by Ganong Bros. Chocolates. It's still available.
- New Brunswick and Nova Scotia boast the highest tides in the world, sometimes 50 ft.

 METRIC CONVERSION CHARTS. First, a simplified list; then, some useful charts: 1 inch = 2.54 centimeters; 1 foot = 12 inches = 30.48 centimeters; 1 yard = 3 feet = 0.9144 meters; 1 ounce = 28.35 grams; 1 pound = 453.59 grams; 2.2 pounds = 1 kilo; 1 U.S. gallon = 3.75 liters; 1 hectare = 2.47 acres; 1 square kilometer = .3861 square miles.

Length

Centimeters	Inches
5	2
10	4 (under)
20	8 (under)
30	11¾
40	15¾
50	19¾
1 meter = 39.37 inches	

Weight

Grams	Ounces
100	3.33
200	6.67
250	8.03
500	16.07
1 kilogram (kilo) = 2.2046 lbs.	

Kilometers Into Miles

This simple chart will help you to convert to both miles and kilometers. If you want to convert from miles into kilometers read from the center column to the right; if from kilometers into miles, from the center column to the left. Example: 5 miles = 8.0 kilometers, 5 kilometers = 3.1 miles.

Miles	Kilometers		Miles	Kilometers	
0.6	1	1.6	37.3	60	96.6
1.2	2	3.2	43.5	70	112.3
1.9	3	4.8	49.7	80	128.7
2.5	4	6.3	55.9	90	144.8
3.1	5	8.0	62.1	100	160.9
3.7	6	9.6	124.3	200	321.9
4.3	7	11.3	186.4	300	482.8
5.0	8	12.9	248.5	400	643.7
5.6	9	14.5	310.7	500	804.7
6.2	10	16.1	372.8	600	965.6
12.4	20	32.2	434.9	700	1,126.5
18.6	30	48.3	497.1	800	1,287.5
24.8	40	64.4	559.2	900	1,448.4
31.0	50	80.5	621.4	1,000	1,609.03

Tire Pressure Converter

Pounds per Square Inch	16	18	20	22	24	26	28	30	32
Kilogrammes per Square Centimeter	1.12	1.26	1.40	1.54	1.68	1.82	1.96	2.10	2.24

Gallons into Liters

U.S. Gallon	Liters
1	3.78
2	7.57
3	11.36
4	15.14
5	18.93
6	22.71
7	26.50
8	30.28
9	34.07
10	37.85

TIME ZONES. The Maritime Provinces use Atlantic time, which is one hour ahead of New York and four hours ahead of California. Newfoundland and Labrador use Newfoundland Time, which is half an hour ahead of Atlantic Time. When it's 3:00 P.M. in New York, it's 4:30 in Newfoundland. During daylight savings time, in effect from the last Sunday in April till the last Sunday in October, the clocks are set ahead another hour.

HOLIDAYS. National public holidays in Canada are New Year's Day, Good Friday, Easter Monday (the Monday following Easter), Victoria Day (the Monday preceding May 25), Canada Day (July 1), Labour Day (the first Monday in September), Thanksgiving Day (the second Monday in October), Remembrance Day (November 11), and Christmas Day. Many holidays are now observed on the closest Monday. Many stores, resorts, and attractions remain open on holidays while banks, schools, and government offices, including post offices, close. The provinces observe the following holidays in addition to the national ones listed above:

New Brunswick: Boxing Day (December 26).

Prince Edward Island: Boxing Day (December 26).

Nova Scotia: Sir John A. MacDonald's Birthday (January 11), Boxing Day (December 26).

Newfoundland: Saint Patrick's Day (March 17), Saint George's Day (around April 23), Discovery Day (penultimate Monday in June), Memorial Day (July 3), Orangemen's Day (July 12), and Boxing Day (December 26).

BUSINESS HOURS. Opening hours for stores, shops, and supermarkets are similar to those in the United States: 9 A.M.–5 P.M., Mon.–Sat. Most shopping malls, now housing the majority of stores (and usually a liquor store), remain open either 9 A.M.–9 P.M. or 10 A.M.–10 P.M., six days a week. Blue laws (enforced Sun. closings) are in effect in much of Canada, so don't expect to get much souvenir shopping done then. Traditionally, Canadian banks are open only 10 A.M.–3 P.M., Mon.–Fri., but the trend is to extended hours and Sat. morning hours. Drugstores and convenience shops in major cities are often open until 11 P.M.

 LIQUOR LAWS. Rules and regulations governing what kinds of alcoholic beverages may be sold, at what hours, and to whom, vary from province to province. The legal drinking age is 18 on Prince Edward Island and 19 in New Brunswick, Nova Scotia, and Newfoundland. Except for consumption on premises, beer and wine are only available from government liquor stores.

 MAIL. As of June 24, 1985, the rate for sending either a post card or a first-class letter weighing up to 30 grams (about 1 ounce) is 34 cents within Canada, 39 cents to the U.S.A., 68 cents to other countries. Areograms are 68 cents each. Stamps can be purchased at post offices in Canada, which are usually open during business hours, Mon.–Fri., and sometimes on Sat.; from your hotel desk; or from vending machines located in transportation terminals, banks, and some shops. They cost the same from a machine as from the post office, but the machines only sell in 50-cent lots.

 TELEPHONES AND TELEGRAMS. Coin-operated telephones are available almost everywhere. To use the coin telephone, just follow the instructions on the phone box. Local calls usually cost 25 cents and can be dialed directly. American coins will not work. If you don't reach your party, your money is refunded to you automatically when you hang up.

For long-distance calls, have plenty of coins available unless you are calling "collect." The operator may ask for enough change to cover the initial time period before she connects you. To place a call outside Canada, dial 0 and ask for the overseas operator. You can, however, dial any point in the United States from most places in Canada directly.

In hotels, your switchboard operator will either place your outside call for you, or tell you how to dial directly from your room. The telephone charges will be added to your hotel bill (although many times local calls are free), and you will pay for them when you check out.

To send a telegram to a destination anywhere within Canada, ask for assistance at your hotel, go to the nearest CNCP telegraph office, or call toll free (800–565–7504 or 800–361–1872). Overseas cablegrams can also be dispatched by CNCP.

 ENTERING CANADA. Customs regulations between the United States and Canada are among the most liberal in the world. Passing from one country to the other is usually a simple matter of presenting some valid and acceptable form of identification and answering a few simple questions about where you were born, where you live, why you are visiting Canada, and how long you will stay.

The identification need not be a passport, although this is certainly acceptable. You can also use a driver's license, birth certificate, draft card, Social

Security card, certificate of naturalization, or resident alien ("green") card. Citizens of Great Britain, Australia, and New Zealand need passports.

Canada allows British and American guests to bring their cars (for less than 6 months), boats or canoes, rifles and shotguns (but not handguns or automatic weapons) and 200 rounds of ammunition, cameras, radios, sports equipment, and typewriters into the country without paying any duty. Sometimes they will require a deposit for trailers and household equipment, but this is refundable when you cross back over the border. (The deposit is to guarantee that you do not sell these items in Canada for a profit.) Needless to say, you may bring clothing, personal items, and any professional tools or equipment you need (if you work in Canada) without charge or restriction. It is also a good idea to carry information about your medical insurance and insurance for boats, vehicles, and personal luggage.

Some items, however, are restricted. You need the contract for a rented car, and, if you are going to return home and leave behind a car you rented in the States, you have to fill out an E29B customs form. Tobacco is limited. Dogs, for hunting or pets, are duty-free, but you must bring a certificate from a veterinary inspector to prove that the dog has no communicable diseases. (Cats may enter without restriction.) All plants must be examined at the customs station to preclude the entry of destructive insects. Most important, Canadian officials are diligent in pursuing smugglers of narcotics and other illegal items.

 LEAVING CANADA. U.S. Customs. American citizens and other residents of the U.S. who visit Canada for more than 48 hours and who have claimed no exemption during the previous 30 days are entitled to bring in duty free up to $400 (retail value) worth of foreign purchases. The items may be intended for personal use or as gifts for those back home. They all count, even if some are personal effects you have already worn.

All your purchases are to accompany you, and it is wise (and simpler when inspection time comes) to try to put everything, or as much as possible, into one suitcase or carryall.

Also try to keep your purchase receipts together and handy, in case you have to produce them.

Members of a family can pool their exemptions; each separate member, including all minors, is entitled to the $400 exemption.

Small gifts under $50 in value may be mailed home to friends duty free, but not more than one package to any one address. Such packages cannot contain perfumes, tobacco, or liquor. The outside of such a package must be marked: "Unsolicited Gift, value under $50," followed by the contents of the package.

Packages mailed to yourself are subject to duty. Your best bet, again, is to carry everything with you. Further information will be provided by the nearest U.S. Customs office or by U.S. Customs Service, Washington, D.C. 20229.

Great Britain. You may bring into the U.K. the following goods duty free: 200 cigarettes, or 100 cigarillos, or 50 cigars, or 250 grams tobacco; plus one liter of alcohol of more than 38.8% proof, or 2 liters of alcohol not more than 38.8% proof, or 2 liters of fortified or sparkling wine and 2 liters of still table wine; plus 50 grams of perfume and ¼ liter of toilet water; plus other goods to the value of £28.

NEW BRUNSWICK

Natural Habitat for Sportsmen

by
COLLEEN THOMPSON

Author of New Brunswick Inside Out, *a native New Brunswicker's view of the province, travel writer Colleen Thompson has journeyed extensively throughout the Atlantic provinces. She is a regular contributor to various U.S. and Canadian magazines and newspapers, a travel columnist for the* Saint John Telegraph-Journal *and a regular commentator on CBC radio.*

New Brunswick is where the great Canadian forest, cut in vast swaths by sweeping river valleys and modern superhighways, meets the sea. It is an old place in North American terms, and the remains of a turbulent past exist in delightfully quiet nooks.

Some 1,400 miles (2,240 km.) of coast surround more than half the province. The violent Bay of Fundy, which has the highest tides in the world, sweeps up the coast of Maine, around the enchanting Fundy Isles at the southern tip of New Brunswick and on up the province's rough and intriguing southern coast. To the north and east, home of the province's French Acadian heritage, it's the gentle Gulf of St. Lawrence that washes up on quiet beaches.

For all that, New Brunswick is also a province of inland attractions. Its land mass and its human side are dominated by the Saint John River Valley—a strip of gentle farmland with sweeping views, and genteel communities with a captivating heritage. The capital, Fredericton, is built on the river's banks and it enters the sea at Saint John, the province's main industrial city.

Although the winter is usually severe with lots of snow, the province is alive with winter sports from late November to late March with skiing leading the list. The province has extensive skiing facilities, both cross-country and downhill, with many annual competitions and championships.

Spring is a glorious time—the greening of the land begins in April. Summer is hot, more so in the inland cities such as Fredericton, where the average temperature of 21°C (70°F) can easily soar to 35°C. (95°F.). In the fall, especially October, the whole countryside is ablaze with some of the most magnificent color in all of North America.

Certain foods and seasons are often well paired in this Maritime province. In the spring, the tourist must sample New Brunswick's delicacy, the fiddlehead, picked fresh alongside the rivers and streams. Eaten as a vegetable (boiled with butter, salt, and pepper), it is delicious. Also in spring, the bony fish, shad and gaspereaux, are popular. Salmon, once the spring staple, is a special treat now that the price is high. Lobster is the Maritimer's favorite dish, eaten on the shore, not at the table. Indeed, all shellfish coming from the Bay of Fundy and Gulf of St. Lawrence waters are especially tasty. Look for oysters, scallops, clams, and crab. And don't overlook dulse, a salty seaweed eaten like potato chips. Wash down these hearty native dishes with rich Moosehead beer, brewed in Saint John (a strictly local brew for decades, it is now a well-known export beer), and you'll have feasted "New Brunswick" style.

A Quiet History

While the red-bearded Vikings may have been familiar with the shores of New Brunswick's Fundy Isles in the Passamaquoddy Bay, history records the first white explorer as Jacques Cartier who traded with the Micmac Indians on New Brunswick's northern shore in 1534 on his way to explore the St. Lawrence River. Some 70 years later, when Samuel de Champlain and Sieur de Monts landed at the mouth of the St. John River they were casually greeted by an elderly Indian chieftain, the same Chief Membertou who had met Cartier on his first North American adventure.

Throughout their exploration of New Brunswick (then part of the area known as Acadia—embracing Nova Scotia, Cape Breton, and Prince Edward Island), the French maintained good relationships with both the Micmacs and the Maliceets who inhabited the St. John River Valley. Hoping to pre-empt the land before the English, they encouraged French settlers, opening up the rich fur trade to them. Their strategy deteriorated, however, when many of the French fought among themselves, a situation that allowed the English to launch successful attacks from Maine and establish their own settlements.

Finally, in 1713, the Treaty of Utrecht ceded Acadia to England. By 1755 there were estimated to be 10,000 Acadians still living in Nova Scotia (the area of New Brunswick and Nova Scotia). Of these, at least 7,000 were expelled by the English, who were concerned about the loyalties of this ever-increasing body should another war break out between France and England. Of the remainder, many were forced to flee to Québec and faraway places, such as Louisiana where the name Acadian has been corrupted to "Cajun." Yet, within 20 years many had returned, settling along the shores, especially in the New Brunswick communities of Cocagne, Shippagan, and Caraquet. Today one third of New Brunswick's population is made up of Acadians and the province is officially bilingual although attempts have only recently been made to familiarize residents with both languages.

The close of the Revolutionary War brought the Loyalists, 50,000 of them, loyal to Great Britain in deed or spirit. Because of the influx, the area known as Nova Scotia was divided into two colonies, and in 1784, the province of New Brunswick came into being.

Three thousand Loyalists arrived at the mouth of the Saint John River on May 11, 1783 . . . a large percentage of them gentlefolk, unaccustomed to deprivation. Here they were forced to seek shelter in tents and hastily constructed shacks, enduring hardships with amazing fortitude. Aged and infirm, women and children suffered deeply and many died of cold and exposure.

In time, settlers spread over the entire country away from the coast though a large number remained at the mouth of the Saint John River, founding the city which now bears that name. The hardy Loyalist spirit and the French persistence have made the New Brunswicker what he is today . . . stubborn, resourceful, fun-loving, sometimes rowdy . . . and fiercely independent.

The Great Outdoors

A province of great geographical variety, New Brunswick claims 1,400 miles of seacoast, including the hauntingly beautiful Fundy Isles, acres of rolling agricultural land along its rivers, and a rugged highland interior—forests, secluded lakes and mountains.

Crisscrossed with rivers, the province is a fisherman's heaven, offering Atlantic silver salmon, speckled trout, and black and striped bass. Especially the latter. New Brunswick offers pretty well the best bass fishing in North America. The season starts in mid-May with the Big Bass Tournament at Mactaquac, upriver from Fredericton. The Miramichi, the Restigouche, and the Nashwaak Rivers are prized by sport fishermen the world over.

Deep-sea fishing is also available for the avid sportsman. Canoeing, hiking, bird-watching—and more recently, whale-watching and wind-surfing—are popular summer pastimes.

New Brunswick is still largely unsettled—88 percent of the province is forested lands. Inhabitants have chosen the easily accessible area around rivers, ocean, and lakes, leaving most of the interior to the pulp companies. In fact, the view from a plane will make you think that New Brunswick is still an unspoiled wilderness with little sign of civilization.

How New Brunswick Makes a Living

Lumbering, a major source of income since the days of pit props and ships' masts, has taken a back seat to the mineral industry in recent times. Zinc, lead, and potash are the major minerals. Fishing remains the major occupation along the shores while the rich agricultural lands of the upper Saint John Valley turn out profitable potato crops each year. Saint John is a major port and industrial city. The largest oil refinery in Canada is located there. Tourism also generates considerable economic activity. Manufacturing is mostly done on the small scale, and it is diverse.

Madawaska

As you cross the Québec border into New Brunswick (a large, new tourist information center has been built here, with displays, audiovisual presentations, etc.), you'll find yourself in the mythical Republic of Madawaska. As we delve into its history, we learn that in the early 1800's the narrow wedge of land which makes up most of Madawaska County was coveted by Québec on one side and New Brunswick on the other. On top of that, the U.S. claimed it as well. Seeking to retain it for New Brunswick, Governor Sir Thomas Carleton found it easy to settle with Québec. He rolled dice all night with the Governor of North America at Québec, who happened to be his brother. Sir Thomas won at dawn . . . by one point. Settling with the Americans was more difficult. The border had always been disputed; even the lumbermen engaged in combat, brandishing peavies as weapons and otherwise harassing each other from both sides of the border. Finally, with the Treaty of Webster–Ashburton, in 1842, the British flag was hoisted over Madawaska county. It is said that one old-timer, tired of being asked which country he belonged to, replied: "I am a citizen of the Republic of Madawaska." So Madawaska exists to this day with its own flag (an independent eagle on a field of white) and coat-of-arms. To be a member of the Republic is a singular honor indeed.

Edmundston, Capital of Madawaska

Edmundston has always depended on the wealth of the deep forest land surrounding it; even today the Fraser Company's paper mill provides the major source of employment. It was in these woods that the legend of Paul Bunyan was born, and the feats of a strong young Madawaskan embroidered. Tales were spread to Maine and even to the west coast. Other lands, other people have tried to claim him for their own . . . but Paul Bunyan was born and raised in the forests and lumber camps of Madawaska County.

Formerly called Petit Sault because of the small rapids which existed here, the town was renamed Edmundston after a visit by Sir Edmund Head, one-time Lieutenant Governor of the province.

Not really an Acadian town, most of the French population has come from neighboring Québec. The first French settlers arrived here in the 19th century, followed closely by the British, especially the Scots. That combination gives this happy, thriving city a unique background. The main language is French, but most people are bilingual, not to mention exuberant. The French from Madawaska are often called "Brayons." The annual midsummer Foire Brayonne festival (lumberjack competitions, folk dancing, handcraft exhibits, and other events) is one of the most popular festivals in New Brunswick. It is held annually during the last week of July.

Examine the two churches which dominate the skyline. The Roman Catholic Cathedral of the Immaculate Conception is regarded as one of the better examples of its particular style of architecture in eastern Canada, and the Church of Our Lady of Sorrows contains some beautiful woodcarvings, notably those of the Fourteen Stations of the Cross created by noted New Brunswick artist Claude Roussel.

At the College of Saint Louis-Maillet, the religious paintings of another native son, Claude Picard, decorate the walls. On the campus too, the Galerie Colline displays touring art exhibitions.

About 20 miles out of Edmundston on Route 120 is a very popular recreation area, the Lac Baker Provincial Park.

For other diversions, skiing is popular on the slopes of nearby Mount Farlagne, the 18-hole golf course is well recommended by residents, and you'll enjoy the old car museum on the grounds of Les Jardins Provincial Park. The new Madawaska Regional Museum has displays on regional history and sports an art gallery.

The Saint John River Valley

The Saint John River Valley is a scenic delight. Rolling hills of rich agricultural land and the blue sweep of the winding Saint John make the drive excellent viewing. From St. Leonard to Woodstock lies New Brunswick's famed potato belt. Note the endless fields of potatoes and the squat, half-underground potato storage houses. Though Grand Falls is itself largely French speaking, from there on down the river, the French tongue is replaced by English everywhere.

At Grand Falls, site of a large and beautiful cataract, you may want to inspect the wells in the rocks, deep holes worn by the action of the water, some with a diameter of 16 feet and a depth of 30 feet. One of the town's interesting features is its wide main street, formerly a military parade ground. As the residents built their homes around it to view the proceedings, it gradually became the center of town.

The legend of Malabeam, part of the town's history, is the story of a young Indian maiden who led her Iroquois captors to their deaths over the falls rather than take them to her village. In memory of her courage, old boats filled with flowers are occasionally sent over the falls during the town's annual celebration of the Potato Festival. Local history is depicted at the Grand Falls Historical Museum.

The Fundy Coastal Region

Route 1, leading along the Bay of Fundy from St. Stephen to Saint John, is one of New Brunswick's most interesting drives. St. Stephen (a small border town named for a surveyor, not a saint) has always enjoyed such good relations with its neighboring American town of Calais that during the war of 1812, while the rest of Canada and the United States were in conflict, St. Stephen obligingly lent gunpowder to Calais for its Fourth of July celebration. Each summer there is an international festival held jointly in the two towns. The Charlotte County Historical Society Museum, describing the area's Loyalist ancestry, is located here.

At Oak Bay, outside St. Stephen, you'll find a little provincial park complete with beach, shaded camping grounds, and barbecue pits stocked with plenty of wood.

Take the jog off Route 1 to St. Andrews, a town every visitor to New Brunswick should see. Long the summer resort of the affluent (mansions ring the town), it's also a fisherman's town. Little has changed in the last two centuries. Of the town's 550 buildings, 280 were erected before 1880. Of these, 14 have survived from the 1700's. Indeed, some ingenious Loyalists who settled here brought their homes with them, piece by piece, from Castine, Maine, across the Passamaquoddy Bay. The Old English character of the town is preserved and enhanced by many of the town's businesses.

A walking-tour map is available from the tourist information center on Water St. . . . follow it to some of the town's most interesting buildings. One of these, Greenock Church, is an architect's delight. Stuart Trueman called it "the church that was born of an insult" in his book *The Fascinating World of New Brunswick*. The church was the result of a remark passed at an 1822 dinner party regarding the inability of the "poor" Presbyterians to have a church of their own. Presbyterian Captain Christopher Scott took exception to the slur. Sparing no expense, he erected an admirable building with a green oak tree carved on its tower in honor of his birthplace, Greenock, Scotland. The new Ross Memorial Museum on Montague Street features one of the finest antique collections in eastern Canada.

A drive up Joe's Point Road takes you to the Huntsman Marine Aquarium, an offshoot of the Federal Fisheries Research and Biological Station nearby. You'll see the shells of the two giant lobsters, Bonnie and Clyde, and be intrigued by the tank holding many varieties of marine life under a sign which says "Please Touch." Playful seals love to entertain the small fry and the film on current off-shore research is thoroughly engrossing.

The blockhouse on the shore is a restoration of one of five built in the area during the War of 1812. It's only 68 miles from St. Andrews to Saint John so take advantage of the route by taking some side trips to the numerous little coastal villages along the way. St. George, for instance, has one of the oldest Protestant graveyards in Canada as well as a fish ladder running up the side of the dam across the Magaguadavic River which flows through the town. And in nearby Lake Utopia (a scenic recreation area) lives the fabled Lake Utopian monster. He's been seen for generations . . . a rival for Scotland's Loch Ness monster.

Black's Harbour boasts the largest sardine cannery in the British Commonwealth. Nearby Pennfield the landing site of the British aviator Mollison, when he made the first nonstop, east-west crossing of the Atlantic.

The Fundy Isles

New Brunswick's Fundy Isles are true escapist retreats. It's hard to beat their windswept hospitable charm. Grand Manan, largest of the three, is the farthest away. It's a two-hour ferry ride from Black's Harbour, but you might see spouting whales, sunning porpoises, or a rare puffin on the trip out. It will be immediately apparent that the island's main preoccupation is fishing. The circular herring weirs dot the coastal waters and fish sheds and smokehouses appear along the shores. Names like Swallowtail, Southern Head, Seven Days Work, and Dark Harbour are as romantic as the island air, and the friendly folk speak with an accent all their own.

Grand Manan

About 20 miles of road lead from Southern Head to Northern Head, each Head with its own lighthouse perched high on jagged cliffs above the rocky surf. The famous American author Willa Cather spent her summers here and some of her novels were written on Grand Manan.

You'll want to visit Dark Harbour where no sun shines until late morning when it finally rises over the high hill that shades the harbor. The home of New Brunswick's dulse industry, it is here that dulse harvesters gather the purple seaweed from rocks left dry at low tide. They dry it in the sun on a natural rocky breakwater, and send it to mainland stores where it is purchased by New Brunswickers who enjoy the salty goodness of dried seaweed. The natives eat it like candy, but the visitor needs a little time to acquire the taste.

At Red Point, you'll find two different geological phenomena. Because of a long ago underwater upheaval, you will stand in one spot and note, on one side, 16-million-year-old volcanic material and on the other, the 6-billion-year-old sedimentary rock of the continental mass.

Welcome bird watchers! The island is known as an ornithologist's wonderland. Even John James Audubon came here in 1831 to study the various species; in fact, the rare puffin is the symbol of Grand Manan. If you'd like a close look at puffins, take a boat trip to Machias Seal Island, about 2 hours away by boat. Bird-watching tour packages are available to Grand Manan throughout the summer months. Contact Tourism New Brunswick for information. Whale-watching expeditions are also available through the Marathon Inn.

Anchorage Provincial Park on Grand Manan offers picnic, camping and hiking facilities. Hiking on Grand Manan generally is a very popular activity for tourists.

At the Grand Manan Museum, formerly the dwelling of Moses Gerrish, one of the first three settlers on the island, you'll be able to see many stuffed specimens of the island's birds as well as a large collection of artifacts from the oceans's bottom—the only residue of vessels wrecked in the waters of the Fundy Isles.

Campobello and Deer Islands

Neatly manicured, preening itself in the Bay, Campobello Island has always had a special appeal to the wealthy and the famous. It was here that the Roosevelt family spent its summers. The home of Franklin Delano Roosevelt, former president of the United States, is now maintained as a lovely museum in his honor. Located in the center of Roosevelt International Park, a joint project of the Canadian and American governments, President Roosevelt's home was the setting for the movie *Sunrise at Campobello*. A few miles away, a gracious mansion known as the Owens home is open to the public, and for overnight guests. Built by Captain William Owens in 1767, it has 21 rooms and nine fireplaces.

Herring Cove Provincial Park has camping facilities and a 9-hole golf course.

Connected to Lubec, Maine, by an international bridge, Campobello may still be approached from the other side by toll ferry from Deer Island.

An easy 20-minute free ferry ride from Letete near St. George brings you to Deer Island for a relaxing visit. You'll enjoy exploring the fishing wharves like those at Chocolate Cove. You'll find the world's largest lobster pound at Northern Harbour (owned by Conley's), and you'll want to walk through an interesting park at Deer Point, where you catch a toll ferry to nearby Campobello. If you listen carefully you may be able to hear the sighing and snorting of "the Old Sow," the second largest whirlpool in the world. If you can't hear it, you'll be able to see it, just a few feet off shore.

Exploring the island takes only a few hours. . . . it's 7½ miles long, varying in width from 3 miles to a few hundred feet at some points. If you decide to spend the night you might be interested to know that Deer Island is located exactly on the 45th parallel and one of the motels at Fairhaven is named just that.

Fredericton, Provincial Capital

The seat of government for New Brunswick's 710,900 residents has been the inland city of Fredericton on the St. John River since 1785. Loyalist to the core and named for Frederick, second son of George III, the city is the pride of the province. Tree-lined, resting sedately on the bank of the river, it was never a true frontier town. From the first town plan, the wealthy and scholarly Loyalists set out to create a gracious and beautiful place.

Its predecessor was the early French settlement of Ste.-Anne's Point established in 1642 during the reign of the French governor, Villebon, who made his headquarters at the junction of the Nashwaak and the Saint John. From Fort Nashwaak—now only a memorial cairn—he launched many successful raids into Maine, which caused great resentment among the English. Villebon left Fort Nashwaak in 1698, but the memory of the English was long and some forty years later a raiding party known as Hazen's Massachusetts Rangers burned the small village to the ground, killed most of the men, and carried the women and children off to Boston. The city of Fredericton rose from the ruins of this small French village.

EXPLORING FREDERICTON

Called the City of Stately Elms, Fredericton became an elegant British garrison town starting in 1825 when the military quarters were established there. A look at the military compound (including officer's quarters, enlisted men's barracks, guardhouse, and parade ground) is a must for any visitor interested in the city's past. Now designated a federal historic site, the military compound has been restored. Although the inside houses government offices, some parts, such as the guardhouse, are open to the public.

At present, the officer's quarters houses the York–Sunbury Historical Museum (largest community museum in the province, displaying many mementos of the past including replicas of 19th-century Fredericton homes), reconstructed with authentic furnishings of the period. You'll also find there the remains of one of Fredericton's legends. Staring at you from its glass case at the top of a staircase is the famous Coleman Frog, allegedly discovered in nearby Killarney Lake by hotelier Fred Coleman. Weighing 42 pounds, it was dispatched to an untimely death by a dynamite charge set by some disgruntled fishermen. Coleman had the frog stuffed; for forty years it sat in the lobby of his hotel on Queen Street where visitors were held spellbound by the stories of how it used to thrive on a diet of buttermilk, June bugs, fireflies, and whiskey fed to it by Fred and his friends. Resurrected from someone's garage after the old Barker House closed, it now holds a place of honor in the museum; and, of course, with a slight smile on its froggy face it never reveals its secret . . . which only Fred Coleman knew. Hoax or miracle? You'll have to decide for yourself.

Because of the gifts showered upon it by former New Brunswicker Lord Beaverbrook, multimillionaire, British peer, and newspaper baron, Fredericton has many fine buildings. On lower Queen Street, just two blocks from the Military Compound, you'll see the Playhouse, a gift of the Beaverbrook and the Dunn Foundation (former New Brunswicker Sir James Dunn, steel magnate and also Beaverbrook's close friend). The Playhouse (home of Theatre New Brunswick), built in 1964, provides year-round professional theater to city and province.

The Beaverbrook Art Gallery across the street will delight you with the wealth of its collection, including works by many of New Brunswick's noted artists as well as Salvador Dali's giant canvas *Santiago el Grande* (a huge painting bought especially for the Gallery's opening in 1959 by Sir James Dunn), canvasses by Reynolds, Turner, Hogarth, Gainsborough, the Canadian Group of Seven, and even works by Sir Winston Churchill. The Gallery houses a large collection of Graham Sutherland (47), and the largest collection in any institution of the works of Cornelius Krieghoff, famed Canadian landscape painter, known for his portrayals of Canadian life in the early 1800's.

The Provincial Legislature, built in 1880, is across the street from the Gallery. Open to the public, it offers guided tours at no cost, except when the Legislature is in session. When the House is in session, the public may view the proceedings from the public gallery, where you must also examine Sir Joshua Reynolds' portraits of George III and Queen Charlotte which flank the Throne.

In the back room of the Legislature, near the handsome spiral staircase, is the Legislative Library which contains two interesting and rare items. The first is a copy of the *Domesday Book*, the first census ever written, commissioned by William of Normandy in 1087. (This edition was printed in 1783.) Then turn to the four-volume set of the rare king-size Audubon bird books, more than three feet high, containing 435 hand-colored pictures (1834).

At the triangle of Queen, Church, and Brunswick Streets, about a block from the Legislative Building, you'll find the Christ Church Cathedral, Fredericton's pride. Completed in 1853, it is a beautiful building, one of the best examples of decorated Gothic architecture in North America and the first new cathedral foundation built on British soil since the Norman Conquest. Inside you'll find a clock known as "Big Ben's little brother" designed by Lord Grimthorpe, probably as the test-run for London's famous timepiece. While there, watch out for the ghost of Mrs. Medley, wife of the first bishop, John Medley. She's often seen crossing the lawn to enter the Cathedral by the west door.

The University of New Brunswick (located at the end of University Avenue on a hill overlooking the city), is ancient by Canadian standards. Established in 1783, when it was called the College of New Brunswick, it later became known as Kings College until 1859, when it became the University of New Brunswick. Today the campus also includes St. Thomas University, a small but steadily growing institution. Site of many firsts, the University of New Brunswick campus had the first astronomical observatory (the Brydon Jack Observatory) in Canada. The building is now an observatory museum called The Brydon Jack Museum. The university initiated the first engineering school in Canada and the second forestry school. With an active enrollment in the sciences and arts as well, the university has come a long way since the first two B.A. degrees were awarded in 1828. Enrollment today is approximately 8,000.

On Woodstock Road, surrounded by spacious lawns, you'll find Old Government House, built in 1828 as a residence for the province's lieutenant governors. The classic old Georgian building has housed many famous guests, for example, the Prince of Wales (later Edward VII) who stayed here in 1860 when he visited New Brunswick as a young man of 19. Dancing all night at one of the city's gaiest balls, he won the hearts of all the women. Unfortunately, now that Government House is headquarters for the RCMP, it is not generally open to the public.

John James Audubon stayed here two years later as the guest of the Governor and painted his famous Pine Finch on the grounds. (You can view it at the Legislative Library.)

A walking tour of Fredericton's historic homes is available at bookstores.

But for a true understanding of New Brunswick's background and history, visit Kings Landing, located about 23 miles west of Fredericton on the Trans-Canada Highway. Challenging the imagination of visitors, this reconstructed village—55 buildings including homes, inn, forge, store, church, school, and working farm—is designed to illustrate life in the central Saint John River Valley between 1790 and 1870. The winding country lanes, creaking wagons, old houses, and the smell of freshly baked bread will pull you back a century or more to when the sound of the motor car was unknown. The costumed staff will answer your questions, and the Kings Head Inn is a friendly spot to rest your feet and quench your thirst with a draft of cold beer or a sip of wine. The restaurant upstairs serves old-fashioned traveler's fare such as cold cuts and hot meat pie. Just around the corner in a barn, the King's Theatre offers some of the funniest "mellerdrama" you've ever witnessed.

PRACTICAL INFORMATION FOR FREDERICTON

HOW TO GET THERE. By air: Both *Air Canada* and *Eastern Provincial Airways* service Fredericton airport at Lincoln (5 miles from Fredericton), with connecting flights from most major airlines.

By car: Follow the Trans-Canada Hwy. from Québec; U.S. 95 and Trans-Canada Hwy. from Houlton, Maine; Hwy. 3 and Trans-Canada Hwy. from Calais, Maine; Trans-Canada from Nova Scotia.

By train: *Via Rail* has daily rail liner service to and from Halifax through Saint John and Moncton. At Moncton it makes connections with the *Ocean Limited* train which travels Halifax–Montréal.

By bus: *SMT* bus service within the province provides regional transportation. Most major bus companies in USA and Canada connect with SMT.

ACCOMMODATIONS. Hotels and motels in and around Fredericton are not luxurious but are adequate with friendly service. A 10% sales tax will be added to your bill. Rates are based on double occupancy as follows: *Expensive,* over $43; *Moderate,* $30–43; *Inexpensive,* under $30.

Most places accept the following major credit cards: American Express, MasterCard, and Visa; others may also be honored. Not all establishments accept credit cards, therefore we suggest you call for information.

The Diplomat Motor Hotel. *Expensive:* Pleasant rooms, many with balconies overlooking pool, good dining room, intimate indoor bar and popular pool bar.

Often patronized by Fredericton residents. Outdoor jazz café in summer. Phone 454-5584. Major credit cards.

Howard Johnson's Motor Lodge. *Expensive:* Rte. 2, Trans-Canada Hwy. Pleasant rooms, good dining area. Indoor court with pool and bar. Phone 472-0480. Major credit cards.

Keddy's Motor Inn. *Expensive:* Forest Hill at end of Princess Margaret Bridge. Pleasant rooms, lively lounge bar, dining room, pool, close to university. Phone 454-4461. Major credit cards.

The Lord Beaverbrook Hotel. *Expensive:* Popular pool bar, good main dining room and steakhouse. River Room bar draws civil servants, politicians, visiting VIPs at lunch and happy hour. Phone 455-3371. Major credit cards.

The Wandlyn Inn. *Expensive:* Prospect St. Pleasant rooms, good dining room, cozy bar. Close to three shopping malls, many restaurants, two theaters. Heated pool. Phone 452-8937. Major credit cards.

The Condor Motel. *Moderate–Expensive:* Woodstock Rd. W. Adequate rooms, small dining room, heated pool. Phone 455-5537. Major credit cards.

The Fort Nashwaak Motel. *Moderate–Expensive.* Homey motel with adequate rooms, small restaurant, three minutes from city center. Also has indoor pool. Phone 472-4411. Major credit cards.

The Fredericton Motor Inn. *Moderate.* Regent St. at the Trans-Canada Hwy. Phone 455-1430. Major credit cards. Excellent value. Nice rooms, good dining room, pleasant décor.

The Sequoia Motel. *Moderate.* Regent St. Better than average rooms, good small dining room, bar, pool, and sauna. Close to shopping centers, restaurants, and theater. Phone 455-9900. Major credit cards.

Fredericton Skyline Motel. *Inexpensive.* 502 Forest Hill Rd. 40 units, licensed dining room. Phone 455-6683.

Norfolk Motel. *Inexpensive.* On Rte. 2 just out of town. 20 units, a quiet and friendly place. Phone 472-3278

 HOW TO GET AROUND. By bus: Fare in city, 75¢. *Fredericton Transit* buses travel across the river to Nashwaaksis, Marysville, Barker's Point and New Maryland. Catch a Fredericton Transit bus by the Military Compound on Queen St. for Silverwood. (An Edmundston bus from the SMT terminal on Regent will take you there too as well as to Oromocto and Lincoln.)

By taxi: As many taxis do not have meters, you could end up sharing a cab with other people. Some meter cabs are available, however.

From the airport: A limousine service is provided to the Lord Beaverbrook Hotel.

 TOURIST INFORMATION. Tourist Office, City of Fredericton, telephone 452–9426. Provincial Tourist Information Centre, on Trans-Canada Hwy., open June to September, tel. 458–8331.

Province: Department of Tourism, 7th floor, Carleton Place, corner Carleton and Kings Sts., P.O. Box 12345, Fredericton. U.S. and Canadian residents call toll-free, 1–800–561–0123.

 RECOMMENDED READING. Fredericton was the home of the late Alden Nowlan, the award-winning poet and novelist. *Bread, Wine and Salt, Between Tears and Laughter,* and *I'm A Stranger Here Myself* are collections of his poems; his book of stories, *Miracle at Indian River,* and his novel *Various Persons Named Kevin O'Brien* offer the most penetrating view available of rural life in the Maritimes. Fredericton has always been a center for writers, from the early Loyalist poet Jonathan Odell to contemporary novelist Kent Thompson *(The Tenants Were Corrie & Tennie)* and a group of poets centered around UNB and *Fiddlehead* magazine. New Brunswick has been more given to poetry and less to fiction than Nova Scotia, but younger writers like David

Adam Richards *(Blood Ties, The Coming of Winter)* and Raymond Fraser *(The Black Horse Tavern)* may be changing that fact. A well-beloved writer of nonfiction is Stuart Trueman *(An Intimate History of New Brunswick, The Fascinating World of New Brunswick).* W.S. MacNutt has written histories of New Brunswick and of the Atlantic provinces generally. *History of Fredericton —the Last 200 Years* by W. Austin Squires gives a readable "human" history of the capital city. Another historian of note is A.F. Bailey *(Culture and Nationality)* who is also a poet *(Thanks for a Drowned Island). New Brunswick Inside Out* by Colleen Thompson is an invaluable handbook for visitors to the province and to Fredericton.

 CITY PARKS. Three hundred acres of wooded land at *Odell Park* off Waggoner's La. Nature trails, picnic tables with barbecue pits and wood, play equipment, duck pond, and deer enclosure. *Wilmot Park* on Woodstock Rd.—picnic tables, wading pool, playground, free tennis courts.

 THE ARTS. Fredericton is a small city (population about 46,000) and its cultural facilities are not extensive, although they are of nationally recognized quality.

The Beaverbrook Art Gallery, in fact, is internationally known, with a collection of works by Turner, Krieghoff, Gainsborough, Dali, the Group of Seven, plus several rotating exhibits.

The Playhouse is the home of *Theatre New Brunswick,* which brings professional live theater to the city. TNB also tours the province.

The *York Sunbury Historical Museum and Officers Square* is the city's main museum. It is part of a downtown historical restoration and features local and military history.

 SHOPPING. New Brunswick is famous for crafts, and Fredericton has many studios and artisans' sales rooms. *Aitkens Pewter,* 81 Regent St., and *Pewtercraft,* 582 Brunswick St., offer beautiful pewter hollowware, goblets, belt buckles, jewelry and authentic reproductions of ancient folk dishes. *Shades of Light Studio and Gift Shop* on Regent St. features stained glass and other local crafts.

The Regent Craft Gallery, 71 Regent St.; wide variety of quality handcrafts of local artists.

The *Boyce Country Market* on George St. operates every Saturday morning offering everything from crafts to home baked doughnuts and breakfast at Goofy Roofy's. An outdoor café, operating out of the market in the summer (in winter it goes indoors), it is an incredible experience as politicians, scholars, actors, musicians and writers come in to partake of Roofy's special omelets.

An elaborate booklet describing crafts in New Brunswick and listing all craftspeople is available from various tourist bureaus and offices.

 DINING OUT. Restaurants in Fredericton have improved a lot in recent years. A few are very good. Price categories are as follows: *Expensive,* over $16; *Moderate,* $11–16; *Inexpensive,* under $11. A 10% provincial tax will be added. Drinks and tip are not included.

Most places accept the following major credit cards: American Express, MasterCard, and Visa; others may also be honored. Not all establishments accept credit cards, therefore we suggest you call for information.

The Coffeemill. *Expensive.* Located in Fredericton shopping mall on Prospect St. Good seafood and generally good food. Phone 454-6376. Major credit cards.

Eighty-Eight Ferry. *Expensive.* 88 Ferry St. Charming old home decor. Excellent food. Friendly owners; drinks served in the garden. Highly recommended. Phone 472-1988. Major credit cards.

The Maverick Room. *Expensive.* Located in basement of Lord Beaverbrook Hotel and open only at night (from 6 P.M.), specializes in steak. The spareribs are excellent, the atmosphere dim, and the wines marked up. Phone 455-3371. Major credit cards.

The Terrace Room, Lord Beaverbrook Hotel. *Expensive.* Specializes in New Brunswick's own foods, like salmon, fiddleheads (New Brunswick's vegetable specialty), and shellfish including Buctouche oysters. Phone 455-3371. Major credit cards.

Victoria and Albert. *Expensive.* Seafood and steaks in Victorian England décor. Phone 455–2524. Major credit cards.

La Vie En Rose. *Moderate.* Old-world café specializing in tempting desserts and exotic coffees.

Mei's Chinese Restaurant. *Moderate.* 74 Regent St., 455–4733; Excellent varieties of Chinese food, moderate prices, understated, comfortable decor. Small.

Pat's Gourmet. *Moderate.* Lower St. Mary's. Excellent Asian food of all persuasions. Phone 472-0992. Major credit cards.

Bar B Q Barn. *Inexpensive.* 540 Queen St. Ribs, fish and chips, and fried scallops. A family spot.

The Luna Steak House. *Inexpensive.* (Soon to be re-named but still to be located on premises of Luna Pizza.) 168 Dundonald St., 455–4020. Leans to Greek style cuisine; brochettes of chicken especially good; great garlic bread.

Ming Restaurant. *Inexpensive.* 1185 Smythe St., good variety of Chinese and Canadian food, excellent for family eating, moderate, pleasant.

NIGHTLIFE. In Fredericton, the most popular spots are the *River Room* at the Lord Beaverbrook Hotel where they feature folksingers; private clubs and discos such as *The Cosmo,* where you have to be signed in at the door. *The Chestnut Inn* has dining and live bands. The *Poacher's Lounge* at the Diplomat Motel on Woodstock Rd. is popular. So is *Hilltop* on Prospect St., a publike spot. The *Riverview Arms,* Lincoln Rd., and the *Rolling Keg* on King St. are taverns serving steaks and featuring loud music.

The Saint John River Valley

At Woodstock, the alternate route to Fredericton (Route 105 on the other side of the Saint John River) takes you through typical small communities over an uncrowded road. It's easy to cross back to the Trans-Canada Highway at Mactaquac where the road leads over the dam. Since the building of the hydroelectric dam over the river, the valley has changed even as far away as Woodstock. While many of the Saint John River islands have disappeared, the area of the headpond has become quite lovely. A provincial park has been established at Mactaquac, probably the most comprehensive in all of New Brunswick. Visitors can enjoy everything from golfing on the 18-hole professional course to swimming, hiking and sailing. The campground is so popular that cars line up, sometimes all night, to claim the first empty camp lot in the morning. Your best bet is to get there early. There are 300 campsites, supervised recreation, two beaches, two marinas, as well as a licensed lodge with dining room. There's an Antique Arms Museum featuring antique firearms, trout fishing pond, and horseback riding nearby. If Mactaquac campsites are full, there are several other good campgrounds in the area.

Load your camera for Hartland. Here you'll find the longest covered bridge in the world—1,282 feet in length. Many of New Brunswick's covered bridges have been destroyed in recent years but the Department of Highways is now seeking to protect the 78 or so that still exist.

Woodstock, population 5,068, named for a novel by Sir Walter Scott, is also called the "hospitality town." It was an axiom in the old days that "no traveller, known or unknown, shall pass through the community without sharing its hospitality." That tradition remains strong today. You'll experience it especially at the annual Old Home Week celebrations in July when most of the Saint John River Valley residents participate.

There is a 9-hole golf course and during the summer months a farmers' market is held on Fridays at the Stewart parking lot where homemade foods may be purchased. Harness racing takes place at Connell Park.

The Old Courthouse (c. 1833) has been carefully restored by an interested community . . . it's been a coaching stop, a social hall, a political meeting place, and the seat of justice for the area. The guides have many tales to tell of famous trials held here.

Just below Woodstock at Meductic, young John Gyles, 9-year-old son of a New England judge, was held captive by the Maliceets for 6 years. His diary, reconstructed by New Brunswick writer Stuart Trueman, makes interesting historical reading.

There are two roads from Fredericton to Saint John. Route 7 is straight and dull for its 68 miles. The other, Route 102, leads along the Saint John River through some of the province's loveliest country. At Oromocto, the site of Canadian Armed Forces Base Camp Gagetown, largest military base in Canada, there's a reconstruction of Fort Hughes, an 1871 blockhouse which stands on the bank of the Oromocto River, and a fine military museum. You'll also find there a shopping mall and a beautifully laid out town, often called Canada's model town.

Along the river you'll notice small car ferries—from Jemseg to Upper Gagetown, Crystal Beach to Westfield, Clifton to Gondola Point, Gagetown to Lower Jemseg, Evandale to Hatfield Point, and Hampstead to Wickham. These cable-ferries are free, will take trailers and pickup campers, and provide you with a little respite from driving or a chance to look at the country on the other side. Grand Lake, for instance, offers camping in a provincial park, with freshwater swimming off sandy beaches.

Closer to Saint John, the Evandale ferry takes you to Belleisle Bay and the Kingston Peninsula—a lovely landscape. At Gagetown, the Steamers Stop Inn provides pleasant dining over the river and rents six rooms.

At Gagetown, stop and have a look at the Queens County Museum, the former home of Sir Leonard Tilley, one of the Fathers of Confederation. While there, stop in at the Loomcrofters, one of Canada's better suppliers of handwoven goods. It's located in a 200-year-old blockhouse. The area is known for its many craftsmen.

Canada's Oldest City

Saint John is old . . . the oldest incorporated city in Canada, with the special weatherbeaten quality of any port city. When Champlain and de Monts landed here in 1604 on St. John the Baptist Day, it must have appeared a primitive spot. But not so primitive as it seemed to the three thousand Loyalists who poured off a ship one May morning in 1785 to find nothing but rocks and forests for shelter. Babies were born in windswept tents that first chill winter as their parents fought to stay alive. But they were a tenacious lot and, by the following year, most had built snug little homes, oddly furnished perhaps, with silver and crystal, damask cloths and lean-to beds. From those beginnings Saint

John has emerged as a thriving industrial and port city, a tribute to its hardy Loyalist forebears. A recent face-lift and a new harborfront development have improved its appearance, and its history is fascinating.

Fiercely loyal to the British Crown, the early residents even laid out King Square in the design of the old Union Jack. Each year in July, a reenactment of the Landing of the Loyalists is held during the Loyalist Day celebrations. A costumed city joins in a colorful event that is the envy of many other communities.

Saint John (the spelling is never abbreviated) has the advantage of a year-round harbor. Ships from all over the world dock here, continually stimulating the economy. Among the outstanding enterprises are those run by the Irving family, descendants of a New Brunswick industrialist, K.C. Irving, who established the Irving pulp mill, the Irving Oil refinery, and a steel and drydock industry.

EXPLORING SAINT JOHN

Urban renewal is on the scene and the old face of Saint John is changing. The Saint John Harbour Bridge is the most conspicuous of the new developments as it spirals into the city in a modern way. But a walk along its historic streets (maps available at the Tourist Bureau on Hazen Street) guarantees you a charming picture of the old city.

Start at the Old Courthouse (1830) and inspect its famous spiral staircase. Built of 100 tons of unsupported stone ascending for three storeys, it is of special interest to architects and engineers.

Walk around the corner, then cross the street and walk down through the old Burying Ground where the first Loyalist settlers are buried. At adjacent King Square, you'll find a strange mass which looks like a piece of meteorite. It is actually a great lump of melted stock from a hardware store across the street which was demolished in Saint John's Great Fire of 1877, when 115 buildings were destroyed.

Just a few blocks along Charlotte Street, you'll come to the low stone walls of Trinity Church, dating back to 1877 when it was rebuilt after the fire. Inside the building over its west door, note the coat-of-arms, a symbol rescued from the council chamber of the Colony at Massachusetts Bay. The coat-of-arms was deemed a worthy relic and set in its place of honor in the church.

Walk down toward the harbor by way of Princess Street, site of an extensive restoration of historic buildings, and you'll come to a most intriguing building. Located on the corner of Princess and Prince William, it's commonly called Chubb's Corner. All around the cornices of the building you'll see carved stone heads grinning at you. They seem to represent an objection to the city council of the day. George Chubb, who commissioned them, had the carver, Mr. McAvity, portray Mr. Chubb, the mayor and members of the Common Council of 1878 in this way. Along the lower part of the building he has delicately carved flowers, fruits, vines, and the faces of the Chubb children. One could stand here fascinated for hours.

Amble down the street, past Market Slip where the Loyalists landed, to Barbour's General Store. This fully stocked 19th-century store was presented to the city as a Centennial project by the Barbour Company of Saint John. Its interior is redolent of smells of the past: tobacco, pickles, smoked fish, peppermint sticks and, on the floor, a big bag of dulse, that tangy edible seaweed New Brunswickers love to chew. No admission charge and the dulse is free. Next to Barbour's is the Little Red School House, a restoration of an 1800's school. Stroll along the boardwalk, visit the pub in the ship, and inspect the posh boutiques in Market Square; then walk up Union Street. At the corner of Union and Germain stands a lovely old Loyalist house. Built in 1810 by Daniel David Merritt, a wealthy Loyalist merchant, the house retains all its past beauty with authentic period furniture and eight fireplaces. Five generations of Merritts have lived there.

But visitors most enjoy the Old City Market. Built in 1876, it runs the full block from Germain to Charlotte. Here's where you'll find red, fresh-cooked lobster, great cheeses, more dulse and the friendly chatter of the marketplace.

Try to visit the New Brunswick Museum—the first in Canada and still recognized as one of the best of its size. You'll see the figurehead from the bad luck ship built in Saint John's famous shipyards—a ship which is said to have killed a man on every voyage.

Along with native animals displayed in natural surroundings, there are costumes, artifacts, even a collection of dolls, and an impressive art gallery to keep you interested for at least an afternoon.

Not far away, you'll note the Martello Tower, high on a hill, built in 1812 as a precaution against American attack. Costumed guides show you its walls 8 feet thick, and pose willingly for pictures. The view from the top of the tower is magnificent as is the one from Fort Howe, a reconstructed fortress on a cliff overlooking the harbor. Reached via a winding road, it is originally the site of Fort LaTour, a French stronghold resolutely defended by Madame LaTour from her absent husband's fur-trading rival. Finally surrendering on the condition that the lives of her men would be spared, the unfortunate woman was betrayed and forced to watch them all put to death. She died shortly thereafter—of a broken heart, it is said . . . a fate befitting her former profession as star of the Paris stage.

The celebrated Reversing Falls Rapids, now somewhat tarnished by the effluent of a pulp mill on its banks, are actually a series of rapids and whirlpools at which, twice a day, the Fundy Tides attempt to push the river water back upstream. When the tide flow weakens and ebbs, the river once again pours out over the rock ledges, and the rapids appear to reverse themselves. Downstream from the rapids is the Wharf Museum featuring marine exhibits.

Saint John also has a small zoo, located at Rockwood Park and year-round harness racing, golf, tennis, and several beaches in the area.

There are a number of side trips from Saint John. One of them along the coastal Route 111 takes you to St. Martins, a delightful seaside village.

Following Route 1 NE from Saint John, you pass the engaging dairy town of Sussex, through rolling countryside to Penobsquis, where you may turn off to Fundy National Park, 80 square miles of sea-conditioned playground skirting the Bay of Fundy.

The coast road up to Moncton takes you over covered bridges and along rocky coasts. At Hopewell Cape, you'll find the famous giant flowerpot, one of many rock formations carved by the action of the Fundy tides.

New River Beach Provincial Park is located right on the southern Fundy shore where rolling breakers come roaring in. New Brunswickers swim in it but—a word to the wise—the Fundy water is usually chilly.

The peaceful hideaway fishing villages of Maces Bay, Dipper Harbour, and Chance Harbour are still much the same as they have been for centuries but residents fear a change since the advent of the nuclear reactor plant at nearby Point Lepreau. If you drive into the area, you'll find a great little tea room, The Fundy Haven, right on the cliffs overlooking the bay. Marvelous, inexpensive seafood!

PRACTICAL INFORMATION FOR SAINT JOHN

HOW TO GET THERE. By air: Both *Air Canada* and *Eastern Provincial Airways* make connections with most major airlines. Airport 10 miles east of city.

By car: From Nova Scotia by ferry from Digby; by road from Nova Scotia through Moncton via Rte. 1, from Fredericton via Rte. 7, from Calais, Me. via Rte. 1.

By train: *Via Rail* has service daily to Fredericton, Moncton, and Halifax. Connections for Montréal can be made at Moncton.

By bus: SMT bus service within the province provides regional transportation. Most major bus companies in USA and Canada connect with SMT.

ACCOMMODATIONS. In the summer, tourist accommodations tend to be at a premium in Saint John so it is best to reserve ahead to ensure a place to stay. Price categories are the same as for Fredericton. Rates are based on double-occupancy as follows: *Expensive,* over $43; *Moderate,* $30–43; *Inexpensive,* under $30.

Most places accept the following major credit cards: American Express, MasterCard, and Visa; others may also be honored. Not all establishments accept credit cards, therefore we suggest you call for information.

The Delta Brunswick Inn. *Expensive.* New downtown hotel atop Brunswick Sq. Dining, bar, banquet and convention facilities. Phone 648–1981. Major credit cards.

Hilton. *Expensive.* Newest part of Market Square overlooking harbor. Mammoth convention facilities, including a Medieval Great Hall. Adjoining shops, restaurants, bars, library. Phone 1–800–361–6140.

Holiday Inn. *Expensive.* Haymarket Sq. Dining room, heated pool. Phone 657–3610. Major credit cards.

Howard Johnson Motor Lodge. *Expensive.* At Chesley Pl. Caters to families. Has special facilities for children. Phone 642–2622. Major credit cards.

Keddy's Motor Inn. *Expensive.* Corner Portland and Main Sts. Heated pool, nice rooms, bar, dining room, and steakhouse. Phone 657–7320. Major credit cards.

Park Plaza Motel. *Moderate.* 607 Rothesay Ave. Dining room and bar. Phone 633–4100. Major credit cards.

Bonanza Motel. *Inexpensive.* 594 Rothesay Ave. Adequate rooms, no dining facilities. Phone 633–1710. MasterCard and Visa.

Fundy View Guest Home. *Inexpensive.* 968 Manawaqonish Rd., in Saint John.

Watt's Tourist Home. *Inexpensive.* 765 Manawagonish Rd., in Saint John West. 2 rooms. No dining facilities. Phone 672–2327.

HOW TO GET AROUND. Airport limousine: Between airport and Delta or Hilton Holiday Inn. $5.

Taxi: individual fares.

Bus: Good community service.

City Guide: Available at Tourist Info. Center, Reversing Falls and at Sydney St. Tourist Bureau.

TOURIST INFORMATION. City: Tourist Bureau, 20 Hazen Ave., telephone 658–2855. Reversing Falls, telephone 672–1198.

SPECIAL INTEREST TOURS. Tours of the University of New Brunswick, Saint John, Moosehead, and Olands breweries can be arranged. Also available: Harbour Tours, and three great walking tours of the city—the Loyalist Trail, Prince William's Walk, and Victorian Stroll. Inquire at Tourist Bureau.

 CITY PARKS. *Rockwood Park,* within the city limits, is an excellent place for kids and adults alike. It surrounds several lakes, has a "children's farm" as well as Atlantic Canada's only exotic zoo, which includes many animals on the endangered species list. Also golf, swimming, and other facilities.

 MUSEUMS. Saint John has a new art gallery and a number of interesting museums.

The *New Brunswick Museum* is the province's largest and also Canada's first established museum. Its galleries of Canadiana, marine display, Loyalist era artifacts, and other exhibits truly evoke early New Brunswick.

Loyalist House, a museum built in 1810, is still in operation.

Barbour's General Store, at Market Slip, is a completely restored old country store that once served farmers in the St. John River Valley.

The *Carlton Martello Tower,* built for the War of 1812, displays weapons, uniforms, and historical objects.

 SHOPPING. As in the rest of the province, it's the little antique stores and craftshops that provide the best shopping. You'll find them sprinkled around the downtown area. Brunswick Square and Market Square in new harbourfront development offer airy shopping with many top quality boutiques. And there's the Old City Market between Charlotte and Germain Streets. It bustles with activity six days a week, and always stocks delicious local specialties such as maple syrup and fresh lobsters.

 DINING OUT. Several good, new restaurants of gourmet caliber have popped up in recent years. Try the ones specializing in seafood. Price categories per person are as follows: *Expensive,* over $16; *Moderate,* $11–16; *Inexpensive,* under $11. Drinks, tax, and tip are not included.

Most places accept the following major credit cards: American Express, MasterCard, and Visa; others may also be honored. Not all establishments accept credit cards, therefore we suggest you call for information.

Turn of the Tide. *Expensive.* In The Hilton Hotel beside Market Square. Elegant dining overlooking the Saint John Harbour. Phone 693–8484. Major credit cards.

The House of Chan. *Moderate–Expensive.* Hilyard Place (near Keddy's and Howard Johnson's). Great luncheon buffet. Good Chinese and Canadian dishes. Lobster and steak specialties. Major credit cards. Phone 693–7777.

Top of the Town. *Moderate–Expensive.* The steakhouse at the top of the new Keddy's Motor Inn has a warm atmosphere and a fabulous view of the city. Good steak and service. Phone 657–7320. Major credit cards.

The Continental. *Moderate.* Level III, Historical Properties, Market Square. European cuisine with pizzaz, served on china and silver. Major credit cards. Phone 642–1157.

Nick's Restaurant. *Inexpensive.* 31 City Rd. Plain-food restaurant.

Grannan's. *Inexpensive.* Market Square. Spills out over sidewalk in summer. Terrific desserts. Nice bar. Raw oyster bar. Phone 642–2225. Major credit cards.

NIGHT LIFE. There are no nightclubs in Saint John but a few places offer entertainment or dancing. *The Mediterranean,* located on Rothesay Ave., is a place where you can dine, dance and drink, usually to hard rock.

The Image at the Holiday Inn is a mirrored discothèque with dancing, sometimes country folksingers.

Sullivan's, in the Delta Hotel, is a piano lounge.

The Squire's Tap, Holiday Inn, quiet friendly bar sometimes featuring singers.

Grannan's, Market Square, Good gathering place in nautical atmosphere.

Tugboat Ocean Hawk II, for oysters, drinks, and socializing. Market Square.

1880 Club, in a restored 19th-century building. Features dancing, dining, and a games room.

EXPLORING THE ACADIAN SHORE

From the Nova Scotian border at Aulac, along New Brunswick's northern shore, across the top of the province to Charlo, the Acadians settled on what is now known as the Acadian region.

Moncton

The city of Moncton has become the unofficial capital of Acadia and much of its history is interwoven with that of the Acadian people. Moncton, settled by Dutch and German families from Pennsylvania, was originally called Petitcodiac by the Indians, meaning the "river that bends like a bow." When the deeply religious Acadians came along they built a chapel and for a while the area was known as La Chapelle. Later it became Le Coude or The Elbow because the river bends so sharply here. Even to this day, one sometimes hears it called "The Bend."

In 1755, Lt. Colonel Robert Monckton finally captured nearby Fort Beausejour, bringing to an end the French occupation of the area. Moncton took his name, dropping the "K" over the years. After the Expulsion, a number of Acadians returned to areas around Moncton, settling most noticeably in Cocagne, Shediac and Grand Digue. Today in Moncton names like Belliveau, Blanchard, and Gaudet are mixed with Steeves (formerly Stief), Trites (Trietz), and Lutes (Lutz).

Once famous for shipbuilding, Moncton gradually became the province's main railway center and is now known as the "hub of the Maritimes" because all railroads seem to lead there. It is a natural center for sales and distribution throughout the Maritimes. A commercial town, its skyline has changed in recent years as economic activity increased.

The population is almost evenly divided between Catholics and Protestants, and churches dot the landscape. It is unfortunate that few historic buildings remain to tell the tale of Moncton's early days. The New Brunswick telephone tower is now the most striking edifice on the horizon and the eleven-storey "Assumption Place" with its adjoining Beausejour Hotel is the newest and most impressive addition to the skyline.

Built on the flat, marshy land on the banks of the muddy Petitcodiac, Moncton was built by railroadmen, sturdy, solid and enduring, but hardly of architectural consequence.

Walk out King Street and around to Mountain Road and you'll find, on Stedman Street, the oldest building in Moncton, a delightful little hall called the Free Meeting House, founded in 1821 by a group who believed in a common place of worship for the residents. Even the little graveyard beside it has been preserved. It has been the home of every denomination in the city, including Protestant, Roman Catholic, and Jewish.

Don't be startled by what you see next! The square modern building across the street has a strange old-fashioned entrance, completely out of keeping with the local architecture. But it happens to be the façade of the original town hall and it has been incorporated into the design of the new Moncton Civic Museum. Once inside the museum, railway enthusiasts and history buffs will delight in the steam engine mementos. And the curator will let you ring the huge cast iron bell. The museum has taken a forward step toward preserving some of the area's past.

One of Moncton's special attractions is the famous Tidal Bore. Viewed best from Boreview Park on Main Street, this low wall of water, which comes in right on time as befits any railroad town, is caused by the tide surging through the narrow entrance of the Petitcodiac River. As it rolls up the river it fills the wide muddy trench from bank to bank.

Moncton's Magnetic Hill—a rare optical illusion—must be seen to be believed. Drive down the hill to the white post. Turn off your motor, but put the car in neutral. As you gaze in astonishment at the steep hill behind you, your car will back up in such a hurry that you may be tempted to use your brake.

At Centennial Park, once more the steam engine reigns supreme. Crawl right up into the cab of the locomotive which is permanently on display there, and pretend your name is Casey Jones.

A drive through the spacious and modern campus of the University of Moncton will take you to the door of the Acadian Museum where you'll find artifacts and historical displays which present a clear picture of what life was all about in the days of the early Acadian settler. The ancient tools and primitive utensils are there along with the interiors of barns, schools and houses, all lovingly and beautifully reproduced.

Following the shore roads from Aulac to Moncton, you'll also follow the Trans-Canada Highway. On the way you'll pass the site of Fort Beausejour, a national historic site. Built by the French in 1751, and captured by the English in 1755, it was originally known as Fort Cumberland—the scene of the final battle for English supremacy in this region.

Sackville, a small university town, with the only harness shop in North America still producing handmade horse collars (and visitors welcome), is worth a short detour to the southeast from Moncton. Home of Mount Allison University, an arts oriented institution, Sackville is reminiscent of many old English villages. Don't miss the Owens Art Gallery on campus. It's open to the public.

Shediac

From Moncton it's only 20 miles to the town of Shediac, home of King Lobster, where each July the Shediac Lobster Festival takes place. The beaches, especially at the provincial park, are long, fine-sanded, and shallow, with water warmer than anywhere else on the coast.

Fishing is the major industry and you can find fresh lobster, cooked or uncooked, at Paturel's Fish Processing Plant; the nearby *Shore House,* run by Paturel's, offers fresh seafood. At Shediac, you can also find excellent and reasonably priced seafood at the *Fishermen's Paradise* just outside town at the Hotel Shediac, and fine dining at *Chez Francoise* in the old Tait Mansion. There are also several very good beaches in the area.

Traveling up the shore towards Bathurst you'll pass through the fishing villages of Cocagne, scene of international hydroplane races in the summer and the Acadian Bazaar, usually in August; Buctouche, noted for the quality of its oysters; Richibucto and Rexton (the latter the birthplace of Andrew Bonar Law, first and only prime minister of Britain to be born outside the British Isles). At Richibucto there's a new museum of local history covering the storied Richibucto River and Kent County.

Kouchibouquac National Park, recently developed, has camping facilities and a marvelous beach, with long miles of sandbar washed by the warm waters of the Northumberland Strait. It also has excellent recreational facilities: canoeing, hiking, and others. Check with the park superintendent about local lobster suppers.

In 1959, 35 fishermen were drowned in a sudden squall off Point Escuminac in one of New Brunswick's worst fishing disasters. A monument created by Claude Roussel, one of the province's foremost artists, has been erected on the shore. It depicts three fishermen starkly outlined against the sea behind them.

Chatham and Newcastle

Chatham and Newcastle, both early lumbering towns, are the exceptions on this Acadian coast, largely retaining the characteristics of the Irish, Scottish, and English immigrants who settled there. Anyone who lives along the Miramichi River is known as a "Miramichier" and proud of it. It's a region of folklore and superstition, of ballads and boisterousness, nourished by pride of ancestry. The hospitality is renowned and the friendly people still wave as you drive by.

Chatham, once a great shipbuilding area, was the home of Joseph and Henry Cunard, who came from Nova Scotia to build wooden ships. At one time the Cunards employed almost everybody, if not in the shipyards, then in the forests, cutting masts for the great ships. Joseph Cunard, flamboyant and wealthy, drove a coach-and-four, ordered peacocks for his lawns, and sent riders ahead to spread the word of his coming whenever he returned from his frequent visits to England. When the coming of the steam engine ruined his business, the area took a long time to regain its former prosperity. The building of a jet training school and air base in the region infused new life into the economy and today Chatham is thriving once again. The history of the area is related through exhibits at the Miramichi Natural History Museum. Loggie House is a late Victorian, Second Empire-style home furnished in antiques from the period. It functions as a cultural center in winter and is open to visitors in summer.

Max Aitken, the son of a poor Presbyterian minister, and later Lord Beaverbrook (a name he took from a brook running near his home), lived his boyhood years in Newcastle. Eventually a multimillionaire, owner of the London *Daily Express,* confidante of kings and politicians, and at one time minister of aircraft production in Churchill's wartime cabinet, Beaverbrook traveled a long way from his early beginnings in New Brunswick. One of his many bequests to Newcastle was his childhood home, the Old Manse, now a functioning library. He encouraged its custodian, the late Dr. Louise Manny, to record the hundreds of folksongs and "come all ye's" of the area and helped her set up an annual folksinging festival which takes place in July every year. His ashes are held in the bottom of his statue in the middle of the town square.

Outside Chatham on Route 11 is the MacDonald Farm, a major restoration of an 1830's working farm.

Three miles west of Newcastle is the Enclosure, the site of the graves of the first settlers, part of a lovely provincial park, largely donated to the province by Lord Beaverbrook.

The shortest route from Newcastle to Bathurst is the inland Route 8 but this route has little of interest.

The road along the shore is more rewarding. You'll pass through small communities with intriguing names such as Burnt Church, named for an ancient English raid; and Tracadie, once a leper colony. The Tracadie Museum, located in the Town Hall, commemorates this part of Tracadie's past. There is a new museum of local history at Tabusintac and a new marine museum at Shippagan, which is a major provincial facility. It depicts the history of the fishing industry and portrays the lives of the area's fishermen. Shippagan, typical of the north shore fishing villages, offers superb opportunities for photographers. This entire shore has fine beaches. You might want to take the free ferry to Miscou Island, where you can beachcomb along deserted beaches. Accommodations there consist of campgrounds and cabins.

Caraquet

Caraquet, a lively Acadian town, is prosperous and busy. You'll find a wooden shipbuilding factory, fish and crab packing plants, and a market on the wharf peddling fish and shellfish fresh from the boats at very good prices.

Down by the Fisheries School, the Acadian Museum perched over the water offers an interesting and informative encounter with area history. You'll even find a small handicraft shop tucked in one corner where you can pick up a hooked rug or a woven napkin for a reasonable price.

West of Caraquet is the Acadian Village, a restoration of 30 buildings, which depicts the Acadian lifestyle in New Brunswick between 1780 and 1880. Also, if you're in Caraquet around mid-August, it's worth staying for the Acadian Festival, a cultural event featuring the Blessing of the Fleet, Acadian folksinging, L'Acadie en fête, and various other unique celebrations. Caraquet is also the province's most popular port for deepsea sport fishing, especially for the bluefin tuna.

From Caraquet to Bathurst the seacoast reminds one of France's Brittany coast, and the design of the occasional house or barn along the way heightens that impression. As you drive along Route 11, the rocky shores of the Gaspé across the Chaleur Bay are clearly visible; at Pokeshaw, notice the curious flat-topped rock. Its dead trees are usually covered with birds, giving it the name "Bird Island."

Bathurst to Dalhousie

Bathurst (population 17,000) has recently found its wealth in mining. Nearby discoveries of iron, lead, and zinc have stimulated industries of all kinds. Always a happy town, it pleased both Jacques Cartier when he visited here in 1534 and also Champlain when he bartered for clothes right off the Indians' backs during his business trip. A century later another tourist from France, Nicholas Denys, liked it so well he settled at the mouth of the Nipisiquit River on Bathurst Bay where he ran a fish and fur-trading business as well as a mill. Bathurst has been a busy town ever since.

In colonial days, the area was known as St. Peters, but religion evidently yielded to politics when, in 1826, the town became Bathurst, after the Earl of Bathurst who was then Colonial Secretary.

As friendly and hospitable a town as it is busy, Bathurst has a special charm. Perhaps it comes from a happy blending of French and English, although the population breakdown always depends on the background of the person asked—English-speaking people say it's 60/40 English and the French say it's 60/40 French. Bathurst also has a war museum operated by the Royal Canadian Legion.

The beach at Youghall, where you'll find a provincial park and camp grounds, winds all the way around Bathurst Bay and the water in summer is warm. That's why Cartier named it *Baie de Chaleur* (Bay of Warmth).

One of the most popular pasttimes in the area is eating lobster on the beach. On a clear night, as you stare out to sea, you might see the phantom ship. All along the Bay of Chaleur from Bathurst to Campbellton, the ship has been sighted. No satisfactory explanation for this phenomenon has been given but descriptions have been pretty much the same: a burning sailing ship, sometimes with sailors scurrying about the flaming rigging; finally the ship disappears, still aglow, beneath the waves. Some say it's the ghost of a French ship lost in the Battle of the Restigouche; others claim it's a reflection of heat waves. Whatever it is, many have sighted it during the years—even a Sunday school teacher and his whole class. So keep your eyes on the Bay of Chaleur. You, too, might see the phantom ship!

Just west of Bathurst on Route 11, there's an Acadian crafts center attached to La Fine Grobe restaurant. At Belledune there's a huge smelter which processes the ores from the mineral fields and looks startlingly futuristic. You'll travel along Jacquet River, where a charming provincial park is situated right on the shore. At Eel River Crossing, you can join right in with your shovel to dig some of the finest clams in the world. Just across the long stretch of sand bar, the local Indians run a small handcraft shop.

In Dalhousie and Campbellton, Scottish and Irish settlers mingled with the Acadians to settle the area. Just as in the Newcastle/Chatham district, it's sometimes hard to pick out the accent. Is it French or Irish?

Dalhousie, a year-round port, is also the home of one of the province's largest industries, the newsprint mill of the New Brunswick International Paper Company. Large ocean-going ships stop here on their way to Europe. The Chaleur History Museum on Adelaide Street features local history of the area.

Campbellton

Campbellton (population about 10,422) retains the charm of a pioneer town. Nestling at the foot of Sugarloaf, a perfectly rounded mountain, it is reminiscent of lumbermen, river drives, and seagoing vessels. Still the headquarters for fishing outfitters for the famous salmon rivers of the region, the town is fast forging ahead into modernity. The new Restigouche Gallery is a major provincial exhibition center. The theater in the modern high school/trade school complex presents plays of professional quality. Theatre New Brunswick also brings its touring productions here where they are always well received.

The all-season Sugarloaf Provincial Park has an excellent ski hill and lodge. Newest winter sport wrinkle is an Alpine slide. Just across the river in Québec, Federal archeologists have been using a diving bell to bring up artifacts from the Battle of the Restigouche, the last naval engagement of the Seven Years' War fought off Campbellton in 1760. A summer salmon festival is held here from late June to early July.

Route 17, known locally as the Stuart Highway, cuts through the central forest where communities are sparse. The road, though narrow, is good, cutting across hills and valleys for 100 miles to the small town of St. Leonard.

PRACTICAL INFORMATION FOR

NEW BRUNSWICK

HOW TO GET THERE. By air: Airports serviced by *Eastern Provincial Airlines* and *Air Canada* at Moncton, Fredericton, and Saint John; EPA also flies to Charlo, near Dalhousie, from Moncton, Chatham and Montréal.

By car: By car ferry from Prince Edward Island, Trans-Canada Hwy. from Nova Scotia, Trans-Canada Hwy. from Québec, Interstate 95 to Houlton, Me., U.S. 1 to Calais, Me.

By train: Regular *Via Rail* passenger service from Moncton to Montréal and Halifax, with links via ferry to Prince Edward Island and Newfoundland. Also from Moncton, daily service to Saint John and Fredericton.

By bus: *SMT* within the province connecting with most major bus lines.

ACCOMMODATIONS. New Brunswick has a number of officially designated "Heritage Inns"—places built mostly in the last century and having some local historic significance. They have either antique china or furniture or some other quaint touch and they provide accommodations that vary from homey to elegant, sometimes in the inexpensive category. They are noted as Heritage Inns in the following listing.

Price categories are based on double-occupancy. *Expensive,* over $40; *Moderate,* $30–40; *Inexpensive,* under $30.

Most places accept the following major credit cards. American Express, MasterCard and Visa; others may also be honored. Not all establishments accept credit cards, therefore we suggest you call for information.

BATHURST. *Expensive:* **Keddy's Motor Inn.** Central. Dining room, bar, coffeeshop. Phone 546–6691; within the province 800–561–0040.

Expensive: **Atlantic Host Hotel.** Swimming pool, dining room. Phone 548-3335.

Moderate: **Danny's Motor Inn.** Comfortable and friendly. Good dining room and coffeeshop. Tennis courts on premises; beach nearby. Phone 548–6621.

Fundy Line Motel. Former seminary, now done up in sexy reds and shag rugs. Dining room. Phone 548–8803.

BUCTOUCHE. *Inexpensive:* **Hilltop Motel.** Rte. 11. Small but adequate. Phone 743–5003.

CAMPBELLTON. *Expensive:* **Howard Johnson Motor Lodge.** Rte. 11. Comfortable and friendly. Dining room. Phone 753–5063; within the province 800–654–2000.

Moderate–Expensive: **Wandlyn Motor Inn.** Comfortable units. Good dining room and coffeeshop. Small bar. Phone 753-7606; within the province 800–561–0000.

Moderate: **Fundy Line Motel.** Adequate units, excellent dining room (open only certain hours for breakfast and dinner). Phone 753-3395; within the province 800–561–7974.

CAMPOBELLO. *Moderate:* **Friar's Bay Motor Lodge.** 10 units, licensed dining room, near the sea. Phone 752-2056.

The Owen House. *Moderate.* Historic old home. Five rooms. Charming bed-and-breakfast. Open June–Oct. Phone 752-2977.

Inexpensive: **Ponderosa Motel and Restaurant.** Beach swimming. Dining room. Phone 752-2100.

CARAQUET. *Moderate:* **The Motel Savoie.** Comfortable and modern. Restaurant on premises. Phone 727–3485.

Motel du Village. Dining room and bar. Phone 732–2982.

Inexpensive: **Hotel Paulin.** A Heritage Inn. Old hotel, est. 1887, no pretensions, undergoing renovations, charming in off-beat other-century way. Dining room has a reputation for good, low-cost seafood. Phone 727–9981.

DALHOUSIE. *Moderate:* **Cedar Lodge Motel.** About 12 miles from Campbellton. Pleasant rooms, some of which overlook the Bay so you can watch for the ghost ship. Excellent dining room, small bar, and dance floor with band. Phone 684–3363.

DEER ISLAND. *Inexpensive:* **The 45th Parallel Motel and Tourist Home.** Restaurant open summer only. Phone 747–2231.

Hartford's Guest Home. Seasonal, 3 units. Situated at Leonardville. Phone 747–2284.

EDMUNDSTON. *Expensive:* **The Wandlyn Motor Inn.** Pool, good dining room, coffeeshop, bar. Phone 735–5525.

Moderate-Expensive: **Howard Johnson Motor Lodge.** Restaurant, licensed dining room, indoor pool. Phone 739–7321.

Moderate: **The Lynn Motel.** Central, coffeeshop. Phone 735–8851.

FUNDY NATIONAL PARK. *Moderate.* **Alpine Chalets.** Seasonal. Phone 887–2848.

Fundy Park Chalets. Seasonal. Good location within park. Phone 887–2808.

Fundy View Motel. Within park. Seasonal. Phone 887–2880.

Many accommodations available at Alma, at gates of Fundy National Park.

GAGETOWN. *Moderate:* **Steamer's Stop Inn.** A Heritage Inn. Seven rooms with a lovely view over the Saint John River. Decorated with steamboat antiques and memorabilia. Good dining room. Phone 488–2903.

GRAND FALLS. *Moderate–Expensive:* **The Pres-du-Lac.** Pleasant rooms, dining room; small bar, heated pool. Phone 473–1300.

GRAND MANAN. Grand Manan Island is a small and very personal place. Expect accommodations to be likewise. A government liquor store operates on the island.

Expensive: **The Marathon.** A Heritage Inn. Hundred-year-old hotel over-looking the ferry landing. Built by a sea captain. Rooms furnished with antique furniture. Heated pool, tennis. Headquarters for whale watching expeditions. Rates include breakfast and dinner. Phone 662–8144.

Moderate: **The Shore Crest Lodge.** A Heritage Inn. An old house by the sea. Homey inn, meals, heated pool and games room. Phone 662–3216.

Surfside Motel. With 25 units, the largest motel on the island. Phone 662–8156.

Inexpensive: **The Compass Rose.** A Heritage Inn. Charming old house by the sea, near ferry landing. Rates include breakfast. Phone 662–8570.

MONCTON. *Expensive:* **Hotel Beausejour.** Main St. The hotel is decorated in old Acadian theme with thick, luxurious carpeting on the floor, plenty of comfortable and attractive furniture. Pleasant bar off lobby, coffeeshop, two dining rooms, pool. Phone 854–4344 or 800–268–9143. Major credit cards.

Howard Johnson's Motor Lodge. Trans-Canada Hwy. Really lives up to the slogan "Your home away from home." Friendly, comfortable, dining room, nice bar, gorgeous pool. Great place for children. Phone 384–1050 or 800–654–2000.

Keddy's Brunswick Hotel. Highfield and Main Sts. Newly renovated. Dining room, lounge/bar, central. Phone 854-6340 or 800–561–0040.

The Park House Inn. Boreview Park. 434 Main St. New part preferred. Great view of bore; good, moderately priced breakfasts. Pool. Phone 382–1664 or 800–565–0201.

Wandlyn Motor Inn. Near Magnetic Hill off Trans-Canada Hwy. Rooms plain but comfortable; pool, good dining room, small bar. Phone 384–3554 or 800–561–0000.

Moderate: **Magnetic Hill Mini Motel.** Magnetic Hill. Coffeeshop, restaurant. Phone 384–3541.

Inexpensive–Moderate: **Hotel Canadiana.** A Heritage Inn in downtown Moncton. Has a fine antique collection, homey atmosphere. Phone 382–1054.

NEWCASTLE. *Expensive:* **The Wandlyn Motor Inn.** Pleasant dining room, sometimes fresh homemade doughnuts for breakfast. Phone 622–3870.

Wharf Inn. Restaurant and licensed dining room. Phone 622–0302.

Moderate: **Riverview Motel.** Overlooks Miramichi River. Phone 622–1727.

OROMOCTO. *Moderate–Expensive:* **The Oromocto Hotel.** Nice bar, good dining room. Phone 357–8424.

SACKVILLE. *Moderate:* **The Marshlands Inn.** A Heritage Inn with an im-pressive collection of 19th-century furniture. You'll enjoy a Marshlands special breakfast. Make reservations well in advance. Phone 536–0170.

Inexpensive. **A Different Drummer.** Bed and breakfast, charming proprie-tors, friendly atmosphere. Phone 536–1291.

SHEDIAC. *Moderate.* **Chez Francoise.** Rooms in old mansion. Some with balconies. Excellent restaurant. Phone 532–4233. *Inexpensive:* **Hotel Shediac.** A Heritage Inn. Grand old hotel of yesterday. Near the finest beaches in New Brunswick. Good seafood restaurant. Phone 532–4405.

SHIPPAGAN. *Moderate:* **Motel Shippagan.** Licensed dining room. Modern surroundings. Phone 336–2276.

ST. ANDREWS. *Expensive:* **Algonquin.** A venerable hotel and a local landmark, 193 rooms, pool, dining room, pub, dance hall, tennis courts. Modified American plan. Phone 529–8823 or 800–268–9411.

The Rossmount Inn. A Heritage Inn. Huge old home, excellent dining room, pool, and lots of crystal and antiques. Phone 529–3351.

Moderate–Expensive: **Tara Manor.** A Heritage Inn. Early American and French Provincial décor. Former home of Canadian politician C.D. Howe. Putting green, lavish bedrooms, coffeeshop. Specify inn or motel. Excellent dining room. Phone 529–3304.

Moderate: **Shiretown Inn.** A Heritage Inn. One of the oldest operating inns in Canada. Large, old, high-ceilinged rooms, dining room, bar, coffeeshop. Old English pub. Homemade bread. Phone 529–8877 or 800–387–3400.

ST. STEPHEN. *Expensive:* **Wandlyn Motor Inn.** Comfortable, good dining room. Phone 466–1814 or 800–561–0000.

Inexpensive: **Haun's Holiday Farm.** Farm vacation home. Run by young German-Canadian family. About 7 miles from St. Stephen. Help with farmwork or just relax, ride the horses, take a picnic lunch and hike. Phone 466–4938.

WOODSTOCK. *Expensive:* **The Wandlyn Motor Inn.** Good dining room, pool. Phone 328–8876 or 800–561–0000.

Inexpensive: **Cosy Cabins.** In town, dining room, pool, beach, studio of Woodstock Weavers. Phone 328–3344.

John Gyles Motor Inn. Trans-Canada Hwy. east. Great view of valley; restaurant, new units. Phone 328–2698.

Shirlee's Tourist Home. Three units, seasonal. Phone 328–6386.

Stiles Motel. In town, good food in tea room. Phone 328–6671.

HOSTELS. Hostels are located in Saint John, Fredericton, Moncton, Shediac, Tracadie, Caraquet, Bathurst, Campbellton, and Edmundston. All operate from 6 P.M. to 9 or 10 A.M., doors closing for the night around midnight—except in Moncton (11 P.M.), Shediac (11:30 P.M.), and Saint John (1 A.M.). Costs less than $5 a night except in Moncton, Fredericton and Saint John, where it is slightly higher. Meals are extra—breakfast, about $1, and some serve dinner early in the evening for under $2. Hostel provides bunk and foam mattress, usually dormstyle. Most have travel information. For details, write New Brunswick Hostel Association, R.R. 4, Douglas, New Brunswick. Telephone: (506) 453–4869 (9–5 P.M.), 472–1597 (evenings and weekends).

TELEPHONES. The telephone area code for all of New Brunswick is 506.

TOURIST INFORMATION. *Municipal Information Centres:* Belledune on Rte. 11, 552–5220; Bertrand on Rte. 11, 727–2126; Buctouche, 743–5719; Caraquet, 727 –6234; Clair, Main St., 992–2181; Dalhousie, Inch Arran Park, 684–5352; Edmundston, 739–8191; Eel River Crossing, 826–3086; Fredericton, 455–3092; Grand Anse, on Rte. 11, 732–5481; Grand Falls, Madawaska Rd., 473–4538; Hampton, Old King's County Jail, 832–3335; McAdam, 784–3574; Moncton, Magnetic Hill, 384–6833; Neguac, on Rte. 11, 776–8907; Oromocto, Miramichi Rd., 357–5730; Plaster Rock, Main St., 356–2196; Richibucto, Legion St., 523–6642; Riverview, Court House, 386–8874; Rogersville, Monument Assumption, 775–2502; Shediac, Corner of Rte. 11 and Rte. 15, 532–1136; Sussex, Four Corners, 433–4553; St. Andrews, Water St., 529–3000; St. George, Brunswick St., 755–3721; Saint John, Hazen Ave., 658–2855; Tracadie, City Hall, 395–9244.

Provincial Tourist Bureaus: At Aulac on the Trans-Canada Hwy., 536–0923; Bathurst, 548–9344; Campbellton at Sugarloaf Park, 753–5413; Campobello,

752–2997; Chatham, 773–5628; Edmundston on the Trans-Canada Hwy., 735–6103; Fredericton on the Trans-Canada Hwy., 455–3092 or 455–3099; Moncton on the Trans-Canada Hwy., 384–8608; Newcastle, 622–0303; Penobsquis on the Trans-Canada Hwy., 433–4326; St. Andrews at Waweig on Rte. 1, 466–4858; Saint John at the Reversing Falls, 672–1198; St. Leonard on the Trans-Canada Hwy., 423–6324; St. Stephen, 466–1139; Woodstock on Rte. 95, 328–3419.

Or write for information to: *Tourism New Brunswick,* Box 12345, Fredericton, New Brunswick, Canada E3B 5C3; (506) 453–2377, 800–561–0123 from Canada and U.S. or 800–442–4442 from within New Brunswick.

TIME ZONE. The province is on Atlantic Time—one hour in advance of Eastern Time.

SEASONAL EVENTS. Food festivals abound all summer, celebrating the harvests of scallops, salmon, lobsters, oysters, clams, and important vegetables like potatoes and Brussels sprouts. Other festivals celebrate heritage, music, crafts, athletics, and old home weeks. For dates and locations, contact *Tourism New Brunswick.* Likewise for schedules of Atlantic Symphony Orchestra performances and art gallery exhibitions.

SPECIAL INTEREST TOURS. At Brunswick Mining and Smelting you can visit "the underground city," almost 3,000 feet down in a mine which produces zinc, lead, silver, and copper.

Boat Tours: Fundy Isles Marine Enterprises, 529–3688. Shediac—Romeo's Marine, 532–6444. Point-du-Chene—Moyak Marine, 532–4098. Dalhousie—Chaleur Phantom, 684–4219. In the Caraquet area there are numerous boat tour operators. Ask for information locally, or from Tourism New Brunswick.

Bird-watching is a special attraction on Grand Manan Island. There are over 240 species of sea birds that nest there. It's also a paradise for rockhounds, painters, nature photographers, and hikers—not to mention whale watchers! Bicyclists contact Carl White, 408 Princess Drive, Bathurst, New Brunswick, for information regarding special bicycle tours. Tours for all of these activities can be arranged by telephoning 800–561–0123.

PARKS AND CAMPING. New Brunswick has two national parks. *Fundy National Park* fronts the Bay of Fundy—about 13 km. (8 mi.) of shore with an inland area of tall timber, lakes, and streams. There is a motel and chalets inside the park. It opens when the fishing season does—the third weekend in May.

Kouchibougouac National Park stretches 25 km. (15 mi.) along the Gulf of St. Lawrence shore. It's a panorama of forest, marshes, tidal lagoons, meandering rivers, sand dunes, and—especially—a vast and sweeping beach along much of its length. Canoes, bicycles, and boats may be rented on site.

Mactaquac, north of Fredericton, is the major provincial park. It has extensive camping facilities, golf, and other summer and winter sports facilities. *Sugarloaf* in the north is a year-round facility with the accent on skiing and other winter activities while *Mount Carleton* offers much wilderness and primitive camping facilities. There are smaller provincial parks throughout New Brunswick.

Miscou Island has camping facilities and cabins. Contact Miscou Island Campground and Cabins, Miscou Centre. Phone 344-8352.

Camping fees in provincial and national parks are generally between $6 and $10, depending on services. Private campgrounds may charge a bit more. The province's accommodations guide lists them all. The Avis Rent-a-Car company also rents tents and camping kits along with cars throughout the Maritime provinces.

FARM VACATIONS. About two dozen farms in the province take on people who wish to experience a farm vacation. Most cater to families, but some will take children alone. Contact *Tourism New Brunswick.*

SPORTS. Golf: New Brunswick has 31 golf courses, most with pro shops and rentals, as well as restaurants and shower facilities. Most are uncrowded.

Fishing and hunting: Charters for deepsea fishing are mostly concentrated in the Caraquet area, where angling for the bluefin tuna is a glamour activity. New Brunswick is also known internationally for its salmon and bass fishing, although its multitude of lakes abound in other freshwater species as well.

Hunting for deer, bear, and small game can be arranged. You will need a licensed guide and a nonresident hunting license for yourself. One outfit (Trius Tours Ltd., 455–8400) organizes bear-hunting expeditions.

Tourism New Brunswick has a fishing and hunting guidebook listing outfitters and other relevant information.

Winter sports: New Brunswick is a growing destination for winter vacationers. It has dependable deep snow and is abuzz all winter with skiing, snowmobiling, ice-fishing, and other activities over great open spaces. Canada East Tours (548-3447) in Bathurst organizes snowmobiling holidays.

Sailing: For the yachting enthusiast, there are the extensive and gorgeous waters of the lower Saint John River and Grand Lake. Yachts can be rented at *Maritime Yachts,* Box 27, R.R. 3, Site 4, Fredericton, N.B. (453–4388) or at *Fundy Yachts,* Dipper Harbour, Box 490, R.R. 2, Lepreau, N.B. (659–2769). Houseboat rentals are available from Houseboat Vacations, P.O. Box 2088, Sussex, N.B. E0E 1P0, or phone 433-4801 or 433-1609. Fredericton Rowing Club, Aquatic Centre, holds clinics and regattas for rowers.

For details on any of the above, contact Tourism New Brunswick, P.O. Box 12345, Fredericton, New Brunswick E3B 5C3; 453–2377, 800–561–0123 from Canada and U.S., or 800–442–4442 from within New Brunswick.

MUSEUMS. The province has a couple of dozen museums apart from the major ones found in Saint John and Fredericton. In particular there's the *Acadian Historical Village* and the *Acadian Museum* in **Caraquet,** plus the *Acadian Museum* at the University of Moncton campus in **Moncton**— all depicting the history of the Acadian people. *Eglise St.-Henri* at **Barachois** is an old wooden church converted to a museum also on the Acadian theme. Most small museums are on local history, but some have specific themes. For example, *Miramichi Salmon Museum,* **Doaktown** the *Central New Brunswick Woodsmen's Museum* at **Boiestown,** the *Automobile Museum* at **Edmundston,** and the *Fundy Antique Car Museum* at **Hopewell Cape,** Hillsborough-Salem Railway operates 1-hour steam locomotive trips in summer the *Antique Arms Museum* at **Mactaquac,** the *Marine Museum* at **Shippagan,** and the *Sportsman's Museum* at **Shediac.** The *Grand Manan Museum* has an interesting collection of birds and geological exhibits. The *Tracadie Historical Museum* pays tribute to those who dedicated their lives to a leper colony that once existed there. The *Moncton Museum* is another fairly large museum of provincial scale.

New Brunswick also has some 9,000 homes designated as "historic." Some can only be viewed from the outside, but some have exhibits and are open to the public. Check the Tourism New Brunswick publication *Historic Faces.*

SHOPPING. Bathurst's one unique store, *Frank's Furs,* specializes in designing and making fur coats in larger sizes.

In **Edmundston,** *Chiasson's Furs* offers stunning furs designed with the French flair. *Henri Nadeau* on the Trans-Canada for handcrafts or *Les Artisinat Handicraft* in nearby St. Basile, specializing in a variety of local works.

Moncton's shopping is some of the best in New Brunswick—five spacious malls and numerous pockets of shops in downtown Moncton. Among the crafts to look for are the yarn portraits of La Sagouine, "the old sage" of Buctouche. The sayings of an old Acadian woman as she goes about her daily chores were made famous in Antonine Maillet's novel *La Sagouine.*

St. Andrews has great English and New Brunswick woolens, lots of English bone china, and marvelous wool yarn at *The Sea Captain's Loft, Cottage Craft,* and *Saint Andrews Woollens.* Rare and out-of-print books, antiques, etc. at the *Pansy Patch,* a stunning old home across from the Algonquin Hotel. Quality crafts are at *La Baleine* on Water St.

Fredericton's artist's studios and craftpeople are noted for their work.

At **St. Leonard,** be sure to visit the studio/store of the *Madawaska Weavers,* whose handwoven items are known the world over. Handsome skirts, stoles, and enchanting ties are some of the items for sale.

At **St. Stephen,** *Quartermain's Ltd.,* a long-standing business where you can browse for hours among quality Canadian and British goods.

In the studio of *Peter Hummel-Newell,* you'll find exquisite pieces of jewelry made from real New Brunswick wildflowers.

The *Directory of New Brunswick Craftsmen & Craft Shops,* available from the Department of Youth, Culture, and Recreation, Handcrafts Branch, Box 6000, Fredericton, N.B. or from tourist bureaus, will direct you to potters, weavers, glass-blowers, jewelers and carvers all over the province.

In summer, handcraft courses are offered at various locations throughout the province.

Shopping hours. Downtown shopping runs from 9 A.M. to 5 or 6 P.M. Monday–Saturday, and up to 9 P.M. on Fridays. The shopping malls are open 10 A.M. to 10 P.M. every day, except in Moncton where they close at 6 P.M. Saturday nights.

Holiday closings during the summer season occur on Victoria Day (3rd Monday in May), Canada Day (July 1), New Brunswick Day (1st Monday in August), Labor Day, Thanksgiving (2nd Monday in October), and Remembrance Day (November 11).

DRINKING LAWS. The minimum legal drinking age in New Brunswick is 19.

 DINING OUT. Expect surprisingly good dining in some places in rural New Brunswick, in others just average. Price categories: *Expensive,* over $15; *Moderate,* $10–15; *Inexpensive,* under $10. A 10% provincial tax will be added to your bill.

Most places accept the following major credit cards: American Express, MasterCard, and Visa; others may also be honored. Not all establishments accept credit cards, therefore we suggest you call for information.

ATHOLVILLE. *Moderate:* **Landry's Steak House.** Good steak.

BATHURST. *Expensive:* **La Fine Grobe.** Located at Nigadoo, near Bathurst. French and traditional Acadian cuisine at its best. Fine buffet; special drink of the house—old Acadian recipe from Prohibition times called Le Caribou. Art and craft gallery with folksingers.

Moderate: **Danny's Restaurant.** Good food, plainly served. Generous lobster cocktails, friendly service in serene dining room.

CAMPBELLTON. *Moderate:* **Fundy Line Motel Dining Room.** Good, plain food. Excellent steak and salmon.

Wandlyn Dining Room. Good food, pleasant surroundings.

CARAQUET. *Moderate:* **Hotel Paulin.** Excellent seafood and home-cooked Acadian dishes.

Le Poirier. A new restaurant with a good initial reputation. Seafoods a specialty.

CHATHAM. *Moderate.* **La Portage.** Good steak.

DALHOUSIE. *Moderate:* **The Cedar Lodge Dining Room.** Excellent food. The apple pie is highly recommended.

EDMUNDSTON. *Expensive:* **Le Baron.** Excellent food; pâté à la maison, crêpe Suzettes flamed at your table.
The Wandlyn. Good food, comparable to Le Baron. Piano bar, dancing.

FORT BEAUSEJOUR. *Moderate:* **Drury Lane Steakhouse.** In Aulac, near Fort Beausejour. Steak, clam chowder with home-baked rolls, steamed clams—all excellent.

GRAND MANAN. *Moderate:* **The Compass Rose.** Seafood in home-cooked style. Afternoon tea.
The Marathon. Dinner at six. Set menu. Bread baked fresh daily. Good food. Homey and friendly.

MONCTON. *Expensive:* **Chez Jean Pierre.** Features Provençal cuisine (stuffed baby pig, quail in raisin sauce, and others). Phone 382–0332. Major credit cards.
The Windjammer. The most elegant dining room in the Beausejour Hotel. Private booths and portholes with real fish swimming around in them. Although expensive, service is slick and food is good. Châteaubriand recommended. Phone 854–4344. Major credit cards.
Moderate–Expensive: **Cy's.** Main St. Noted seafood restaurant which richly deserves its reputation. The seafood platter, one of the specialties, will amaze you with its quality and quantity. Lobster a specialty, of course, and a great view of the tidal bore from a window table. Phone 382–0032. Major credit cards.
Papa Joe's. Fair food. Fiddleheads available, steaks are good; try some of the flaming coffees. Phone 854–9947. Major credit cards.
Moderate: **Ming Garden Restaurant.** Interesting Cantonese-Canadian food, the best in the Maritimes. One dish, chunks of fresh lobster, wrapped in thin slices of chicken, deep fried and served with oyster sauce should be tried. Open till 2 A.M. weeknights, 3 A.M. weekends. Phone 855–5433. Major credit cards.
Vito's. Mountain Rd. Good Italian food, popular. Phone 382–5003. Major credit cards.
Moderate–Inexpensive: **Le Cave à Pape.** Excellent French and Acadian cuisine. Phone 855–0581. Major credit cards.

NEWCASTLE. *Moderate:* **The Wandlyn Dining Room.** Small, cozy, good.

PERTH-ANDOVER. *Moderate:* **York's Dining Room.** Deserves special mention. A uniquely New Brunswick establishment, York's serves gargantuan helpings of excellent home-cooked foods in an unassuming dining room.

SACKVILLE. *Expensive–moderate.* **Marshlands Inn.** Fine old inn serving traditional English and New Brunswick foods such as steak and kidney pie, seafood, fiddleheads, in mahogany panelled dining room with antique lined walls.

SHEDIAC. *Expensive–Moderate.* **Chez Francoise.** Glowing old-fashioned dining rooms in old mansion. Cuisine *a la francais* with accent on fresh seafood of the region.
Moderate: **Paturel's Shore House.** At Cape Bimet a few miles east of Shediac. Lobster and seafood.

Shediac's Fisherman's Paradise. Good seafood in the heart of lobster country.

ST. ANDREWS. *Expensive:* **The Algonquin.** Excellent lobster dinners on weekends. Open dances in the Casino on some Saturday nights.

Conley's Shore House. Good fresh lobster in all forms, boiled, stewed or on rolls.

L'Europe. King Street. Superb dining—excellent food, good service (529–3818).

The Rossmount. Elegant décor, reservations suggested. Excellent food. House specialties—lobster and Bay of Fundy fish.

Moderate to Expensive. **Tara Manor.** Good dining room with friendly service.

Moderate: **The Shiretown.** Fairly good food. Lunchtime buffet interesting and hearty, local area food. Licensed. English inn atmosphere.

Smugglers' Wharf Restaurant. Seafare with a view over St. Andrews Harbour. Licensed.

ST. STEPHEN-MILLTOWN. *Moderate.* **Wandlyn.** Small, cheerful dining room with good average fare.

WOODSTOCK. *Expensive:* **The Wandlyn Dining Room.** Large pleasant room, good food.

Inexpensive–Moderate: **Stiles Home Town Tea Room.** Home cooking.

NIGHT LIFE. In **Edmundston**, some of the hotels that offer live entertainment are *Charlies Bar* at the Wandlyn Motel, *Rita's Motel* bar, *The Riverside* and the *New Royal* (the last two have been known to offer strip shows), or the bars at the *Praga* tavern atmosphere with canned music.

In **Moncton** for dressed-up stepping out, the hottest spot is the *Cosmopolitan Club* in the old courthouse on Main St. *The Beaus and Belles* lounge in the Beausejour Hotel is an attractive spot decorated in Gay Nineties style where you can have a snack with your drink. *The Coach Room Lounge*, Keddy's Motel, dark, quaint and quiet. Perfect spot for a quiet tête-à-tête. *Lamplighter Room* in the Howard Johnson's Motor Inn, pleasant, congenial, and quiet.

In **St. Andrews**, two swinging bars in the Algonquin Hotel offer nightly entertainment. Quiet drinking in the *Shiretown Inn*, Water St., like a small English pub.

PRINCE EDWARD ISLAND

Garden of the Gulf

by
ALAN FREEMAN, RALPH SURETTE,
and
COLLEEN THOMPSON

Ralph Surette is a freelance journalist living near Dartmouth N.S. He writes for a number of Canadian magazines and is a regular commentator on Canadian Broadcasting Corporation Radio.

In the Gulf of St. Lawrence, off the coasts of New Brunswick and Nova Scotia, Prince Edward Island is Canada's smallest province, but in many ways its most captivating. The Micmac Indians, the island's original inhabitants (still represented here on four reservations), called the Island *Abegweit,* meaning "cradled on the waves." French explorer Jacques Cartier, sighting the island in 1534, described it as "the fairest land 'tis possible to see." More than two centuries later, the British were sufficiently enchanted to name the island after Edward, Duke of Kent, father of Queen Victoria. Today, tourist brochures refer to it as "the Garden of the Gulf," a tribute to the wide variety of fresh fruits and vegetables brought daily to the table from the Island's farms.

Red Cliffs—Green Fields

Prince Edward Island is characterized by an abundance of natural beauty. The southern coastline is a harmonious blend of red sandstone cliffs topped by rich green fields and trees. Summer visitors arriving by ferry across the Northumberland Strait will get their first impressions of the island from this shore.

The north shore, on the other hand, is famous for its white, silky sand. Inland, immaculate communities form a part of the gently rolling landscape.

That the island has been able to retain its popular appeal over the centuries is a tribute not only to its enduring attractiveness, but also to the friendly, hardy residents (many of them descendants of the early settlers), who live and work harmoniously while maintaining their individual heritages. Although a scant 140 miles long and from 4 to 40 miles wide at any given point, Prince Edward Island is the permanent home of 123,000 Islanders.

The island appeals to its inhabitants, who serenely weather the sometimes bitter winters, in much the same way as it attracts visitors, offering lovely land, a low-key style of living, clean environment, and a satisfying range of diversions. Throughout the island, the people have industriously developed the agricultural and coastal resources, and built good schools that do much to encourage succeeding generations to remain on the island. At the same time, they have retained an almost stubborn pride in their heritage—British, French, Scot, and Micmac Indian. You will find evidence of this in the many local museums that dot the island and in a number of cultural festivals held throughout the summer.

Agriculture

Prince Edward Island has been described as two huge beaches separated by potato fields. An oversimplification, of course, but not entirely inaccurate. Agriculture is the island's most important industry, and about 60,000 acres of potatoes, the major crop, are planted each year. Waving fields of barley, oats, wheat, and other grains provide a feast for the eye with their summer hues of brown, yellow, and green. Although potatoes are more profitable, more acreage is planted in grain, some of which is exported. Tobacco is a relatively new crop and is internationally known for its high quality. Many vegetables as well as strawberries, blueberries, apples, and raspberries are among the other crops under cultivation. The island has a healthy livestock population, too.

Tourism Is Number 2

As a source of revenue, tourism follows agriculture. Facilities accommodate more than half a million visitors annually. The Island is readily accessible via ferry service from New Brunswick, Nova Scotia, and the Magdalen Islands, and by plane from nearby major cities of the mainland. The tourist season is generally compressed into the summer months, owing to the island's North Atlantic locale; the accommodations are numerous, if modest. The range of vacation activities is broad: from fishing, boating and other watersports on both inland and coastal waters to golf (ten courses), horseback riding, professional sulky races, festivals, repertory theater, and an informal but frequently lively night life. Add to this good sightseeing at museums, art galleries, historic homes, and, for the children, a surprising number of amusement parks, animal enclaves, wildlife centers and youth-appeal museums within minutes of most major crossroads.

What the visitor will find distinctive, however, are the historic and personal elements: the enduring French Acadian influence; the vestiges of Micmac, English, and Scottish settlements; vacation farms that are a unique and refreshing experience for visitors who want to share the accommodations—and chores—of their farm family hosts; home/studios of local craftsmen (and there are many) where travelers can stop awhile and talk with the artists and, of course, buy their works; the serenity of the low inland hills, rarely more than a few miles away but seemingly far from the main routes; and, above all, an essentially rural island personality that sets this locale apart from similar but more commercial holiday destinations.

The sense of remoteness, in fact, is one of the island's most charming features; as a result many of the facilities here are oriented to the natural environment. Despite the island's minute size, it encompasses 3,700 miles of paved road that make all communities easily accessible. Camping and trailer sites are numerous in the official provincial as well as privately operated parks scattered along the coast and inland. Prince Edward Island, in effect, begs to be explored.

To facilitate sightseeing, there are three scenic motor routings, each marked with distinctive symbols, called Lady Slipper Drive, Blue Heron Drive, and Kings Byway. Each follows the coastline of the island's three major land divisions, which are naturally sectioned by indentations of bays and rivers. These divisions are also the approximate boundaries of the province's three counties, Prince, Queens, and Kings.

Local officials encourage visitors to allot at least one day for each drive, and point out that side trips should be the rule rather than the exception since distances between attractions are short and almost every side road eventually leads to a major highway. Each drive features access to beaches, parks, camping grounds, scenic lookouts, towns, villages with notable historic or special attractions, and places where you may buy fresh seafood and vegetables.

Although Prince Edward Island is very much part of the modern world, the province has retained a good deal of the slow pace and human qualities of an earlier age. Islanders are not only friendly but thoroughly hospitable, preferring unpretentious comfort, homey accommodations and plain, traditional food from land and sea. Food should be a treat, as a mainstay of the dinner table is the lobster, brought in daily from the deep waters off the coast when the season permits. The lobster supper, a Prince Edward Island tradition, is a unique dining experience and should be sought out when touring along the North Shore. Other popular local foods (in season) are oysters from the famed farming beds in Malpeque Bay, strawberries, cranberries, and blueberries, which thrive on the island's sandy soil, apples and cherries from native trees, and the plenteous home-grown farm vegetables that invariably surprise the visitor because of the island's limited size and growing season.

Fishing is P.E.I.'s third industry, with lobsters the most profitable of the more than 30 varieties of fish yielded up by the waters surrounding and crisscrossing the island.

History Is Sparsely Recorded

Except for scattered monuments, restorations, re-created villages (some frankly commercial), gravestones and the like, there are few visible reminders on Prince Edward Island of the earliest European settlements. But the island did experience a history of quarrelsome confrontations between those early rivals France and England in the race to exploit and colonize North America. The heritage of both remains.

The French came first but took their time in settling here. Jacques Cartier discovered Prince Edward Island in 1534, but the French did not establish an outpost on the Île St. Jean, as they named it, until 1663. A more complete settlement came along in 1720 when Compte St. Pierre and a band of 300 established Port La Joie, across the harbor from what is now Charlottetown, the capital. (Today, the site of Port La Joie is part of Fort Amherst National Historic Park.) France hoped that the new settlement would draw from the Acadian (French) settlements in what is now Nova Scotia, but there was little migration until the French were forced to leave, following the fall of Louisburg on Cape Breton Island to the English.

Capitalizing on this maritime foothold, the English continued to rout the French when Lord Rollo brought four ships and 500 men to take possession of the island. Following the British takeover in 1763, the name was Anglicized to the Island of Saint John. In 1799 it was changed again—this time to Prince Edward Island in honor of Prince Edward (later the Duke of Kent). In 1769 the island was separated from Nova Scotia.

Micmac Means "Allies"

There is little indication of any major strife here between the early French settlers and the Island's Micmac Indians. The tribe, made up of small groups, each with its own chief, did not live in permanent villages, preferring instead to move from place to place as hunters and fishermen. Today, about 400 Micmac Indians remain on the island's four reservations where they have found it difficult to maintain their native culture. By comparison, descendants of some of the early Acadians also remain on the island but retain their identity in a number of ways, notably in their food, their music, and their language. The Acadians are often considered to speak a debased form of French. They do not. Though many English words have crept into their speech over the years, their language is still basically good 18th-century provincial French, just as the distinctive accents of Newfoundland often prove to be pure 18th-century Devon or Dorset.

The population of the island grew during the American Revolution, particularly at its end when British Loyalists were forced to leave the newly established United States and flee to Canada. It was during this period that the island officially became a Crown Colony and was re-named Prince Edward Island. One of the more durable settlements was established by Scotland's Lord Selkirk, who arrived in 1803 with three ships of pioneers from the Scots Highlands. Restored log cabins and other shelters, as well as the group's church built in 1824, may be seen in the Belfast district of the island, where there are also a number of descendants of the original settlers.

For most visitors, the island's development in the first half of the 19th century has a more visible significance since a number of the homes, churches, government structures, monuments, and sites of historic or colorful interest can actually be seen and visited. Province House, in Charlottetown, is probably the most revered of these, having been the site of the 1864 conference of Confederation planners. Their deliberations led, three years later, to the union of all the British North American colonies into a united Canada, although P.E.I. did not join the Confederation until 1873. The imposing structure still serves as the province's legislature and still dominates the architecture of downtown Charlottetown.

A more contemporary symbol is Green Gables House, which served as the setting for Lucy Maud Montgomery's well-known novel *Anne of Green Gables.* Situated at Cavendish, in the center of the island's North Shore, the house should be visited by devotees of the book and other works by the author, although in other respects it is an unremarkable island farmhouse. Nearby, Green Gables Post Office is the island's most popular center for stamps and postmarks during the summer.

Other sites associated with Mrs. Montgomery and her works are Rainbow Valley, an amusement center which features, among other things, three-dimensional reproductions of the author and her fictional characters; Mrs. Montgomery's birthplace in New London; heroine Anne's House of Dreams, furnished in the style of the early 1900's, at French River; and Silver Bush Museum in Park Corner, where Mrs. Montgomery was married in 1911.

EXPLORING CHARLOTTETOWN

The provincial capital and Prince Edward Island's only city, Charlottetown, reflects its Loyalist heritage even in its name (after Charlotte, stylish consort of England's George III). It is often referred to as "the cradle of Confederation," a reference to the conference held here in 1864 that led to Canada's unification.

Essentially a small city (population 15,300), Charlottetown has no smokestack industry in the traditional sense. Its main activities center around government, tourism, and private commerce, and in these capacities it functions as a service center for the surrounding districts. Although new suburbs are springing up, the core of Charlottetown remains virtually unchanged. In fact, the waterfront is being restored to recapture the tempo and appearance of another era.

In addition, the façades of the old red brick buildings and the gingerbread architecture of the wood houses lining its side streets are pleasant reminders of the past. The Prince Edward Island Museum and Heritage Foundation has strengthened this image by restoring an entire block of row housing on Great George Street across from St. Dunstan's Basilica.

The exceptionally handsome and modern Confederation Centre of the Arts, opened in 1964, as Canada's national memorial to the Fathers of Confederation, houses an art gallery, art workshops, a museum library, Children's Theatre, memorial hall, and the 1,100-seat Charlottetown Theatre. During July and August, the Confederation Centre's Summer Festival offers excellent professional entertainment, including the annual world-famous musical version of *Anne of Green Gables.*

Across the street from the Centre is the old Hughes Drug Store, officially designated a national historic site as Canada's first drugstore. Much of the original interior is still in place, including its elaborately carved woodwork. Protruding from the sidewalk in front of the store is a cannon barrel, now used only as a flower receptacle.

Two nearby churches are particularly noteworthy. St. Paul's Anglican Church, east of Province House, is the oldest (1747) Protestant church on the island. Its baptismal register includes the name of Margaret Gordon, sweetheart of author Thomas Carlyle and heroine of his masterpiece, *Sartor Resartus.*

St. James Presbyterian Church, better known as "the kirk," has impressive stained-glass windows and ancient relics from the island of Iona, one of the earliest sites of Christianity in Scotland. A block of granite resting on a marble slab embedded in the north wall of the kirk, in fact, came from St. Mary's Cathedral on Iona. It also has an intriguing legend. On the day in 1853 when the ship *Fairy Queen* went down in Northumberland Strait, the kirk was empty, but the kirk's bell, so the story goes, was heard to toll many times. A townsman who heard it claimed to have seen three women, bareheaded and barefoot, disappear through the locked doors of the kirk. Later it was learned that three female members of the congregation were lost in the wreck.

South of Province House, on Great George Street, stands St. Dunstan's Basilica, seat of the Roman Catholic Diocese in the province. It is not only one of the largest edifices of its kind in eastern Canada, but contains an impressive altar along with many beautifully executed Italian carvings.

St. Peter's Cathedral, in the northwest corner of Rochford Square, was erected in 1879 and consecrated by the Lord Bishop of Nova Scotia. The church chapel (1888) was designed by W.C. Harris, with murals by his famous brother, Islander Robert Harris.

Victoria Park, overlooking the expanse of water in Charlottetown Harbor at the southernmost tip of the city, is the setting for several notable buildings. Located on a hill between white birches is the old Government House, a mansion built in 1835 as the official residence for the province's lieutenant governors. Next to the mansion stands Beaconsfield, a house designed by W. C. Harris, brother of artist Robert Harris, and an excellent example of Victorian architecture. Built in 1877 and named Beaconsfield for a nearby lake, the house is now the headquarters of the Prince Edward Island Museum and Heritage Foundation. Island artifacts are on display, and the interior design of this gracious old home is worth a visit.

Also in Victoria Park and overlooking the harbor is Fort Edward, built in 1805. It is one of a series of fortifications constructed along the Charlottetown Harbor entrance, and has a six-gun battery. From here one can look across the harbor mouth to Fort Amherst, now a National Historic Site.

The University of Prince Edward Island is located in the capital and is a popular gathering place for young Canadians throughout the summer months.

Exploring Routes Near Charlottetown

For a rewarding coastal drive, take Route 1 out of Charlottetown and Route 19 around Fort Amherst National Park, site of the old French fort. On the way, you'll drive through Cornwall, a spot where the locals swear a mermaid came ashore one day. Described "as big as a small girl," she talked to no one and allowed no one too close. After about an hour in the July sun, she slipped back into the ocean.

At New Haven on Route 1, Fairyland is one of P.E.I.'s many attractions that cater especially to children.

At Hampton, watch for Route 116, which takes you to the shore and to Victoria Provincial Park. No matter where you travel in this section, the scenery is delightful. Nearby Victoria is a quaint old English community. When you're here, take a drive around Augustine's Cove.

EXPLORING PRINCE EDWARD ISLAND

The best way to see all three sections of the island is via the Scenic Drives. These comprehensive routings are described in the brochure *Prince Edward Island Scenic Drives Tour Guide,* and outlined in the P.E.I. tourist map. Both are available from tourist information offices in Charlottetown and other locations throughout the Island and also at some car-rental agencies. Each Drive is color-coded in the literature, and easy to follow on the road because of the frequently posted symbols. Each is more or less a continuous circle, so the driver may start or stop at any point or travel in either direction. All together, the Drives tour the entire coast of Prince Edward Island and also provide easy access to inland areas and communities. Most highways are paved, with some short stretches of smooth red clay; with few exceptions, all roads are evenly surfaced and well maintained, for comfortable drives.

Blue Heron Drive

Circling Prince Edward Island's center segment, Blue Heron is the shortest of the three Drives, and in many ways a cross-section of the entire island. Highlights along the routing are the North Shore beaches, Anne of Green Gables country, scenic rural areas, the red sandstone seascapes along the southern shore, and a number of historic sites. It takes its name from the stately blue herons which you're likely to see along the route. The guide marker is a white square with blue border and blue heron in the center. Here is a suggested routing:

Driving north from Charlottetown in a counterclockwise direction, follow Route 15 to Brackley Beach, a pivotal intersection for access to the roughly 40 kms. (25 miles) of North Shore beaches that comprise the National Park. Symbols on the road map will advise you of available facilities (campsites, beaches, day-use parks, fishing).

Lobster Suppers

This is also the region where you must sample the island's distinctive lobster supper. Popular places for lobster suppers are Howe's Hall at

Brackley Beach (you will also have a great breakfast here), New London, New Glasgow, St. Ann's Church in Hope River, Fisherman's Wharf in North Rustico, and Stanhope Beach Lodge.

At Brackley Beach, Blue Heron Drive turns left and follows Route 6 across Oyster Bed Bridge to South Rustico with its historic Farmer's Bank, chartered in 1864. Farmers and fishermen were its directors, and it prospered for 30 years by providing cheap credit to help the people of this predominantly Acadian community gain economic independence. Rustico, in fact, took its name from one of its early French settlers, René Rassicot, who came from Normandy. Townsfolk claim that the world's first automobile was driven in this community in 1866 when Father Belcourt drove around in a "strange, noisy contraption."

South Rustico is also the home of Jumpin' Jack's (admission $1.00, children under 12 free), an authentic old country store that dates back to the 1800's and features cracker barrels, fish barrels, egg crates, a checkerboard, potbellied stove, and countless other old items purchased and used by the residents' forefathers.

"Anne of Green Gables" Country

Farther along Route 6 is Cavendish and the farmhouse which served as the setting for Lucy Montgomery's *Anne of Green Gables.* Situated on the edge of the challenging 18-hole Green Gables Golf Course, the house is open to the public (admission is free) and offers bilingual guide service. The Green Gables Post Office, located on Route 6, offers all current postage stamp issues, including first-day covers, mint sets, plates, corner blocks, and sheets. Lucy Montgomery is buried in the Cavendish Cemetery, where you'll also find the graves of 21 American sailors who drowned when their ship, *Yankee Star,* sank many years ago off the Cavendish coast.

Blue Heron Drive continues along Route 6 for about 11 kms. (7 miles) to New London (you may want to see the white cottage where Lucy Montgomery was born) and then turns north onto Route 20. For an interesting side trip, turn off the Drive at Springbrook and turn left on Route 234 for the short drive to Long River. Here, look for the Old Mill Museum, containing amusing antique items such as a 100-year-old hand-pumped organ, an 80-year-old carriage, and a dog-powered butter churn. Built in 1820, the mill also houses a collection of old bottles, some the size of a thimble.

Returning to Springbrook, resume the drive north along Route 20 to the French River district near New London Harbor, where there are two pioneer-era cemeteries, Yankee Hill and Sims, located within 300 yards of each other. They contain inscribed tombstones of a number of residents who died between 1816 and 1843. Farther along the highway is Park Corner, where those who have read the stories of Pat of Silverbush (more of Lucy Maud Montgomery) might enjoy a visit to the Anne of Green Gables Museum at Silverbush. Lucy Maud was married here and many personal effects are on display.

Historic Malpeque

Crossing over from Queens to Prince County you come to Malpeque, one of the truly historic corners of Prince Edward Island. The French settled in this area in the early 1700's; before them, the wandering Micmac Indians camped here. Traces of their weapons and implements can still be found in Malpeque. In 1765, when the English sent Captain Samuel Holland to survey the new colony, he recommended that "Princetown," as he called the settlement, be made capital of Prince County (although it subsequently reverted to the Indian name). Five years later came the first sizable migration of Scots; many of their descendants live here today. The famous Malpeque oysters farmed in adjacent Malpeque Bay are shipped from here to seafood distribution centers throughout North America.

From Malpeque, follow the route to the southern coast and watch carefully for the Blue Heron Drive signs since the highway route numbers change several times. At Cape Traverse, east of Borden, you'll find a monument to the ice boat—the only way to travel to the mainland in the winter before 1917. Still farther east is Augustine Cove, an exceptionally attractive inlet, and beyond that Victoria, a quaint Old English community. Across the harbor is Victoria Provincial Park, a scenic setting for camping and picnicking.

Just beyond is DeSable and from here there are two major routings back to Charlottetown. The Blue Heron Drive continues along the red sandstone coastline to the end of the peninsula that faces Charlottetown south of its harbor. Just before this point is Fort Amherst National Historic Park, site of Port La Joie, the first French settlement and, later, of Fort Amherst (English), built in 1758. Today only the earthworks of the fort remain, but the Visitor Centre provides a social, political, and military history of the area.

At the tip of the peninsula is Rocky Point and the Micmac Indian Village. Displays at the village include birchbark wigwams and canoes, handmade hunting and fishing implements, and life-size sculptures of Indians and animals. Of special interest is the museum, which holds actual tools and weapons used by the first inhabitants of the island.

The final leg of Blue Heron Drive backtracks a short way down the north side of the peninsula, then crosses the West River, and continues to Cornwall, where it connects with the Trans-Canada Highway back to Charlottetown.

The alternate return from DeSable is more or less an inland drive along National Route 1 (Trans-Canada Highway) and is generally more entertaining as well as scenic. At Bonshaw, just beyond DeSable, is the Car Life Museum, with a collection of vintage gas pumps, handsomely restored autos from the Roaring Twenties era, and old farm equipment. Farther along the highway is Strathgartney Park, a scenic area for tenting with a stunning view of the surrounding countryside. Route 1 continues through New Haven and Fairyland, an attraction for children; then it rejoins the Blue Heron Drive at Cornwall for the last several miles into Charlottetown.

Lady Slipper Drive

The region encircled by Prince County's Lady Slipper Drive is considered one of the less developed areas of the island for tourism purposes. It is made up of small and very old villages (with the exception of Summerside, the largest P.E.I. community designated as a town, and second in size to Charlottetown), still adhering to a more traditional way of life. The area is also the home of the Island's Acadians, descendants of the original French settlers.

The Drive might be likened to a misshapen figure-eight, and is named for the lady slipper orchid that blooms in late spring and is the official Provincial Flower. The Drive marker, appropriately enough, is a white square with a red border and a red orchid in the center. In addition to the Acadian presence, Indians, farms, Irish moss and oysters are pronounced influences in the region.

At Summerside

Again, there is no official starting point for Lady Slipper Drive, but a logical place to begin is Summerside. An annual event here is the eight-day Summerside Lobster Carnival in mid-July. The Carnival is actually a combination fair and festival, with exhibits of livestock, agriculture, and handicrafts as well as parades, beauty contests, harness racing, a midway and, of course, lobster suppers (chicken too). Specific dates of the Carnival are available from the Island's Visitor Information Centres or from the Summerside Area Tourist Association.

From Summerside follow the Lady Slipper Drive signs on Route 1A to St. Eleanor's; then turn west on Route 2 to Miscouche. Here, the Acadian Museum has a collection of artifacts dating from before the 1800's which relate to Acadian lifestyles over the years. There are household and farm implements as well as other domestic items. The red stone monument behind the museum stands over a collective Acadian grave transferred from River Platte in 1839.

Following the northern route of the Drive, proceed up Route 12 to Rosehill, then turn right onto Route 123, and continue along the road that curves around the cape—jutting into Malpeque Bay, center of the island's oyster-farming industry. The road rejoins Route 12, which then winds along the western shore of the Bay, across rivers and harbor inlets and through small and large ports serving as harvest centers for other catches of the Island's important fishing industry.

Green Park, a Provincial Historic Park at Port Hill, merits a visit. There is a mansion here that was the onetime home of a shipbuilding family named Yeo, and the park area is now a permanent museum. The mansion, built in 1865, has been restored and refurnished. An interpretive center houses displays and artifacts from those early wooden ships, and there is also a shipyard with a display of a wooden vessel under construction. Guided tours are available at no charge and the park has campgrounds.

Much farther north is Alberton, one of several major deep-sea charter fishing ports along Lady Slipper Drive (others included are Skinner's Pond and Conway Harbor Inlet). Deep-sea fishing outings can be a family affair and all you need are warm clothing and a lunch. Most trips last four hours, with cod, mackerel, halibut, herring, and hake the usual catches. Cost is $10 per person or more. The cost for tuna chartering is usually $300 per 8-hour day for upwards of six persons, and there are often special rates for children. The boat captain will supply all the tackle and bait and you don't need a license.

Leavitt's Maple Tree Craft Shop in Alberton specializes in turned Bird's-eye maplewood products. The craftspeople here are always ready to talk with visitors, and Bird's-eye maple blanks can be purchased for home lathes. There is also a variety of finished wood products. Also in Alberton, the Alberton Museum features local and provincial artifacts and relics, housed in an old renovated barn. It focuses on the silver fox industry, which thrived here in the early part of this century, but also has Indian relics, farm and trade implements, glass, china, books and other artifacts.

At nearby Northport is Sea Rescue Park overlooking Northport Harbour. The park is the site of the restored lifeboat station from which Northport seamen performed a daring rescue of survivors from a floundering sailing vessel during a storm in the fall of 1906. There are picnic tables, washrooms, water tap, and a children's playground.

North Cape

Lady Slipper Drive continues past Cape Kildare, where French explorer Cartier reportedly first took a close look at the island, then proceeds to the northwesternmost tip of the island named, appropriately, North Cape. Motoring down the western coastline you will drive through Skinner's Pond and, a bit farther south, Miminegash at the head of the river of the same name, considered one of the better inland fishing areas in the western part of Prince Edward Island.

The next 48 kms. (30 miles) or so of Lady Slipper Drive follow the quietly attractive western and southern coastline. For a more sightworthy routing, leave the Drive at Campbellton and take Route 145 to Route 2, turning right at Bloomfield to St. Anthony, and right again on Route 143 to Howlan, where there is a blacksmith shop. From Howlan, Route 148 takes you to the farming community of O'Leary, which has a museum.

At Coleman, you are again on Lady Slipper Drive and should take the southern routing back to Summerside in order to visit the Acadian Pioneer Village at Mount Carmel. The restoration includes a church, priest's house, blacksmith shop, homes, barn, and store. The buildings are furnished with artifacts and restored items relating to the life of the French settlers of the early 19th century. To enjoy Acadian food, visit the restaurant on the site and try Acadian soup or a potato dish. Prices are reasonable.

Kings Byway Drive

The Kings Byway takes visitors through some of the oldest and most interesting areas of Prince Edward Island. Many of the attractions recall early days of the island and the pioneering spirit which the settlers brought with them. There are also red-banked as well as white sand beaches, highly photogenic lighthouse points, tobacco farmlands, fisheries, and the "Tuna Capital of the World" at North Lake. This is also a considerably longer routing than the other two Drives and visitors wishing to enjoy it at a leisurely pace should think of making one or two overnight stays along the route. The Kings Byway symbol is a white square bordered in royal purple with a crown in the center.

There are many major sights and attractions along the way, beginning at Charlottetown and heading south. The agricultural heritage of the island's rural communities is highlighted at Orwell Corner, an officially designated Historic Site near Orwell. A living farm museum, the site contains a combined store, post office, school, church, farmhouse, and barns. Farming methods are those of former years, and there are old-fashioned musical evenings and hayrides. Farm life of the early inhabitants is also highlighted at Macphail Provincial Park at nearby Orwell. The home of Sir Andrew Macphail, a noted Prince Edward Island physician and author, is surrounded by picnic grounds open to the public.

Still another village tribute to the past, and one of the island's most historic, is the Lord Selkirk Settlement at Eldon. A memorial to the Scottish settlers who arrived here in 1803, it features several reproductions of shelters and cabins that served as the first homes of these pioneers. Farther along the route is Flat River, where the Flat River Crafts Studio specializes in good pottery. Visitors may chat with the craftsmen as they watch them at work.

Continuing along the coast, Kings Byway circles Murray Head peninsula, the southeasternmost tip of the Island, and passes through a number of special communities lining the large Murray Harbour inlet. At the community of Murray Harbour is the Log Cabin Museum depicting the lifestyle of the island during the last century, with many well-preserved implements and household necessities of both local and European manufacture. The building itself is made of logs and finished with hand-split island shingles. In Murray River, the Handcraft Co-op Association shop on Main Street is one of the largest and most complete handcraft retail outlets on the island. And at Murray Harbour North, at the upper corner of the bay, wildlife fanciers may want to seek out Seal Cove Campground from which to view a natural seal colony just offshore.

Just beyond the crossing at Sturgeon River, which happens to be a popular waterway for rainbow trout, Route 317 will take you to Milltown Cross and two of the island's more unique wildlife attractions. At Buffaloland Provincial Park, there is a small herd of North American buffalo, an imported species here, which grazes on a 100-acre enclosure. Nearby is Moore's Migratory Bird Sanctuary, a refuge for thousands of wildfowl, including black duck, American widgeon, blue-wing and green-wing teals, ringneck duck and, of course, Canada goose. Although privately operated, the sanctuary is free.

Rejoin Kings Byway by taking Route 4 from Milltown Cross north to Montague, where the Garden of the Gulf Museum features an interesting collection of old firearms, along with displays of farm tools and household items. Waterways cut deep into this eastern coast of Prince Edward Island north of Montague, forming a number of unusual seascape peninsulas. One of the more popular views is bordered by the Brudenell and Cardigan Rivers, the site of the 1,400-acre Brudenell Provincial Resort.

Since the Byway follows the heavily indented coastline north, duplicating scenery and sights, you may want to bypass part of this by taking Route 4 north to Dingwells Mills, then turning right on Route 2, which rejoins the Byway at Rollo Bay West. Moving more directly up the coast, you should not overlook the Basin Head Fisheries Museum, established in 1973 to preserve the heritage of the island's fisheries, notably that of the inshore fishermen. Displays and photographs illustrate how the small boats were used and the types of fish they caught. Replicas of the fish shacks have been constructed, and an old lobster canning plant by the water adds to the authenticity. There are excellent sandy beaches in this area.

Tuna Fishing

The Byway now proceeds to the tip of the island, East Point, then around to North Lake, major port for the island's big-game fishermen who battle the giant bluefin tuna. Some of the giants run to almost 1,200 pounds and can fight for hours before being brought to gaff. The

North Lake Tuna Charter Association at North Lake has a number of properly equipped tuna boats which charter for about $250 per day for a maximum party of eight. Most charters leave at 10 A.M. If you want to try standby, show up early at the wharf and you may be able to join a party for a share of the cost. Take a lunch and warm clothing; if a tuna is on the line, you may be out long past the normal 6 P.M. returning time. The tuna is the property of the boat captain. The angler gets a photograph of himself and the fish after the weigh-in as his trophy.

It has been said that the railroad on Prince Edward Island was built and paid for by the mile, wandering along for many miles without getting very far. Although the passenger service no longer operates, there is a railway museum which preserves the memories. A gift of Canadian National Railways, the Elmira Railway Station dating from 1911 has been refurbished and features photographic displays and railroading artifacts. Elmira is a short side trip south of North Lake, on Route 16A.

The Kings Byway routing back to Charlottetown follows the North Shore of Kings County, crossing the Morell River (good salmon fishing), and crossing back into Queens County at St. Andrews. If you're in a hurry, you can skip a portion of the Byway by remaining on Route 2, rejoining the Byway at Dunstaffnage. For antique car buffs, the Spoke Wheel Museum here has a 1916 Buick believed to be the only one in existence. This private collection also includes many models and vintages.

On the final leg of the Byway, flower fanciers may want to turn off at Rte. 25 for a very short detour to Jewell's Country Gardens, at the village of York. Specialties at these formal gardens are begonias and fuchsias; there is also an antique glass museum, old country store, and a children's playground.

PRACTICAL INFORMATION FOR

PRINCE EDWARD ISLAND

HOW TO GET THERE. By air: *Eastern Provincial Airways (EPA)* has direct flights to Charlottetown Airport from Toronto, Montréal and Halifax daily. *Air Canada* has one-stop (Ottawa) service from Toronto and also from Boston and New York, stopping at Halifax where you change to EPA for the short flight to the island. Schedules and other information are available from both airways. Many of the larger hotels and resorts in Prince Edward Island will meet guests at the airport if prior arrangements are made. A "limo service" will take passengers from the airport to major motels in Summerside.

By car ferry: Two ferry systems link Prince Edward Island with the mainland, providing service from New Brunswick via Borden and from Nova Scotia via Wood Islands. Each ferry has a snack bar and newsstand. Ferry service also connects with the Magdalen Islands via Souris.

By rail: Transports passengers by bus to the train in Moncton, N.B. from Charlottetown and Summerside.

ACCOMMODATIONS. Double-occupancy rates in Prince Edward Island are categorized as follows: *Expensive,* $50 or more; *Moderate,* $35 to $50; *Inexpensive,* under $35. The 10% provincial sales tax is applied to all accommodation rates. Reservations should be made in advance through any

P.E.I. tourist bureau. A listing of all accommodations, including the many comfortable guest homes and cottages on the island, can be obtained from P.E.I. Visitor Services Division, P.O. Box 940, Charlottetown, P.E.I., Canada C1A 7M5. You can make reservations by calling toll-free (1–800–565–7421) from Nova Scotia or New Brunswick from mid-May to mid-September.

Most places accept the following major credit cards: American Express. MasterCard and Visa; others may also be honored. Not all establishments accept credit cards, therefore we suggest you call for information.

ALBERTON. *Moderate:* **Westerner Motel.** Plain, comfortable accommodations. Housekeeping cottages and motel units. large play area; trout fishing. Open year-round. Off-season rates September 30 to June 1. Pets allowed. Phone 853–2215. Major credit cards.

BRACKLEY BEACH. *Moderate:* **Shady Spruce Tourist Home & Cottages.** 8 housekeeping cottages (one and two bedrooms) three miles from the beach. Phone 672–2264. No credit cards accepted.

Centennial Cottages. 9 two-bedroom cottages; housekeeping; nearly 6 kms. (3½ miles) from beach; surrounded by active farm with animals; 8 kms. (5 miles) to 18-hole golf course. Lobster suppers nearby. Phone 672–2729. Major credit cards.

Inexpensive: **Bayview Farm Apartments and Cottages.** On Rte. 15, 2 km. (1 mile) from National Park. Seven housekeeping cottages. Clam digging, picnic tables, swings and barbecues on premises. No credit cards.

BRUDENELL. *Inexpensive–Moderate:* **Fraser's Deluxe Housekeeping Cottages** River beach on the property. Open June 1 to October 31. Pets permitted. 10 housekeeping units. Phone 838–2453.

CARLETON. *Inexpensive:* **Carleton Motel.** Housekeeping cottages and motel rooms, weekly rates, near beach. Pets permitted. Coffeeshop serves breakfast and lunch. Open year-round. Phone 855–2644. Visa only.

Jenny's Cottages. Spartan; babysitting; near ocean beach. Pets permitted. Phone 855–2341. No credit cards accepted.

CAVENDISH. *Expensive:* **Bay Vista Motor Inn.** Social gathering spot, overnight and housekeeping units, lounge, pool, 3 miles to beach and golf course, excellent restaurant. Phone 963–2225. Major credit cards.

Cavendish Motel. Pool, housekeeping accommodations. Phone 963–2244. Major credit cards.

White Eagle By the Sea. 21 two-bedroom housekeeping cottages, ocean view, near 18-hole golf course. Also, 4-bedroom house for rent, nearby. Phone 963–2361.

Moderate–Expensive: **Green Gables Bungalow Court.** Adjacent to golf course; tennis courts, babysitting arranged. Housekeeping bungalows from bed-sitting rooms to 3 bedrooms. Pets on leashes. Phone 963–2722. No credit cards accepted.

Inexpensive: **Marco Polo Inn.** Farm home with 6 rooms, babysitting services, large campground. Pets permitted. Phone 963–2351. Major credit cards.

CHARLOTTETOWN. *Expensive:* **Charlottetown Hotel.** Central; restaurant, lounge. Guests may use pool at Prince Edward Sheraton Convention Centre. Phone 894–7371. Major credit cards.

Prince Edward Sheraton Convention Centre. Central; restaurant, lounge, indoor pool, sauna. Phone 566–2222. Major credit cards.

Rodd's Confederation Inn. At the junction of Rtes. 1 and 2 in West Royalty. Heated outdoor pool. Lounge, licensed dining room. Pets permitted. Phone 894–2481. Major credit cards.

The Inn on the Hill. Babysitting arranged; trained pets permitted. Phone 894–8572. Major credit cards.

The Kirkwood Motor Hotel. Nice units; indoor pool. Pets permitted. Phone 892–4206. Major credit cards.

The Rodd Royalty Inn. Excellent accommodations, pool, games room, sauna; pets in motel only. Phone 894–8566. Major credit cards.

Wandlyn Inn. Heated outdoor pool. Pets on leashes. Phone 892–1201. Major credit cards.

Dundee Arms Motel and Inn. Near golf course, harness racing, theater, historic sites, and ocean beach. Good dining room, antique furnishings. Phone 892–2496. Major credit cards.

MacLauchlan's Motel. Sauna, indoor swimming pool, beauty lounge, barbershop. Pets on leashes permitted. Phone 892–2461. Major credit cards.

Moderate: **Caroma Lodge.** 9 units near downtown. 2 kitchens for use of guests, laundry facilities. Major credit cards. Phone 894–9039.

Inexpensive: **Auld's Tourist Home.** One room. Located near theater and shopping. Phone 892–2730. No credit cards accepted.

Gateway House. 3 rooms; near harness racing. Small pets only. Phone 894–9761. No credit cards accepted.

KENSINGTON. *Inexpensive:* **Duggan's Bed & Breakfast.** 4 rooms and basement apartment. 13 kms. (8 miles) to ocean beach, 18 kms. (11 miles) to golf course. Phone 836–3444. No credit cards accepted.

KINGSBORO. *Moderate–Expensive:* **Seabreeze Motel.** Well-maintained and comfortable. Has a view over Basin Head Harbour, near the Fisheries Museum. White sandy ocean beach nearby. Motel will arrange deep-sea fishing charters. Dining room is good and features home-style cooking with fish as the specialty. Open year-round. Phone 357–2371. Major credit cards.

MONTAGUE. *Moderate:* **Lobster Shanty North.** One of the better places to eat and stay on the King's Byway. Features good dining with seafood specialties in a rustic licensed dining room which extends into the lounge bar overlooking the Montague River, 27 kms. (17 miles) to ocean beach and 11 kms. (7 miles) to Brudenell golf course. Open year-round. Quiet pets permitted. Phone 838–2463. Major credit cards.

Inexpensive: **Lane's Tourist Court.** 9 housekeeping units. Near center of Montague. Quiet, scenic atmosphere. Children's playground. Phone 838–2433. Major credit cards.

NORTH LAKE. *Moderate:* **Bluefin Motel.** Clean, comfortable accommodation near the North Lake tuna fishing area. Ocean beach 152 meters (500 feet) from the motel. Open mid-June to mid-Oct. Small pets permitted. Phone 357–2599.

NORTH RUSTICO. *Moderate:* **St. Lawrence Motel.** Weekly or nightly rates, babysitting arranged, games room, barbecues, golf range, bicycle rentals, supervised ocean beach. Pets permitted. Phone 963–2053.

POOLES CORNER. *Moderate:* **Kingsway Motel.** Small, modern motel. Licensed dining room, good food, home cooked variety; cozy lounge bar. The river beach and golf course at Brudenell Resort are 5 kms (3 miles) away. Open year-round. Leashed pets. Phone 838–2112. Major credit cards.

RUSTICOVILLE. *Expensive.* **Pines Motel.** 8 overnight and 3 housekeeping units, dining room. Open May 1 to Oct. 14. Phone 963–2029.

SOURIS. *Inexpensive:* **Souris West Motel & Cottages.** Small, comfortable motel and cottages overlooking Colville Bay. On parle français ici. Open year round. Pets okay. Off-season rates before June and after Sept. 15. Phone 687–2676. No credit cards accepted.

SUMMERSIDE. *Expensive:* **Garden of the Gulf Motel/Quality Inn.** Heated outdoor pool, 9-hole golf course and bay beach on property. Babysitting arranged. Adjacent restaurant. Open year-round. Off-season rates Sept. 30 to June 1. Leashed pets okay. Phone 436–2295. Major credit cards.

The Linkletter Motel. Downtown area. Tuna and deep-sea fishing charters, car rental agency, and travel agency. Coffeeshop and dining room. Open year-round. Off-season rates Jan. 1 to May 31. Phone 436–2157. Major credit cards.

Inexpensive: **Cairns' Motel.** Open year-round. Golf, riding academy, drive-in theatre nearby. Phone 436–5841.

Gallant Tourist Home. Small place with friendly hosts. Bilingual. Breakfast provided on request. Open May 1 to Sept. 30. Phone 436–3897. No credit cards accepted.

MacQuarrie's Lighthouse Motel. Housekeeping and overnight units. Near shopping, golf, beaches. Phone 436–2992. Major credit cards.

Sunny Isle Motel. Golf nearby. Open May 1 to Nov. 1. Off-season rates before June 25 and after Sept. 15. Phone 436–5665.

TIGNISH. *Inexpensive:* **Murphy's Tourist Home & Cottages.** Housekeeping and overnight units. Breakfast served on request. Spacious playground. Pets on leash. Visa accepted. Phone 882–2667.

UIGG. *Inexpensive–Moderate:* **Dunvegan Farm Motel.** Noted for the friendly hospitality of owners Dorothy and Harold MacLeod. On a working farm with cows, horses, poultry, and pets. Motel equipped for housekeeping. Rooms available in farm home. Breakfast served on request. Free horseback riding for guests. Open year round. Phone 651–2833. No credit cards accepted.

VICTORIA. *Moderate:* **Victoria Village Inn.** Licensed dining room. Open year round. Phone 658–2288.

WOOD ISLANDS. *Moderate:* **Meadow Lodge Motel.** Clean, comfortable accommodation. Near picnic area and ocean beach at Wood Islands Provincial Park. Open May 15 to October 10. Small leashed pets okay. Phone 962–2022. Major credit cards.

YORK. *Inexpensive:* **Vessey's Housekeeping Units.** Quiet place only 8 km. (5 miles) from Charlottetown. 3 overnight units, one housekeeping apartment. No dogs allowed. No credit cards. Open June 15–Sept. 15.

HOSTELS. *Canadian Hostelling Association's* main hostel is at 151 Mt. Edward Rd., Charlottetown. Showers, kitchen facilities. $5 for members, $7 for non-members. Open late May to Oct. 5. Phone 894–9696.

TELEPHONES. The Island has one long-distance telephone area code throughout (902).

HOW TO GET AROUND. By bus: Double-decker London-style buses tour Charlottetown and visit the North Shore daily, with departures from Confederation Centre.

By limousine: Service is available by reservation to South Shore points of interest, with departure from Charlottetown Hotel.

By taxi: City tours are $15 per hour or $1 per mile.

On foot: In Charlottetown, most attractions are within walking distance of one another. A booklet entitled *Walks in Charlotte Town* is a useful guide. It's available in many bookstores or at the P.E.I. Heritage Foundation.

By car: As tour operations in Prince Edward Island are not extensive, visitors arriving by air in Charlottetown might best tour the province by rented car. Rental agencies such as *Avis, Budget, Hertz,* and *Tilden* are located at the

Charlottetown Airport. Some car-rental agencies maintain small branches in Summerside. During the summer months, it is advisable to book your car rental in advance through a travel agency or the local branch of the rental agency.

How to Reach the Blue Heron Drive. *By car:* From Charlottetown (following the blue heron sign), continue in a counterclockwise direction on Rte. 19, or take 15 north to Rte. 6 at Cavendish.

How to Reach Lady Slipper Drive. *By car:* From Charlottetown, take Rte. 2 to Summerside. Rte. 2 intersects Lady Slipper Drive at the tiny village of Traveller's Rest. Follow the red signs showing the silhouette of a lady slipper plant.

By ferry: The ferry service from Cape Tormentine, New Brunswick, docks at Borden, P.E.I., about 27 kms. (17 miles) from Lady Slipper Drive. From the ferry, turn west onto Rte. 10 to join the drive at Reads Corner. For ferry information, contact CN Marine, Borden, P.E.I. The service from Cape Tormentine takes 45 minutes. From June 21 to Sept. 3 there are hourly crossings from 6:30 A.M. to 8:30 P.M. then at 9:45, 11:30 and 1 A.M. Reduced crossings the remainder of the year. Reservations are not required. Tickets may be purchased at drive-through kiosks entering the ferry terminal area.

By bus: *Island Transit Co-Operative Ltd.* operates a bus service from Charlottetown to Tignish, a distance of 141 kms. (88 miles), daily except Sunday.

How to Reach Kings Byway Drive. *By car:* From Charlottetown, take Rte. 1 [the Trans-Canada Hwy.] east across Hillsborough Bridge and follow the purple crown Kings Byway signs. From Cavendish and the National Park area, take Rte. 6 east and go around Kings Byway drive in a clockwise direction. The ferry from Caribou, Nova Scotia, to Wood Islands, Prince Edward Island, lands visitors about 1½ kms. (1 mile) from Kings Byway. Turn east or west at Wood Islands. For ferry information, contact Northumberland Ferries Limited, 54 Queen St., Charlottetown, P.E.I., C1A 7L3. During the summer season—June to September—the ferry crossings run from 6:30 A.M. to 7:20 P.M. and at 8:15 P.M. and 9:50 P.M. if needed. Reduced hours from Sept. 3 to Dec. Reservations are not required.

FACTS AND FIGURES: Prince Edward Island is by far the smallest of all the Canadian provinces, covering only 2,184 square miles. The capital of P.E.I. is Charlottetown. The province has a population of about 123,000.

TOURIST INFORMATION SERVICES. The Charlottetown Visitor Information Centre is located at the Royalty Mall on University Avenue. Call 902–892–2457 long distance, or just 892–2457 locally. Or write to Visitor Services Division, P.O. Box 940, Charlottetown, P.E.I. C1A 7M5. The Visitor Information Centre at the Borden ferry terminal is open from May to Oct. Lady Slipper Visitor Information Centre at Summerside operates from June to September and the Alberton Centre from June to mid-Sept. There are also Visitor Information Centres at Brackley, Aulac, Cavendish, Kensington, Souris, Stanhope, and the Wood Islands Ferry Terminal (open May to Oct.). The Kings Byway Visitor Information Centre is open from June to October at Pooles Corner, almost 5 kms. (3 miles) north of Montague.

Dial-the-Island reservations and information system: This arrangement makes it easy for you to call ahead to plan your trip, secure any information you may need and to make reservations. Just call the central reservations office while en route to the Island. From New Brunswick or Nova Scotia, dial toll-free 1–800–565–7421. Once on the Island, a network of two-way radios at Visitor Information Centres gives you valuable assistance with reservations and other travel needs day by day.

RECOMMENDED READING. Prince Edward Island is the home of Atlantic Canada's most famous and successful author, the late Lucy Maud Montgomery, whose *Anne of Green Gables* and its successors are worldwide favorite books for girls. Montgomery's life and work are the basis of a small sub-branch of the tourist industry in P.E.I.

Réshard Gool, who teaches at the Island's university, is a poet, novelist *(Price)* and essayist *(Portraits and Gastroscopes,* with Frank Ledwell) and publisher. His Square Deal Press publishes many Island poets and playwrights; it has also published Christopher Gledhill's *Folklore of PEI* and the reminiscenses of a folksy former premier, Walter Shaw's *Tell Me the Tales.* A recent comic novel is Jeffrey Holmes' *The Highjacking of the PEI Ferry.* A worthwhile memento of an Island visit is *Prince Edward Island Photographs,* by Wayne Barrett and Edith Robinson.

TIME ZONE. Prince Edward Island is on Atlantic Time (one hour ahead of Eastern Time).

FESTIVALS AND EVENTS. Alberton. The *Prince County Exhibition* takes place in late August.

Cardigan: *Canada Day parade,* entertainment and craft display.

Charlottetown: The *Charlottetown Summer Festival,* one of Canada's summer highlights, takes place each year from June to September, presenting a series of plays in the Confederation Centre of the Arts. Two full-scale musicals play in repertory six nights a week, Monday to Saturday along with that perennial musical favorite, *Anne of Green Gables,* are among the performances. Special exhibitions of art are presented in the Art Gallery. For information on the summer season, write to: Confederation Centre for the Arts, P.O. Box 848, Charlottetown, Prince Edward Island, C1A 7L9.

May to October is harness racing season. Details available from local tourist bureaus.

Natal Day, a regatta takes place in mid-June.

Country Days and Old Home Week is held in early August.

Eldon: *Highland Games and Gathering of the Clans* take place in early August.

Montague: *Welcome to Summer Celebrations* is held in late June.

O'Leary: The *Prince Edward Island Potato Blossom Festival* takes place in late July.

Oyster Bed Bridge: Stock car races in mid-July. Drag races in early Aug.

Summerside: The *Cape Egmont Yacht Race* is held in June.

In late July the *Lobster Carnival and Livestock Exhibition* takes place.

Tyne Valley: The *Oyster Festival* occurs in early August.

Exact dates of festivals and events change yearly. Check dates and details in *1986 Events,* a free brochure available on request from P.E.I. tourist information centers.

TOURS. *Abegweit Sightseeing Tours* offer a *Charlottetown Tour* of the old and new capital city on a double-decker London-style bus; 6 one-hour tours daily, including Sunday; adults, $3.75, children under 12, $1.00. They also offer a *South Shore Tour* by limousine (reservations required) and a daily *North Shore Tour* by bus leaving the Charlottetown Hotel at 10:30 A.M. and returning in late afternoon. Adults, $15; children under 12, $7.50. Price includes all admissions.

PROVINCIAL PARKS. Along the Kings Byway, a small herd of North American bison is the feature attraction at the 100 acre *Buffaloland Provincial Park* on Rte 4, 6 kms. (4 miles) south of Montague. There is also a small picnic area.

Fantasyland Provincial Park on Rte. 348, near Murray River, has a nice picnic area, swimming, clam-digging, and boating facilities. For the children, there are giant replicas of fairytale characters and a playground.

The *Lord Selkirk Provincial Park,* on Rte. 1, east of Eldon, has a campground, picnic area, swimming, posted hiking trails, and clam-digging flats.

An excellent beach with supervised swimming is available, at the *Panmure Island Provincial Park* on Rte. 347, off Rte. 17 on the south side of Cardigan Bay. This recreation park also has campsites, picnic area, clam-digging flats, and a laundromat. Good for small-boating.

Sir Andrew MacPhail Provincial Park at Orwell is a day-use park on Rte. 1, 32 kms. (20 miles) from Charlottetown. The 143 acres of natural woodland has nature trails, fishing in the pond, a picnic area.

Near the Wood Islands Ferry Terminal is the *Wood Islands Provincial Park.* A day-use park, it overlooks the ocean and has a picnic area and a children's playground.

The *Marie Provincial Park* is another day-use park on the bank of the Marie River 3 kms. (2 miles) east of Morell on Rte. 2. Picnic and small recreational areas along the green riverbank.

Red Point Provincial Park and *Campbell's Cove Provincial Park,* both on Rte. 16, offer tenting sites and swimming for visitors to King County. Supervised beach.

The Northumberland Provincial Park is a complete camping and day-use park with supervised swimming and bathing houses with showers on the sheltered salt water beach. There are picnic areas, a children's playground, a laundromat, recreation hall, and clam-digging flats. On Rte. 4, 3 kms. (2 miles) east of Wood Islands Ferry Terminal.

In the Island's rugged North Cape along Lady Slipper Drive, the *Anglo Provincial Park,* a day-use park, has a good beach and playground for children. Rte. 12, just north of Tignish.

Another day-use park with a playground is *Bloomfield Provincial Park* on Rte. 2 near St. Anthony. Picnic area, washroom, and shower facilities.

A great picnic site with a view is *Campbellton Provincial Park* on the high cliffs overlooking Northumberland Strait, 2½ kms. (1½ miles) south of the junction of Rtes. 14 and 145 at the village of Campbellton.

Cedar Dunes Provincial Park, 18 kms. (11 miles) south of O'Leary on Rte. 14 at West Point, has a long sandy beach, playground, evergreen groves, tenting and trailer sites.

Jacques Cartier Provincial Park honors the French explorer who landed here in 1534. On Rte. 12, 8 kms. (5 miles) north of Alberton. Facilities include campground and beach, with a clam-digging and trout fishing area nearby.

Green Park Provincial Park in Port Hill near Tyne Valley has a interpretive center and a shipbuilding museum. Also a campground with shower and washroom facilities.

Cabot Provincial Park on Rte. 20 has a sandy beach, campground, 24-hour supervision and laundromat on the premises.

Along Blue Heron Drive, *Victoria Provincial Park* on Victoria Harbour, Rte. 10, has a good picnic area. There is swimming here and also at *Argyle Shore Provincial Park.*

Bonshaw Provincial Park on Rte. 1 offers a 32-km. (20-mile) hiking trail. Beginning at West River Bridge near St. Catherine, it goes on to Victoria, winding through large woodlots, fields, and country roads. Never far from roadways, the trail may be hiked in sections. *Strathgartney Provincial Park,* nearby, offers picnic and tenting facilities, as well as a 9-hole golf course.

The *Devil's Punch Bowl Provincial Park* near Granville, on Rte. 254, is a day-use park with a short hiking trail which leads to the spring from which the park got its name.

Scales Pond Provincial Park, Rte. 109, is the site of the Island's largest hydroelectric operation which began in 1798 and closed in 1963.

The Prince Edward Island Visitor Information Centres supply information, locations, opening and closing dates for other smaller day-use and camping provincial parks with picnic, beach, swimming, and other attractions.

GARDENS. Good red earth has made the entire province a garden spot during summer months. *Jewell's Gardens and Pioneer Village* at **York,** off Kings Byway on Rte. 25, specialize in begonias and fuchsias. An antique glass museum, an old country store, and a children's playground are nearby. Open daily, mid-June to mid-Oct., 9 A.M. to 5 P.M. Open until dusk during July and August. Admission: adults $3.50, children under 12 $1.50. pre-schoolers free.

Malpeque Gardens on Rte. 20 features brilliant varieties of dahlias and dozens of floral arrangements. An old-fashioned windmill irrigates the gardens. Open June 25 to August 31, daily 9 A.M. to dusk. 9 A.M.–5 P.M. during September. Admission: adults $2; children under 14, $1; preschoolers free.

FARM VACATIONS AND FARM TOURIST HOMES. For visitors seeking less commercial accommodations, farm vacation and tourist homes offer both an economical way to spend a holiday and an opportunity to meet the people of an area and live among them for a time. Farm tourist and vacation homes take guests on a daily or weekly basis. Some of the homes are on working farms; others are in rural areas. Guests stay in spare rooms, share meals, activities, and even chores with the host family.

Daily rates, ranging from about $15 to $20 per day for two people, may include home-cooked country meals and a snack before bed. Most farm homes have special rates for children.

In general, farm pets do not welcome visiting pets. Check before you come. Bring old clothes and shoes or boots for everyone, especially the children. Farm families usually go to bed early and rise early. Pay for your farm holiday in advance—it's easier to do business before you've become friends.

The P.E.I. Visitors Information Centres have complete listings of farm vacation and tourist homes with rates. Make reservations well in advance directly with the farm family hosts, especially for an extended stay.

RESORTS. *Very Expensive:* **Dalvay-by-the-Sea** at Grand Tracadie north of Charlottetown by the P.E.I. National Park. 25 rooms in manor surrounded by rolling green lawns, 2 cottages. American plan with American and French cuisine in dining room. Babysitting arranged. Two tennis courts, bowling greens, ping pong, driving range, canoeing and trout fishing on premises. Ocean beach 200 yards. Open mid-June to mid-September. Phone 672–2048. Major credit cards.

Expensive: **Brudenell Resort** at Roseneath on the east end of the Island. Probably the best known resort in P.E.I. and an excellent family holiday location. All chalets, most with housekeeping facilities. The complex has been developed on spacious grounds overlooking the Brudenell River. Supervised heated outdoor pool, trail riding, lawn bowling, river beach, 18-hole championship golf course, volley ball and tennis courts, shuffleboard and giant checkers. Supervised children's playground. Gift shop. Deep-sea fishing charters arranged for guests. Open June 1 to the second Monday of October (Canadian Thanksgiving). Phone 652–2332. Major credit cards.

CHILDREN'S ACTIVITIES. Beaches, playgrounds, and parks throughout the province offer excellent activities and facilities for children. Other points of interest include:

Burlington near Kensington: *Woodleigh Replicas,* displays scale models of famous castles and cathedrals, including the Tower of London. Some are large enough to enter and walk around in.

Bonshaw: *Bonshaw 500* has karting for all members of the family. Children drive their own karts. Picnic tables; playground.

Cavendish: *The Royal Atlantic Wax Museum* has life size wax figures of famous people from Josephine Tussaud.

Green Gables House is the famous farm home in Lucy Maude Montgomery's *Anne of Green Gables.*

Rainbow Valley as described in L.M. Montgomery's *Rainbow Valley,* has a Children's Farm, a playground, Fantasy Area, Flying Saucer, and boating lakes.

DeSable: *House of Dolls* exhibits miniature dolls of famous people from many nations. Also, children's corner.

Harrington: *Pinehills Playground* has large play area with long slide, maze, haunted cave, swings, Indian area, and prehistoric animals.

North Rustico: *The Wildlife Park,* complete with picnic area, has fine collection of native animals and wild birds.

Rocky Point: *Micmac Indian Village* has Indian Trail and authentic Indian Village.

Stanley Bridge: *Marineland Aquarium and Manor of Birds* has fine collection of mounted birds; fish tanks; seal pool; butterflies.

Also check under *Festivals and Events, Provincial Parks,* and *Camping* in this section.

SPORTS. P.E.I. is sports-oriented. On an island of **golf** courses, one of the best known in Atlantic Canada is the championship Brudenell Golf Course, located in the resort complex at *Roseneath.* The Belvedere course in *Charlottetown,* the Mill River championship course on Lady Slipper Drive, and the Summerside Golf Club Course (all are 18-hole courses) are also among the best.

The Green Gables Course, part of the National Park, surrounds the home of the storybook character Anne of Green Gables, in the *Cavendish* area.

The *Rustico* Golf Course is flanked by trees and waterholes overlooking Rustico Bay. An 18 holer, it is near recreational activities of all kinds.

The *Stanhope* Golf and Country Club is situated near Prince Edward Island National Park.

A 9-hole course, the Glen Afton, is located on the south coast near the historic *Fort Amherst* site. Another 9-hole course, Forest Hills Golf Course, is located on Rte. 6 in *Cavendish.*

The *Strathgartney* links offer a par three, nine-hole course.

Bicycling. Its small size and veinwork of quiet country roads make P.E.I. a natural attraction for the cyclist. Bicycles can be rented at MacQueen's Bike Shop, 430 Queen St., *Charlottetown* (892-9843) or at Summerside Advance Rental, 133 Water St., *Summerside* (436-3867); cost: about $12 daily, $30 weekly at both places.

Canoeing is also growing in popularity in the province's many meandering tidal estuaries—a delight of rolling sandbars and quiet havens. Visitor information bureaus can tell you where to rent canoes.

Hiking and cross-country skiing are a pleasure on the low rolling terrain of Prince Edward Island. There are hiking trails and numerous nature walks.

Devil's Punch Bowl Trail—one mile long, located between the Rattenbury Rd., Rte. 254, and South Granville—down an old horse and carriage road through hardwood forests. Easy enough for children.

Bonshaw Hills Trail—20 miles long, from West River Bridge (near St. Catherines) to Victoria, not far from Borden.

P.E.I.'s national park has several trails. And in winter there are four loop-style cross-country ski trails.

Information on hiking and cross-country ski trails is available from the P.E.I. Department of Tourism.

Fishing. The Island has some of the best salt- and freshwater fishing in eastern Canada. *Freshwater fishing* for brook trout and white perch is usually no more than a few minutes' walk across a field. The trout season runs from mid-April to September 30, with a limit of 20 trout a day. Non-resident fishing licenses cost $12, obtainable from the Fish and Wildlife Division in Charlottetown or any other license vendor; guides are not required. All the inland fisheries are fine places to catch brook trout. For rainbow trout, fish the Dunk, Cardigan, and Sturgeon Rivers and two inland lakes—Glenfinnan and O'Keefe.

Saltwater or deep-sea fishing can be a family outing. Most trips last 4 hours and most fishing ports have boats available for charter. The cost is about $10 per person. The boat captain supplies all tackle and bait. Boats listed by the Visitor Information Centres have passed rigorous safety standards set by the federal government. Reservations can be made in advance by phone. A boat list is available at the nearest Visitors Information Centre or at a wharf displaying the deep-sea fishing sign.

Tuna fishing is serious sport in P.E.I. The North Lake area on the Kings Byway is still the giant bluefin capital of the island. On the Blue Heron Drive, North Rustico, and Malpeque Harbour are tuna fishing ports. On King's Byway there are two other tuna ports: Morell Harbour and Savage Harbour.Tuna charters are roughly $250. Further information on tuna charters and other deep-sea fishing arrangements is available from any P.E.I. Visitors Information Centre. Or write Tourism Services Division, P.O. Box 940, Charlottetown, P.E.I., C1A 7M5. The Fish and Wildlife Division, P.O. Box 2000, Charlottetown, P.E.I., Canada C1A 7N8 will also have any additional information you need.

Along with golf and fishing, another top sport is **harness racing.** Many residents race their own horses at the small racetracks throughout the province. Two major tracks—at Charlottetown and Summerside—feature competitions from all over Canada and the U.S.

Other popular sports are tennis, swimming, boating, and horseback riding, available at a good number of resorts, campgrounds, and at the national park.

 CAMPING. For a small island, P.E.I. has a good number of private and provincially operated campgrounds for tenting, trailering, and camping. Check open dates for each campground. Unless stated otherwise, reservations may be made directly with the camping area.

Along the Kings Byway, at Roseneath, near Brudenell Resort, is the *Brudenell River Provincial Park,* on Rte. 3 between Pooles Corner and Georgetown. The 90-acre park has 94 unserviced sites and 12 two-way hookups. Campers can use the 18-hole Brudenell golf course and the fresh water beach on the Brudenell River. Open mid-May to mid-October. Reservations not accepted.

For campers who prefer saltwater beaches, *Seal Cove Campground* at Murray Harbour North has a saltwater beach on the premises and another ocean beach just a short distance away. Located 16 kms. (10 miles) from Murray River via Rtes. 4 and 17, the 25-acre campground has 17 unserviced sites, 25 two-way hookups, and 60 three-way hookups. Open June 1 to Oct. 15.

For the camper with an interest in history, the *Lord Selkirk Provincial Park* commemorates the Scottish settlers who broke the land here in 1803. Located 1½ kms. (1 mile) east of Eldon, just off the Trans-Canada Hwy., the 50-acre camping portion of the park has 52 unserviced sites and 20 two-way hookups. Among other amenities is the nearby reconstructed Lord Selkirk Settlement, saltwater beach, picnic sites, marked hiking trails, and clam-digging flats within the park. Open from the beginning of June to September 6. Reservations not accepted.

Jacques Cartier Provincial Park has 24 unserviced sites and 12 two-way hookups on 22 acres. Located 6 kms. (4 miles) from Alberton off Rte. 2 at Kildare Capes. Ocean beach on premises. Reservations not accepted. Open June to Labor Day.

One of the best ocean beaches is at *Cedar Dunes Provincial Park,* 24 kms. (15 miles) from O'Leary. The 100-acre park has 36 unserviced sites and 10 two-way hookups. Reservations not accepted.

Green Provincial Park, which includes a wooden shipbuilding museum and restoration, is 32 kms. (20 miles) west of Summerside, on Rte. 12. There are 66 unserviced sites and 24 three-way hookups with an ocean beach on the premises. Reservations not accepted. June to Labor Day.

About 6½ kms. (4 miles) west of Summerside on Rte. 11, *Linkletter Provincial Park* has 52 unserviced sites and 32 two-way hookups. Saltwater beach on the premises. Reservations not accepted. Open mid-May to mid-September.

Along Blue Heron Drive, beach camping is excellent in the campsites of Cavendish, Brackley, and Stanhope, all part of the National Park. The privately owned Cavendish Sunset Campground has a swimming pool, tennis courts, ocean beach, and a miniature golf course. Reservations accepted.

At *Blythwood Trailer Park,* Cavendish, pets permitted on leash, mini-bikes not permitted; ocean beach, and 18-hole golf course.

At *Rustico Island Campground,* a section of the national park, 5 kms. (3 miles) west of Rte. 15 on Gulf Shore Rd., you'll find 113 developed acres and 148 unserviced sites. There's an interpretative program, outdoor theater, ocean beach, and 18-hole golf course. Reservations not accepted.

The *Prince Edward Island National Park* runs 25 miles along the coastline and beaches of the North Shore. Excellent beaches, campgrounds, and sporting facilities.

Another section of the national park at Stanhope on Gulf Shore Rd. has 5 developed acres with 103 unserviced sites and 14 three-way hookups. An interpretive program, ocean beach, and 18-hole golf course are available. Washing machines on site. Reservations not accepted.

Camping fees range from $5.50 to $12 daily, depending on the type of site. Private trailer park daily rates average $8 a day.

Note: Camping on Prince Edward Island is restricted to organized camping grounds. It is against the law to camp on a beach or on property not designated as a camping area.

The P.E.I. Visitors Information Centres have listings of campgrounds with rates at their bureaus.

 MUSEUMS AND HISTORIC SITES. P.E.I. Tourism's brochure *Visitor's Guide* describes and illustrates museums and historic sites by County, and is available by request, at no charge from the provincial tourism department. Some highlights—In **Charlottetown,** historically important *Province House* now houses the province's legislature; *Beaconsfield* is headquarters for the Prince Edward Island Museum and Heritage Foundation; and *Old Charlottetown* houses a wide variety of old shops, museums, stores, craft centers, restaurants, churches, and homes.

The Kings Byway Dr. will take you through many attractions that recall the early days of the Island and the early settlers' pioneering spirit. (See *Kings Byway Drive* section earlier in this chapter for additional Museums and Historic Sites.)

The agricultural heritage of rural P.E.I. is re-captured at the *Rural Life Museum* near **Orwell.** Open for the summer season, 10 A.M. to 6 P.M. Admission: adults $1.50; children 5¢.

The Lord Selkirk Settlement at **Eldon** features reproductions of settlers' shelters and cabins. Open 9 A.M. to 7 P.M., July and August; 9 A.M. to 4 P.M., June 19 to September 11. Admission $2.25 per adult, children under 16, $1.00. The *Polly Gift Shop* is on the premises.

The Log Cabin Museum at **Murray Harbour** depicts the Island's 19th-century lifestyle. Open July 1 to Labor Day, 9 A.M. to 7 P.M. daily. Admission: adults, $1; children, 50¢; under 6, free.

An interesting collection of old firearms is one of the features at the *Garden of the Gulf Museum* in **Montague.** Open June 27 to September 16, 9:30 A.M. to 5 P.M., Monday–Saturday, 1 to 5 P.M. Sundays. Admission: adults, about $1.00; children under 12, 50¢. Displays and photographs in the *Fisheries Museum at Basin Head* show how small boats were used by early fishermen.

Antique car buffs might visit the *Spoke Wheel Car Museum* at **Dunstaffnage.** Open June 1 to September 15, 9 A.M. to 7 P.M., during July and August; 10 A.M. to 6 P.M., the remainder of the season. Admission: adults $3.00; children 1 to 6, $1.00; pre-schoolers, free.

Along Lady Slipper Drive, *Green Park Provincial Park* at **Port Hill** commemorates a 19th-century shipping complex. Admission: adults $1.00, children under 12 free. Open daily 10 A.M. to 6 P.M. June 25 to September 6. Check for hours after September 6. A campground is also part of the park.

At **Northport,** *Sea Rescue Park* has picnic tables, washrooms, water tap, and a children's playground. Sea Rescue Park is open from June 1 to October 31, from 9 A.M. to 10 P.M. daily. Free.

The *Acadian Museum* at **Miscouche** has an impressive collection of 17th- and 18th-century household, farm, and other domestic implements portraying the Acadian lifestyle over the years. Open from June 24 to September 20, Sundays 1:00–5:00 P.M. and rest of week, 10 A.M.–6 P.M. Adults, $2.00; children, $1.00; under 12, free.

(See *Lady Slipper Drive* section earlier in this chapter for additional information.)

Blue Heron Drive passes the historic *"Farmers' Bank"* (chartered in 1864) at **South Rustico.**

At **Long River,** Rte. 234 off Rt. 20, the *Old Mill Museum* contains antiques and a collection of bottles. Adults, $2.00, children, $1.00. Hours: 10 A.M.–5:30 P.M.

The **French River District** has two pioneer era cemeteries, *Yankee Hill* and *Sims.*

At **Bonshaw** just beyond DeSable is an interesting *Car Life Museum.* Open May 24 to mid-Sept.; July and August, 9 A.M. to 9 P.M. daily, May, June and Sept. 10 A.M. to 5 P.M. Admission: adults, $3.00; children 6–14, $1.25; pre-schoolers, free.

At **Rocky Point** across the harbor from Charlottetown, the earthworks of the historic *Fort Amherst* (formerly Port La Joie, 1720) are a reminder of 18th-century occupation.

One mile east on Rte. 19, a *Micmac Village* has been re-created . . . birchbark canoes, wigwams, and an Indian craftshop.

  ART GALLERIES. *The Confederation Centre Art Gallery and Museum* at the Confederation Centre in Charlottetown, is one of Canada's premier art museums. It is dedicated to the work of Canadian artists and hosts major exhibits from Canada, the U.S. and overseas. Its permanent collection includes the country's largest collection of paintings by Robert Harris (1849–1919), Canada's foremost portrait artist. Admission is $1, family $2. Open 10 A.M. to 8 P.M. July and August; 10 A.M. to 5 P.M. (and closed Mondays), September to June.

The Great George Street Gallery at 88 Great George St., Charlottetown, is a nonprofit gallery run by artists and supported by the national and provincial governments. It provides a program of exhibitions by local and regional artists, plus some special events. Admission free.

 THEATER. During July and August, the **Charlottetown** Festival at the Confederation Centre for the Arts includes that P.E.I. perennial, *Anne of Green Gables,* plus a number of other, usually musical, productions. Feature plays are staged six nights a week in the 1,100-seat *Main Stage Theatre.* International concert artists are featured Sunday evenings on Main Stage. The adjacent *Cameo Theatre* cabaret productions of Canadian musicals six nights a week.

The King's Playhouse at **Georgetown** on Rte. 3, 30 miles (50 km.) east of Charlottetown, provides professional summer theater. Three plays in repertory plus variety concerts. Open daily, July 5–August 28.

The Governor's Feast at *The Barn* restaurant on Rte. 1 near **Charlottetown** is light dinner theater featuring the governor of 1842 and retinue. Similarly, there's *The Prohibition Feast,* bouncing 1930's stuff, at *The Brothers Two* restaurant on Rte. 1A near **Summerside.**

SHOPPING. Since colonial times, handcrafted items have been valued by P.E.I. inhabitants and craftspeople excel at jewelry making, wood carving, pottery, enameling, leather work, quilting, and weaving—just a few of the crafts executed with great skill. The P.E.I. Craftsmen's Council, Inc., P.O. Box 1573, Charlottetown, P.E.I. C1A 7N3 (tel. 892–5152), or the P.E.I. Visitors Information Centre can supply full information on outlets and types of crafts available.

Along Lady Slipper Drive, look for turned Bird's-eye maple wood products at the Leavitts' Maple Tree Craft Shop in **Alberton.** Open year-round, 8 A.M. to 5 P.M., Monday–Saturday.

Lennox Island Indian Arts and Crafts on **Lennox Island,** Rte. 163, has MicMac beadwork, moccasins, masks, turtle rattles and other crafts.

One major stop is the Acadian Pioneer Village at **Mont Carmel,** a restored early 19th-century community. Also visit the restaurant on the site and try an Acadian soup or potato dish. The restaurant is open from 10 A.M. to 11 P.M. daily. Prices are reasonable. The museum village is open from mid-June to mid-Sept., 10 A.M. to 7 P.M. daily.

For good pottery, visit the Flat River Crafts Studio on Kings Byway Drive. Open year-round, daily, 9 A.M. to 9 P.M.

One of the largest and most complete handcraft shops in P.E.I. is the Wood Islands Handcraft Co-Op on Main St. in **Murray River.** All the Island crafts are represented in this retail outlet on Kings Byway, which is open from June to Sept.

In **Charlottetown,** there's the Island Craft Shop located at 146 Richmond St. This shop contains a wide selection of island crafts. Open year-round from Monday to Saturday, 9 A.M. to 5 P.M. In July and August it's Monday to Saturday, 9 A.M. to 8 P.M.

Shopping malls are open 10 A.M. to 10 P.M., Monday to Saturday. Other stores throughout the province generally open at 9 A.M. and close at 5 or 5:30 P.M. On Friday evenings, most stores stay open until 9 P.M. Country stores generally open earlier and close later.

Holiday closings: Good Friday, Easter Monday, Victoria Day (in mid-May), July 1 (Canada Day), Labor Day (September 3), Thanksgiving (October 8), and Remembrance Day (November 11).

DINING OUT. The Island offers plenty of plain, wholesome, home-cooked food with friendly (often slow) service in an informal setting. In Charlottetown, however, good formal dining can be had in at least half a dozen restaurants.

The legal drinking age is 18. Liquor stores are open six days a week for about 12 hours a day.

Restaurants are categorized on the basis of full course dinners; drinks, tax, and tip are excluded. *Expensive,* over $15; *Moderate,* $10–$15; *Inexpensive,* under $10. A 10% provincial tax will be added to all meals over $2.00.

Most places accept the following major credit cards: American Express, MasterCard and Visa; others may also be honored. Not all establishments accept credit cards, therefore we suggest you call for information.

Every effort is made to ensure that the list of restaurants is up to date, but they come and go so quickly that it is always a good idea to call before going far out of your way.

CAVENDISH. *Moderate:* **Chez Yvonne.** Good food, all home cooking; has its own garden, fresh vegetables. Phone 963–2070.

Fiddles & Vittles. Fresh shellfish, chowder, and steak. Open 4–9 P.M.; licensed. Phone 963–2225.

Marco Polo Inn. Well-known; good food. Phone 963–2351. Major credit cards.

Inexpensive–Moderate: **Cavendish Arms.** Steak and seafood, licensed; Irish and modern music; dancing. Phone 963–2732.

CHARLOTTETOWN. *Expensive:* **The Confederation Dining Room,** Charlottetown Hotel. Elegant surroundings, pleasant food. Phone 894-7371. Major credit cards.

Griffin Dining Room in the Dundee Arms Inn. Situated in a Victorian home. Checked tablecloths, fireplace, good food. Licensed. Swiss-French cuisine. House specializes in fondue Bourguignonne and has a special knack with locally caught fish. One of the best. Phone 892-2496. Major credit cards.

Minnie's. Seafood specialties—scampi, sole, excellent scallops wrapped in bacon, lobster. Homemade cheesecake and strawberry crêpes. True gourmet dining. Many people call Minnie's the best restaurant on the island. Call for reservations. Phone 894-7232. Major credit cards.

Lock Stock and Barrel at the Confederation Inn. Good but not ritzy. Phone 892-2481. Major credit cards.

Moderate: **Caesar's Italy.** Italian foods plus local steaks and seafoods. A casual place with a salad and soup bar. Phone 892-9201. Major credit cards.

Off Broadway Cafe. Tucked away in old Charlottetown. Homemade specials. Phone 892-0632.

The Dispensary. Early Canadian atmosphere. Located in historic building. Fondues a specialty. Has a good reputation. Phone 892-5195. Major credit cards.

MacLauchlan's Motel. Scottish atmosphere. Home-style cooking. It has gained popularity in recent years for its accent on traditional island dishes. Phone 892-2461. Major credit cards.

The Rodd Royalty Inn. An uncomplicated but fairly attractive menu of steaks and seafoods. Phone 894-8566. Major credit cards.

The Showboat Dining Room. Home-style cooking. Accent on seafood. Live entertainment, large dance floor. Phone 892-7998.

Inexpensive: **Casa Mia.** Situated in old home. Quiet. Italian and Canadian food. Phone 892-8888. Major credit cards.

CORNWALL. *Moderate:* **Bonnie Brae.** Good family restaurant. Phone 675-2241.

GRAND TRACADIE. *Expensive:* **Dalvay-By-The-Sea Hotel.** Located 3½ miles off Rte. 25 (near Stanhope). One of the Island's most elite eating places. Built as a summer home for a wealthy American who later sold it to his coachman (in lieu of 7 years' wages, according to locals), it has a large staircase and elegant interior. Excellent seafood. Reservations preferred but not always necessary. Phone 672-2048. Major credit cards.

KENSINGTON. *Moderate:* **Recreation Center.** Homemade food; not elegant but good.

KINGSBORO. *Moderate:* **Seabreeze Motel.** Good dining room, licensed; features home cooking with seafood specialties. Open year-round. Phone 357-2371.

MONTAGUE. *Moderate–Expensive:* **Lobster Shanty North.** One of the best places to eat on the Kings Byway. Dining room has rustic décor that extends into the lounge bar overlooking the Montague River. Licensed, and features seafood, particularly lobster. Open year-round. Phone 838-2463.

MONT CARMEL. *Moderate:* **Étoile de Mer** in the Acadian Pioneer Village. Specializes in Acadian dishes—rapure and meat pies. Try Acadian soup or a potato dish. Open mid-June to mid-September, 10 A.M. to 11 P.M. daily.

MORELL. *Moderate:* **Village Diner.** Features home-cooked meals and specials every day. Overlook the rough atmosphere and enjoy the food. Licensed with adjacent lounge bar. Open year-round.

POOLES CORNER. *Moderate:* **Kingsway Motel.** Licensed dining room, good food and a cozy lounge. Open year-round. During off-season—dancing. Phone 838–2112. Major credit cards.

ROSENEATH. *Expensive:* **Brudenell Resort Restaurant.** Usually good service and good food in the resort complex. Licensed. Two lounge bars adjacent. Open June 1 to September 30. Phone 652–2332. Major credit cards.

RUSTICO. *Moderate–Expensive:* **Fisherman's Wharf Restaurant.** Open mid-May to October. 7 A.M.–10 P.M. daily. Seafood and special mussel chowder. Phone 963–2669.

SOURIS. *Moderate:* **Bluefin Restaurant.** Plain food in unpretentious surroundings. Licensed with adjacent lounge bar featuring entertainment. Open year-round. Phone 687–3271.

SOUTHPORT. *Moderate–Expensive:* **The Barn.** Features beef and seafood. Rustic atmosphere. Phone 569–2228.

SUMMERSIDE. *Moderate–Expensive:* **Brothers Two.** Steaks and seafood, scallops a specialty. Open and airy atmosphere, pleasant service. Licensed. Dancing. Also "Prohibition feast," specializing in Island seafood served by a cast of talented performers who dine, dance and perform during feast. 6 P.M. to 9 P.M., Monday to Saturday. Phone 436-9654.
Moderate: **Linkletter Motel.** Licensed; specialty is good buffet at noon weekdays & on Friday evenings. Phone 436–2157. Major credit cards.
Papa David's. Seafood, mostly in a cozy waterfront setting. Phone 436–4606. Major credit cards.

LOBSTER SUPPERS: You must sample the lobster suppers; usually served in church halls or community centers, they are an Island tradition.
Brackley Beach Lobster Suppers, open June 21–September 6, daily, noon–9 P.M., phone 672–2352 or 672–2718, on Rte. 15 in Brackley Beach at Howe's Hall, manager, Gordon MacCallum.
New Glasgow Lobster Suppers, open June 4–Oct. 23, daily 4 P.M.–8:30 P.M., phone 964–2870, New Glasgow on Rte. 224, manager, Ralph Dickieson.
New London Lion's Club Lobster Suppers, open June 5–Oct. 3, daily 4 P.M.–8:30 P.M., phone 886–2599, New London on Rte. 6, manager, Nelson Roberts.
St. Ann's Church Suppers (licensed), open June 20–September 10, daily 4 P.M.–9 P.M., phone 964–2351 or 964–2385, Hope River on Rte. 224, manager, Rev. E. Van De Ven.
Stanhope Beach Lodge, Lobster plus smorgasbord. Also rolls, salads . . . all you can eat for about $17. June 30 to September 5.
Fisherman's Wharf Lobster Suppers, North Rustico, 963–2669.

 NIGHTCLUBS, BARS, LOUNGES. A lounge in P.E.I. is a fully licensed bar which usually has some live entertainment part or all of the week. Some lounges also have a limited food menu during certain hours of the day. All are closed on Sundays.
Charlottetown: *The Tudor Lounge,* Charlottetown Hotel, is quiet, popular on Friday evenings. *The Smuggler's Jug,* Confederation Inn. Rustic beams, quiet background music. *Page One,* Rodd Inn. Cozy, dim and attractive, small lounge. *The Gallows Lounge,* small, built on Gallows Hill with rather macabre gallows décor; daily happy hours. *Prince Edward Lounge* and *WR's Place.* Often feature local entertainers who have now achieved national recognition—Anne Murray, Stompin' Tom Connors, John Allen Cameron, Ryan's Fancy. *Showboat Dining Lounge.* Nightclub-like atmosphere, big dance floor, entertainment, popular and rock music. *The Tackroom.* Small bar, great drinks. *Mrs. K's,* Kirkwood

Motor Hotel. 1920's decor, lively crowd. *Sea Shell Lounge* (large and plush) and *Crossed Keys Bar* (small and intimate), both in Prince Edward Hilton hotel.

Summerside: *Regent Lounge.* Disco to 2 A.M. weekends, 1 A.M. weeknights. *Scrooge's Lounge* above Clovie's Restaurant, closes at 1 A.M. *Papa David's Lobster Trap Lounge,* disco to 2 A.M. weekends, 1 A.M. weekdays. *Friday's Lounge* and *Capt. Grady's Pub* are both in Brothers Two restaurant.

NOVA SCOTIA

Old Legends—New Attractions

By
ALAN FREEMAN and RALPH SURETTE

Alan Freeman is a travel writer based in Nova Scotia and New Bruns-wick.

Nova Scotia! The name itself—Latin for "New Scotland"—evokes the magic rhythms of the sea. Sometimes serene, sometimes violent, the sea encircles all but the narrow isthmus which attaches the province to New Brunswick and the Canadian mainland. The coast, unspoiled and accessible almost everywhere, is one of grand rocky sweeps and intimate coves, clifftop views, and gentle beaches. The sea winds its way, too, through the province's economy, its long history—and its legends.

The Vikings may have seen its shores around A.D. 1000. One of the oldest European settlements in North America was established at Port Royal, on the Bay of Fundy, in 1605. And the area was of pivotal importance during the French-English wars of the 17th and 18th centuries that determined the future of Canada. The French fortress at Louisbourg, Cape Breton, one of the most ambitious historical reconstructions ever undertaken in Canada, and the Citadel which dominates downtown Halifax are but two of the many fortified remains of that period. It was an epoch, too, that gave rise to a rich lore of ghost ships, buried treasure and other pirate tales that form a constant theme in the province's many museums.

But Nova Scotia is more than a coastline encompassing history and legend. Its inland parts are also compelling—from the apple orchards and farmland of the Annapolis Valley to the beautiful highlands of Cape Breton and through all the lakes, streams, fields, and forests in-between and beyond.

Despite the attractiveness of field and shore, it is the capital, Halifax, that provides one of the province's most intriguing sides. The modern pressures of development have marked it, yet Halifax has preserved the essentials of its architecture and traditions. Its mix of old and new, history and modernity, is considered among the best in North America.

The Tides of History

As early as 1518 and again in 1523, French expeditions tried—with no success—to establish permanent settlements in the area. The first Europeans to colonize the region were French explorers de Monts and Champlain who secured their "Habitation" in 1605 near present day Port Royal and called it Acadia. Eight years earlier, British navigators John and Sebastian Cabot had stopped briefly on the northern tip of Cape Breton, claimed the entire continent for England, and then moved on. It was not until 1621, when King James I of England and VI of Scotland granted the province to Sir William Alexander, that the British made their first attempt to settle in Nova Scotia, the first British colony to possess its own flag. Derived from the original arms presented by King James, it is made up of the blue cross of St. Andrew with a shield depicting the red lion of Scotland. A new order of knighthood— the Baronets of Nova Scotia—was created and each knight was awarded a grant in the new territory. Although the scheme to colonize the area failed after a few years, the Order still exists.

The French were more successful at colonization but less so at retaining their territory. The entire region was the scene of continuing French/British conflict for supremacy over all of Canada in the 17th and early 18th centuries until the Treaty of Utrecht transferred Nova Scotia to British rule in 1713. Cape Breton Island (a separate province until 1820) remained French for a short time thereafter.

Although the French struggled to preserve their beachheads in the British part of the province, disaster struck in 1755 when they were driven from the province by British troops who questioned their loyalty. Some journeyed to Quebec, Prince Edward Island, or Cape Breton Island; others set out for Louisiana where their descendants are known today as "Cajuns," a corruption of "Acadians." Henry Wadsworth Longfellow, 19th-century American poet, immortalized the tragedy of the forced evacuation in *Evangeline:* "Waste all those pleasant farms and the farmers forever departed!" In return Acadians immortalized both Longfellow and *Evangeline.* There are stone monuments to the poet and his creation in the Grand Pré National Historic Park, although according to historians Longfellow never set foot in Nova Scotia.

The Acadians' lands were quickly settled with thousands of New England "planters," who were British Empire Loyalists escaping the American Revolution. The Acadians who managed to return to their former holdings found them occupied. Moving further down the Nova

Scotia coast, they settled the area between Yarmouth and Digby—where the Acadian language and traditions are maintained to this day.

The Treaty of 1763 gave Britain permanent possession of Nova Scotia and most of what is now eastern Canada; France relinquished all claims, including Cape Breton Island, except for the tiny islands of St. Pierre and Miquelon which remain French Departments to this day.

Until 1784, Nova Scotia included what is now the province of New Brunswick. Following the influx of tens of thousands of United Empire Loyalists to the enlarged Nova Scotia, the separation of the New Brunswick portion was accomplished.

Early in 1800, the Highland Scots began to arrive; within 30 years more than 50,000 had settled in Cape Breton, and Pictou and Antigonish counties. Present-day Scots have maintained their Highland tradition, taking a fierce pride in the Gaelic language, the kilt, bagpipes, and traditional dances. Today, no parade in Nova Scotia is complete without a pipe band, (bagpipe, that is), and throughout the summer there are numerous Highland Games, gatherings, and concerts.

After the American Revolution, about 25,000 American colonists, with strong ties of allegiance to England, migrated to Nova Scotia where they founded Shelburne. In the war of 1812, Nova Scotia was the leading British base in North America.

The colony became the first one in British North America to achieve representative government—government elected by the people. That happened in 1758. In 1848 it became the first part of Canada to achieve "responsible" government—in which the cabinet was chosen from the elected members rather than appointed by the crown.

Today, Nova Scotia has become a stable meld of the various peoples and nationalities who made up the original settlements. Various areas remain Acadian; in the Lunenburg area, the people are Dutch or German; the Scots are dominant in the eastern part of the province. Indeed, it is said that there are more clans represented in Nova Scotia than in Scotland itself. And 5,400 of the original people, the Micmac Indians, still live on a number of reserves around the province.

Industry in Nova Scotia

Nova Scotia has a highly diversified economy. Manufacturing takes many forms—from electronics to textiles to steel—in both large and small plants. Fishing is obviously a major activity, but so are forestry, agriculture, and even tourism. One interesting note with regard to forestry is that the county of Lunenburg is considered the Christmas tree capital of North America. Hundreds of thousands of cultivated firs are shipped from there every autumn. Manufacturing is dominated by the French multinational company, Michelin Tires Ltd., which has three tire-making plants in the province. Another dominating installation is the steel mill at Sydney, which employs several thousand people. Sydney is the only other city in the province apart from Halifax and Dartmouth, which form one metropolitan area. Shipbuilding and ship repair are also important throughout the province, while Halifax, of course, is a major Canadian port and naval base.

Mining has been an up and down affair over the decades. There was a short-lived gold rush in the late 1800's, then a decline, and now there's a revival in mining generally. Around the turn of the century, Nova Scotia was a major gold producer. Today there is evidence of this prosperity in heaps of mine tailings and abandoned pits on remote back roads in areas such as Moose River Gold Mines off Highway 7, or at The Ovens, near Lunenburg, where there's a local museum on gold mining.

Coal mining has had a checkered history in Nova Scotia, bringing vast fortunes to a few industrialists and little more than bitter memories to the miners early in the 20th century. As oil became more common, the collieries declined, and in 1969, the Canadian government set up the Cape Breton Development Corporation to wind down the mines and transfer the miners to other work. After the rapid rise in oil prices since 1973, coal has again become a valued resource. Several new mines have been opened in the Cape Breton coalfield, employing thousands of miners.

Tourists may take mine tours in Springhill, a town built above the deepest coal mines in Canada, and in Cape Breton at Glace Bay and Sydney Mines. The Miners' Museum at Glace Bay has an excellent layout and display area, including reproductions of typical early buildings from the mining towns.

History Preserved and Polished

The province abounds in historic homes, building sites, and other attractions that have been maintained or restored by the provincial and federal governments. There are eight specially designated tourist routes that cover most of the areas of interest. These follow mostly the old trunk highways that wind their way through the villages and towns. Traffic is usually light on these roads, since the province also has a network of modern superhighways for through traffic.

The South Shore (Lighthouse Route) between Halifax and Yarmouth is often called the quintessential Nova Scotia. It features intriguing fishing villages and small towns nestled in a sometimes rugged, sometimes gentle coastline loaded with seafaring tradition. Near Mahone Bay, for instance, there's the famous Oak Island money pit—an ingeniously designed pit believed to have held pirate treasure but which defies sure explanation to this day. Peggy's Cove—the province's showpiece fishing village—is on this route. So is Lunenburg, site of the Fishermen's Museum, a small town which is pretty well the Canadian capital of the fishing tradition.

The Annapolis Valley route (Evangeline Trail) takes you past Annapolis Royal, the site of Samuel de Champlain's 1605 settlement; the entire downtown has recently received an historic facelift with numerous old buildings being restored. Nearby is North America's first tidal power plant on the Annapolis River. The valley is also a very scenic drive.

The Fundy Shore (Glooscap Trail) runs along the site of the world's highest tides, where ships rest on the bottom and fishermen collect their catch on foot at low tide. The cliffs contain a wealth of fossils, especially near Joggins. And Cape Blomidon Provincial Park located here is as lovely a spot as you'll find anywhere.

The Eastern Shore (Marine Drive) follows the ever-captivating Atlantic coast from Halifax to Cape Breton, with a high point at Sherbrooke Village, the province's main 19th-century reconstructed historic village.

The Northumberland Shore (Sunrise Trail) has plenty of beach and warm water for swimming—the only part of the province that has it.

Cape Breton has three trails. There's the Cabot Trail with its breath-taking views—one of the most gripping marine drives on the continent. The Fleur-de-Lis Trail goes to the reconstructed fortress at Louisbourg and some Acadian parts of Cape Breton, while the Ceilidh (pronounced *kay-lee*) Trail takes you to places like St. Ann's, Baddeck, and other centers of the province's rich Scottish-Gaelic heritage.

The Climate

Weather in Nova Scotia depends on the area. Inland, the temperatures tend to be more extreme, roughly -10 to $-1°C$. in January and 11 to 29°C. in summer (13–30°F. in January and 52–75°F. in summer), than temperatures along the coast. Along the coast, weather tends to be more variable, particularly in winter, changing as much as 23°C. (45°F.) over an eight-hour period. Precipitation may be snow inland and rain along the coast. While the ocean causes variable weather, it also warms the land, keeping the province relatively warm in winter and cooler in the summer.

Each season brings its own pleasures. In the spring (mid-April to the end of May), days are mild, nights are cool. A season of crocuses, tulips, and budding trees. Average temperatures: 7 to 14°C. (45–58°F.).

Summer (June, July, August) is time for fun in the sun. Even the hottest summer day is cooled in the evenings by soft ocean breezes. Be prepared for the occasional summer shower and, for comfort, take a light sweater for evening. Temperatures range from 18 to 32°C. (65–90°F.).

No part of Nova Scotia—54,390 sq. kms. (21,000 square miles)—is more than 56 kms. (35 miles) from the sea. During July, August, and even into early September the many sandy beaches are well used. For comfort, saltwater swimming should be restricted to the Northumberland Strait coast where water temperature will reach up to 21°C. (70°F.). On the other coasts the water temperature is distinctly cool, and so cold in the Bay of Fundy as to be dangerous to swimmers. A number of beach areas on all coasts have been developed by the provincial government and several have supervised swimming areas. These vary from year to year. Check with the Department of Tourism for an up-to-date list.

Indian Summer (September) is one of the favorite times of year for travelers to Nova Scotia. Days are warm, but not hot; evenings crisp, but not cold. Expect temperatures from 18 to 23°C. (65–75°F.), cooling to 15°C. (60°F.) at night.

Autumn (October) brings on Nova Scotia's most colorful season. Leaves turn first in the inland areas; then, in a predictable 2-week period, the vibrant colors spread to the coast. Temperatures hover between 13 and 18°C. (55–65°F.), cooling at night.

Autumn travel has become more popular in recent years. During July and August, accommodations and the better service facilities are usually taxed to the limit, and charge high season rates. After September 1, the traffic flow dwindles considerably and travel operations become less crowded.

Particularly in the Cabot Trail region of Cape Breton and certain sections of the Annapolis Valley, the brilliant autumn leaves combined with clear, crisp weather bring out native Nova Scotians as well as visitors. The best fall colors can usually be seen during the first two weeks of October, depending on the preceding weather.

In winter, November days are blustery and snowfalls begin in time for a white Christmas. Snows are intermittent and rarely predictable from December through March.

Cape Breton/Cabot Trail

With dramatic seascapes, rugged highlands, and lovely, old fishing villages, Cape Breton, the island part of Nova Scotia, is the province's most popular tourist area. The Cabot Trail, some 278 kms. (172 miles) of mountain and sea on a circular loop, is one of the most spectacular day drives in North America in any season. The controversy that rages as to whether one should drive the trail in a clockwise or counterclockwise direction is usually settled in favor of the clockwise direction. This puts the sun to the side of the car or behind it, and allows driving on the "inside"—next to the mountain rather than the cliff, so that the steepest grades are descended rather than climbed. Part of the Cabot Trail lies within the Cape Breton Highlands National Park, but no entrance fee is required unless specific Park facilities are to be used.

The Bras d'Or Lakes form a large inland salt lake which has become popular with yachting enthusiasts. Most of them headquarter at the Baddeck Yacht Club and spend days cruising the sheltered inland sea.

Cape Breton has a history of chronic unemployment due to the unsteady fortunes of the coal and steel industries. As a result, much of the Sydney–Glace Bay industrial area and environs have acquired a permanently depressed appearance. Yet the people are friendly and the place has its own rough charm. The traditions of steelworking and coalmining are cherished despite the hard times they evoke.

The Scottish tradition is still very strong in Cape Breton, particularly around the Baddeck-Iona region. Many people still speak Gaelic and the Gaelic College in St. Ann's is unique on this continent with its summer courses in piping, highland dancing, and Gaelic language.

Say "Hello" and Find a Friend

Nova Scotians, like most Atlantic Canadians, are quiet people who appear to have a touch of shyness. Often it is the visitor who must say the first "hello" or ask for help. But once the ice is broken, the visitor has a new friend—ready to give directions, lead the way, offer advice, or explain the fine points of a local attraction. Meeting Nova Scotians will be one of the greatest pleasures of your visit.

EXPLORING HALIFAX/DARTMOUTH

Founded in 1749 by Lord Cornwallis, Halifax—capital of Nova Scotia, largest city in the Atlantic Provinces, and one of the oldest cities in Canada—today combines the best of the colonial heritage with contemporary life.

Originally a military and naval base designed to defend the British colonies and also to counteract the defenses raised by the French at Cape Breton Island at Louisbourg, Halifax—built on a small peninsula —protected its harbor by a series of fortifications including the Citadel, which became the mightiest fortress in British North America and is now an historic site.

A Spectacular Harbor

Enjoying the benefits of one of the finest harbors in the world, Halifax is joined to the city of Dartmouth to the northeast by two suspension bridges. The "old bridge," the Angus L. Macdonald Bridge, was opened in 1955 and is some 1597 meters (5,239 feet) long. The "new bridge," the A. Murray McKay Bridge, was opened in 1970. The toll on both bridges starts at 25¢ for cars in either direction. The tollbooths are on the Dartmouth side of the bridges.

At the foot of both cities is the harbor where the shipping of the world ties up. The busy container port often operates around-the-clock. While one ship may be loading grain for eastern Europe, another is off-loading automobiles from the Orient at the Autoport.

Halifax/Dartmouth is the home of the Canadian Forces Maritime Command (Atlantic), and the sleek gray warships are a common sight under the two massive suspension bridges spanning the harbor.

Together, Halifax and Dartmouth form the largest metropolitan area east of Montréal. With a population of some 280,000 people, they are the major urban center for almost half of Nova Scotia as well as the business, financial, educational (also medical; most of the major hospitals are located here), and shopping center for Atlantic Canada. The area is also the seat of provincial government and headquarters for most government offices, both federal and provincial.

"Historic Properties"

The combination of old and new in Halifax is nowhere more apparent than in and around the area known as *Historic Properties*. Only one block away is the ultramodern Scotia Square, a shopping-office-apart-ment-hotel complex. High-rise office and apartment buildings spear the skyline in downtown Halifax, yet Historic Properties is only a few steps away. A joint development of the City of Halifax, Historic Properties Ltd., a Halifax company, and the federal department of Indian and Northern Affairs, the area has 12 buildings, of which several date back to the early 1800's.

When the area was originally built in the 1800's, it was the center of business for the young city. The Privateer's Warehouse was a stone building which housed the cargoes captured by Nova Scotia schooners serving as privateers until the captured ships and cargoes could be auctioned off by the Admiralty.

Collins Bank was the headquarters of Nova Scotia entrepreneur Enos Collins. When Collins died in 1871, he was reported to be the richest man in British North America.

The block of North American Renaissance buildings on Granville Street, between Duke and Buckingham, was constructed after the great Halifax fire of 1859, which razed the area. Designed by William Thomas, architect, of Toronto, the buildings were not all built at the same time but all exhibit a common theme and exterior format. Some of the storefronts which still remain were fabricated of cast iron and were probably designed by Bogardus. The only way to tell if they are metal is to test with a magnet. While many of the details of the architectural extravagances of the 1870's have been obliterated by time, the original elegance may still be seen in the tall windows and storefront designs. That part of Granville Street is now a strictly pedestrian area.

Between June and October in Historic Properties you can hear the town crier, take water tours, walking and bus tours, *Bluenose II* tours, and enjoy numerous special events.

Saved by the People

Early in the 1960's, the Historic Properties area was slated for demolition to make way for a superhighway along the waterfront. A successful campaign by civic groups saved the area from the wrecker's ball and the City of Halifax, which owns most of the property, called for redevelopment plans to restore the buildings to their original appearance on the exterior, while retaining commercially usable interiors.

The buildings have nooks and crannies in interesting locations, arches and odd-shaped windows, stucco and wooden beams—all of those beautiful "useless" architectural appendages which modern designers seem to eliminate in their functional steel and glass buildings.

The buildings of Historic Properties once again hear the footsteps of Haligonians (inhabitants of Halifax) and visitors alike walking the old cobblestone streets and shopping for wares in shops featuring handmade articles—leather, wood, glass, and ceramic. There are law offices, federal and provincial government offices, the campus of the Nova Scotia College of Art and Design, and restaurants and pubs. Nova Scotia's floating ambassador, the schooner *Bluenose II,* docks at Privateer's Wharf, just as vessels tied up there 200 years ago. Instead of loading the exotic plunder of faraway countries, *Bluenose II* lowers the gangplank for visitors to enjoy a cruise out in Halifax Harbour during summer afternoons and evenings.

One block up from Historic Properties is the new Barrington Hotel, which continues the tradition of revitalizing old buildings. Its exterior was rebuilt with the original granite from the façade of an entire city block, but the interior contains a modern hotel and two levels of boutiques, craftshops, restaurants, and some of the city's finest stores. It is also linked to Scotia Square, the main downtown shopping, hotel and office complex.

A couple of blocks to the south along Upper Water Street is a new waterfront development that includes the Maritime Museum of the Atlantic. Displays that describe Nova Scotia's golden age of sail, when the province's flag was seen in ports around the world, dominate. The main display is docked outside, however. It's a 900-ton hydrographic ship, the *Acadia,* which charted the Labrador and Arctic coasts early in this century.

Between the museum and Historic Properties, the Halifax–Dartmouth ferries chug in and out of a new terminal. It's a cheap (35¢) sightseeing tour in itself.

Plenty of Open Space

With such development in the middle of the downtown core, one might assume that the Halifax/Dartmouth metro area is not an entirely relaxing place in which to live and work. Although there is the hustle and bustle associated with any city, both cities are blessed with hundreds of acres of open green park and recreation space as well as salt-

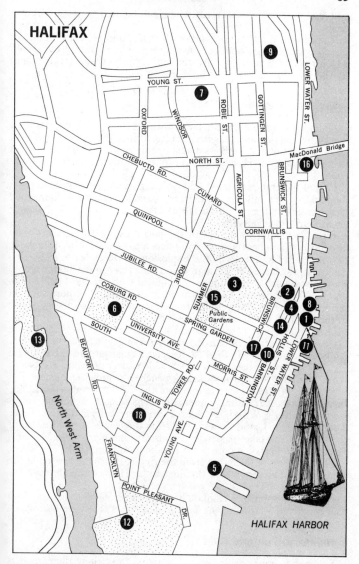

HALIFAX

Halifax—Points of Interest
1) Bluenose II Wharf
2) Chateau Halifax
3) Citadel
4) City Hall
5) Container Port
6) Dalhousie University
7) Exhibition Grounds
8) Fisherman's Market
9) Fort Needham
10) Government House
11) Maritime Museum
12) Martello Tower
13) Memorial Tower
14) Neptune Theater
15) Nova Scotia Museum
16) Old Dutch Church
17) St. Mary's Basilica
18) St. Mary's University

and freshwater recreation areas which can be used by the area's residents.

The North West Arm, Halifax Harbour, and Bedford Basin are dotted with pleasure boats of all shapes and sizes during the season which runs from spring to "frostbite" time in November. Dartmouth has no less than 22 lakes within the city limits.

No Longer Drab

Halifax was once appropriately known as the "gray city." Its dour and somber appearance has been replaced since the mid-60's with the establishment of new business and shopping centers, a night life which is interesting, and the vibrant atmosphere associated with a growing city.

Part of the drab reputation that once tagged the city comes from its long history as a military port. Here, roaming press gangs kidnapped unsuspecting young men from the streets and forced them into service aboard British naval ships.

Fort Needham, a long hill in the north end of Halifax, has been developed as a memorial park and offers a panoramic view of the area devastated in the Great Halifax Explosion on December 6, 1917. The explosion, the largest single man-made blast prior to the atomic bomb, was caused when a munitions ship collided with another vessel in the harbor. Two thousand fatalities were recorded, 10,000 more suffered serious injuries, 25,000 were left homeless, and the shockwave was felt in the town of Truro, more than 60 miles away.

One of the most pleasant spots in summertime Halifax is the Public Gardens on Spring Garden Road. Preserving much of the original landscape design (1753), the 18 acres have formal gardens, a large pond for ducks, geese and swans, lawns, a wide variety of exotic plants and trees, fountains, and plenty of park benches for quiet enjoyment.

Most visitors to Halifax take one of the excellent water tours. The famous *Bluenose II* sailing schooner takes passengers on harbor cruises from Privateer's Wharf, as does a company called Halifax Water Tours. Harbour Island Tours leaves from the new Marine Museum of the Atlantic and takes passengers to historic and mysterious McNab's Island at the harbor mouth for a two-hour walking tour.

The best view of the city is from the ring-road around the top of the Citadel, the old fort which dominates the Halifax skyline near the waterfront.

Fairview, a suburb of Halifax, has its own recollections. It was here that recovered victims of the *Titanic* disaster (1912) were buried.

Halifax in Sun and Rain

Summer evenings bring out locals and visitors along the pathways of the Commons in the center of Halifax to enjoy amateur sports or just to walk about.

Halifax is a quiet, clean, and pleasant city but a couple of cautions are in order. Food and accommodations can be expensive and parking is a problem in the downtown area of Halifax. The best bet is to head for either the Scotia Square Parking Garages which usually have some space, or the Historic Properties parking area on the waterfront.

In the rain, take refuge in the provincial pioneer and military museums inside the Citadel and the Nova Scotia Museum on Summer

Street; the latter features natural history and has supervised programs, mainly for children. The new Marine Museum of the Atlantic on Lower Water Street displays the seagoing tradition of the east coast. The Dartmouth Heritage Museum exhibits early history, while the suburban Cole Harbour Heritage Farm features agricultural history. Art galleries at St. Mary's, Dalhousie, and Mount St. Vincent universities, as well as the New Art Gallery of Nova Scotia, have regular exhibitions.

One can even don rainwear on damp days and walk to Point Pleasant Park's Black Rock to watch ships come and go only a few hundred yards away. Ship watching is equally pleasant in fine weather. Be sure to look for some of the Scottish heather here—apparently the only location in North America where the plant grows wild. The seeds came from mattresses shaken out by British sailors many decades ago.

Halifax is a city to explore. The old and new stand side by side in a fine blend. The only shots to be fired from the Citadel are the cannon announcing the arrival of noon each day—a custom which is still preserved, much to the shock of unwary passersby.

PRACTICAL INFORMATION FOR HALIFAX/DARTMOUTH

HOW TO GET THERE. By air: *Air Canada* operates flights into the Halifax International Airport from all major and some minor points in the Atlantic Provinces and the rest of Canada; also from Boston and London, England. *CP Air* flies Montréal–Halifax and Halifax–Amsterdam. *Eastern Provincial Airways* flies from Toronto and most airports in the Atlantic Provinces.

By car: Most highways in Nova Scotia lead to Halifax/Dartmouth. Hwys. 3/103, 7, 2/102 and 1/101 terminate in the twin cities. Hwy. 104, the Trans-Canada Hwy. from Amherst at the New Brunswick border joins Rtes. 2/102 at Truro.

By bus: Within Nova Scotia, Halifax is served by *Acadian Lines Limited;* along the South Shore only, service is operated by *MacKenzie Bus Lines.* Through interconnecting lines, most major North American bus lines serve Nova Scotia. At Amherst, intraprovincial bus lines link most major communities.

By train: *Via Rail* passenger services serve Halifax from most major Canadian centers. From the United States, *Amtrak* connections may be made in Montréal.

ACCOMMODATIONS. Accommodation in Halifax/Dartmouth is generally comfortable and reservations are a necessity any time of year. Reservations can be made by calling the toll-free numbers listed in the *Tourist Information* section. Hotel/motel rates in Halifax/Dartmouth, based on double occupancy, are categorized as follows: *Expensive,* $44 or more; *Moderate,* $33 to $44; *Inexpensive,* less than $33.

The 10% provincial sales tax is added to all hotel/motel rates.

Most places accept the following major credit cards: American Express, MasterCard and Visa; others may also be honored. Not all establishments accept credit cards, therefore we suggest you call for information.

HALIFAX. *Expensive:* **The Delta Barrington.** Barrington at Granville Sts. Part of a shopping and convention complex incorporating the reconstructed façade of an entire historic city block. No charge for children under 18 sharing parents' room. Phone 429–7410, 800–268–1133. All major credit cards.

Halifax Sheraton. New, elegant, on the harborfront. Contains The Café Maritime, a fine restaurant. Lobby is a lounge featuring live piano entertainment. 1919 Upper Water St. Phone (902) 421–1700.

Chateau Halifax. 1990 Barrington St. in Scotia Square. A CP Hotel with 305 rooms. Rooms are better than average but corridors are dark and narrow. Heated indoor-outdoor pool, sauna, dining room, pub and lounges. The best part of this hotel is that it is part of the big Scotia Square shopping-office complex. Phone 425–6700, 800–268–9411. All major credit cards.

Citadel Inn. 1960 Brunswick St. 189 rooms, quiet lounge and dining room. Rooms are excellent; patronized by businessmen and sales personnel. Phone 422–1391, 800–565–7162. All major credit cards.

Dresden Arms Motor Hotel. 5530 Artillery Pl. 94 rooms in pleasant surroundings off the main street but still downtown. Dining room usually good. Pool, sauna, whirlpool and exercise area. Phone 422–1625. Major credit cards.

Holiday Inn. 1980 Robie St. at the Willow Tree. Better than average Holiday Inn with 237 rooms, indoor pool, sauna, rooms for the handicapped, dining room, lounge and pub. Phone 423–1161. All major credit cards.

Hotel Nova Scotian. 1181 Hollis St. at the railway station. A local landmark. Facilities for the handicapped. No charge for children sharing parents' room. Phone: 423–7231, 800–565–7164. Major credit cards.

The Lord Nelson Hotel. 1515 S. Park St. opposite the Public Gardens. A local landmark. 320 rooms. Phone 423–6331. Major credit cards.

Wandlyn Motor Inn. No. 2 Hwy. at Fairview. About 15 minutes from downtown. Water-view rooms have a good view over Bedford Basin. 74 rooms, coffee bar, licensed dining room. Off-season rates January to June, October to January. Pets permitted. Phone 443–0416, 800–561–0000. All major credit cards.

Moderate: **Carleton Hotel.** 1685 Argyle St. 68 rooms, 40 with bath. Licensed lounge and dining room; free parking. Phone 423–7111. Major credit cards.

Keddy's Motor Inn. 20 St. Margaret's Bay Rd., Armsdale. About 15 minutes from downtown. Part of a chain. 132 rooms (7 efficiency) of adequate quality; pool and sauna. Off-season rates November to May. Phone 477–5611. All major credit cards.

Inexpensive: **YMCA.** 1565 S. Park St. 68 pleasant rooms for men with full use of Y facilities: sauna, pool, gym, and squash. Downtown location. Phone 422–6437. Visa only.

YWCA. 1239 Barrington St. 12 pleasant rooms for women, with use of Y facilities. Phone 423–6162. No credit cards accepted.

DARTMOUTH. *Expensive:* **The Atlantic Inn.** 739 Windmill Rd. 92 units near Dartmouth Industrial Park. Coffee shop, licensed dining and lounge. Off season rates October to April. Phone 469–0810. All major credit cards.

Holiday Inn. 99 Wyse Rd. at MacDonald Bridge. 120 rooms with no surprises; dining room with less than adequate food and lounge. Outdoor pool. Off-season rates October to May. Phone 463–1100. All major credit cards.

Keddy's Dartmouth Inn. Mic Mac Rotary. One of the better mmebers of this chain with 82 rooms and 36 motel units. Efficiency units available. Licensed dining and lounge. Phone 477–5611. All major credit cards.

 HOW TO GET AROUND. Walking is a good way to get around many areas of downtown Halifax and Dartmouth. In downtown Halifax, in particular, parking may be a problem during the business day.

By taxi: Taxi rates start at $1.20 and meter up based on mileage and time combined. A crosstown trip should cost about $4.00 to $5.00, depending on traffic. Hailing taxis on the street is often difficult. Call a stand and have the taxi pick you up.

By bus: The *Metropolitan Transit Commission* operates a bus system covering the entire metropolitan area. Basic fare is 60¢, and exact change is needed. Call 426–6600 for information.

By ferry: The *Dartmouth Ferry Commission* operates two passenger ferries from the George Street terminal in Halifax to the Portland Street terminal in Dartmouth. Ferries operate from 6 A.M. to midnight on half-hour and hourly schedules. Fare for a single crossing is 35¢. Call 466–2215 for schedules and information.

TOURIST INFORMATION. *For Nova Scotia.* Write Nova Scotia Department of Tourism, P.O. Box 130, Halifax, Nova Scotia, Canada, B3J 2M7. Phone: (902) 424–4247.

Call-toll free: in continental U.S.A. (except Alaska and Maine), 1–800–341–6096; in Maine, 1–800–492–0643; Canada-wide, 1–800–565–7166; in the Maritime Provinces, 1–800–565–7105; in Newfoundland and Québec, 1–800–565–7180; in Ontario, 1–800–565–7140; in British Columbia, 112–800–565–7166. You can also make hotel and motel reservations through these numbers.

Tourist information desks are located on the ferries to Nova Scotia from Port-aux-Basques and Argentia, Nfld. At Bar Harbour and Portland, Me., tourist-information desks are inside the ferry terminals. These ferries go to Yarmouth on a daily basis. And the N.S. Department of Tourism operates a tourist information center at Port Hastings on the Cape Breton side of the Canso Causeway (625–9991), and at Pictou, a few miles from the landing of the Wood Island Ferry from P.E.I. (485–6213).

You will find provincially operated tourist bureaus at Yarmouth and Digby near the ferry wharves; at Antigonish on the Trans-Canada Hwy.; near the Halifax International Airport; at Amherst near the New Brunswick border; and at the Pictou Rotary a few miles from the ferry landing from Prince Edward Island. Most are open from 8 A.M. to 8 P.M. from mid-May to the end of October, and at the Red Store, Historic Properties, Halifax, year-round. You're generally no more than 15 miles from a tourist bureau anywhere in the province.

For Cape Breton: Write The Cape Breton Tourist Association, 20 Keltic Dr., Sydney River, N.S., Canada B1S 1P5. Telephone (902) 539–9876.

From June to September the Tourist Association distributes a free monthly guide to events and places called *What's Happening,* which you'll find in restaurants, motels, and tourist bureaus.

Park information centers are located at both the Ingonish and Cheticamp entrances to Cape Breton Highlands National Park.

The Red Store, Historic Properties, Halifax—The *City of Halifax,* the *National Parks Department* and the *Nova Scotia Department of Tourism* all operate information centers in the Red Store. For city information, call 421–8736; for provincial information call 424–4247; for national parks information call 426–3436. Offices open year-round. Also, there's a year-round information center at Halifax International Airport (861–3184).

The City of Dartmouth operates a tourist bureau on Thistle St. from mid-May to mid-October. Call 421–2319 during the open season, and 421–2220 off-season.

Throughout the province there are some 40 tourist information bureaus run by local municipalities and boards of trade.

RECOMMENDED READING. The novels of Thomas Raddall (and, to some extent, Will R. Bird) give a vital and colorful account of the province's rich history. Raddall's *Halifax: Warden of the North* has been called a model of local history. The speeches, essays and poems of Joseph Howe are compiled in several anthologies; Howe was the greatest political and intellectual leader in 19th century Nova Scotia. Thomas Chandler Haliburton's *The Clockmaker* set out to scourge the Bluenoses for their want of thrift and industry; it became the first Canadian book to achieve international fame. Haliburton learned his satiric trade in part from Thomas McCulloch, a pioneer clergyman, satirist and educator (among other things, he was the first president of Dalhousie University), whose sharp satiric portrait of Pictou, *The Stepsure Letters,* is still in print and still funny.

The fiction of Ernest Buckler (particularly *The Mountain and the Valley* and *Oxbells and Fireflies*) and of Charles Bruce *(The Channel Shore)* are meditative, beautifully written portrayals of the traditional Nova Scotian lifestyle. Helen Creighton's *Bluenose Magic* and *Bluenose Ghosts* reveal the depth of folklore in the province.

Recent Nova Scotia fiction includes Chipman Hall's *Lightly,* Alistair MacLeod's *The Lost Salt Gift of Blood,* and Susan Kerslake's *Middlewatch.* Recent nonfiction may be represented by Harry Bruce's *Lifeline,* the story of the Maritime ferry system, and by Silver Donald Cameron's account of the great fishing strike of 1970/71, *The Education of Everett Richardson.* Jim and Pat Lotz have written a comprehensive volume, *Cape Breton Island. Nova Scotia in Your Pocket* by John Prince is a good general guide.

 BUSINESS HOURS. Most stores are open between 9 or 10 A.M. until 9 P.M., Wednesdays, Thursdays, and Fridays. From Monday to Saturday, they close at 6 P.M.
Banks are open 10 A.M. to 3 P.M. generally; most stay open until 4 P.M. Thursdays and Fridays, while some stay open until 5. A few banks in the shopping centers keep shopping center hours.

 SEASONAL EVENTS. Every year the N.S. Department of Tourism publishes a *Calendar of Events,* free on request, which describes provincial festivals and events. Some highlights:
May: Antique Show & Sale, Halifax; Late May: Apple Blossom festival, Kentville area (one of the major Nova Scotia festivals: it includes dances, parade, sports, entertainment).
June: Mid-June: Annual Summer Antique Sale, Halifax; the Nova Scotia Tattoo, Metro Centre, Halifax.
July: In Dartmouth, the Festival of Piping; later in the month, Halifax Natal Day (road races, rock concerts, band concerts, parade in the morning, children's program, barbecue, sports events, rock dance, fireworks).
August: Halifax and Dartmouth Natal Day Celebrations; Mid-August: Halifax Citadel Festival of History.
September: The Joseph Howe Festival (oratorical contest, pony express ride, pancake breakfasts, open-air and craft markets, dances, concerts, beer fests, parade, whaler races, bazaar, multicultural concert, and town crier championships).
October: Antique Show and Sale, with paintings by maritime artists, Halifax; International Town Crier Championship at Halifax.

FREE EVENTS. The programs listed in the *Childrens' Activities* section are free. So is entry to all the city's museums and other public cultural facilities. Participation in the various cultural festivals is without charge. And the Sunday-afternoon band concerts at the Public Gardens are free as well.

 TOURS. Both the *Metropolitan Transit Commission* and *Gray Line* (operated by Acadian Bus Lines) have coach tours of Halifax, each lasting about two hours. The Gray Line tour may be boarded at the Acadian Lines terminal on Almon Street, and at most major hotels. For times and information call 454-9321. *Halifax Transit* tours may be boarded at Historic Properties. Call 421–6600 for full information. Cost of both tours is about $4.00 ($1.50 for children).
Halifax Water Tours operates an excellent 2-hour boat tour of Halifax Harbour and the Northwest Arm leaving from Privateers Wharf four times daily, June 16–September 9, with fewer tours daily starting June 1 and lasting to Oct. 13. The tour boat is comfortable and licensed; commentary by the hostesses is very good. For information and times call 423–7783 or 425–1271. The cost is about $6.00 per person ($2.00 for children).
During most of July, August, and September, visitors may enjoy a sail on a Halifax Harbour cruise aboard *Bluenose II,* the 143-foot replica of the famous Nova Scotia sailing schooner. A 2-hour sail costs about $9.00 per person ($4.00 for children, $4.50 for senior citizens) and the vessel leaves from her wharf at Historic Properties. For information on sailing times, call 422–2678, or 424-4247.
One unique package involves a sail to McNab's Island, at the mouth of Halifax Harbour, for a 2-hour walking tour. The name of the company is

Harbour Island Tours, and it leaves twice daily through most of the summer from near the Maritime Museum of the Atlantic. Phone 422–9523.

Further information on day charters, boat rentals and cruises can be obtained from the Nova Scotia Department of Tourism's publication, *Sports and Activities,* P.O. Box 456, Halifax, N.S. B3J 2R5.

The Halifax, Dartmouth, or Provincial tourist bureaus have details of a number of well-organized self-drive tours of the area. Walking tours of historic sites in downtown Halifax and Dartmouth are available.

A non-guided tour of Halifax Harbour is as simple as taking a trip on the Dartmouth Ferry on a bright, sunny day. The round trip costs 50¢ and takes 45 minutes to an hour. Passengers can sit outside on the top of the ferry.

A Cyclist's Guide to Nova Scotia is available from N.S. Tourism and local sports stores. Halifax is an easy city to explore by bike.

PARKS. *Point Pleasant Park* covers the entire tip of the peninsula of the City of Halifax. As it is a natural woodland park, automobile traffic is banned. Surrounded on three sides by saltwater, there are trails, picnic areas, a swimming beach, and a number of partially ruined fortifications.

Fort Needham, a hill in the north end of Halifax, has been developed as a small park.

Fleming Park on the North West Arm is known locally as "The Dingle." The area was donated to the city by Sir Sandford Fleming, a railroad builder who also invented Standard Time. The tall tower was built to commemorate the first elective assembly held in the British colonies. The view from the top of the tower overlooking the Arm and the City makes the many steps well worth your while.

The Citadel as well as *Horseshoe Island Park* in Halifax are also pleasant.

Many of the 22 lakes in Dartmouth have small parks, beaches, and picnic areas along the shores.

The Halifax Commons is a large area in the center of the city with children's playground, wading pool, ball fields, tennis courts lighted for night play, and lots of grassy area.

GARDENS. The *Halifax Public Gardens,* 18 acres of color in the heart of the City, is a favorite spot for relaxation for visitors and Haligonians. Landscaped originally in 1753, these gardens are among the oldest on the continent. In addition to trees and shrubs from every corner of the globe, there are fountains, a bandstand, and a large pond with various waterbirds. One corner has been set aside as a children's area.

The gardens are open mid-May to mid-November, 8 A.M. to sundown daily. No admission charge.

CHILDREN'S ACTIVITIES. During July and August, the Halifax and Dartmouth Recreation Departments operate summer programs at *school playgrounds,* the *Halifax Commons,* and at the *Dartmouth Lakes.* The playground facilities, including swings and other equipment, wading pool and playground fields at the Halifax Commons may be used without charge.

Dartmouth and Halifax have supervised swimming at many of the lakes and Halifax has supervised salt water swimming at *Point Pleasant* and *Flemming Parks.*

The Nova Scotia Museum on Summer Street in Halifax has special children's programs throughout the year. Call 429–4610 for information.

For children of all ages, fishing from a waterfront wharf or breakwater on the incoming tide usually yields some small but interesting specimens of salt water fish.

For complete information, call Halifax Recreation at 426–6426; or Dartmouth Recreation at 469–9211.

SPORTS. Halifax is the home of the American Hockey League *Nova Scotia Voyageurs,* a farm team of the Montréal Canadiens. The team plays more than 20 home games from November to April against international competition. For information on game dates and tickets, call 453-4015.

College-level sports events take place throughout the school year. For full information, contact the Halifax Tourist Bureau.

Hard surface *tennis* courts, lighted for night play, are available at the Halifax Commons. For *sailing* enthusiasts there are five yacht clubs in Halifax/Dartmouth. *Canoeing* is a popular sport in Dartmouth and is centered on Lake Banook and Micmac Lake.

Bicycle tours available from Bicycle Nova Scotia, 5516 Spring Garden Road, P.O. Box 3010 Halifax, N.S. B3J3G6 Phone: 425-5450.

For full information on all sports in the Halifax/Dartmouth area, contact the tourist bureau in either city.

 HISTORIC SITES. Halifax has three surviving military installations, all of British origin, which once served as essential elements of the defense against the French threat at Louisbourg. The *Citadel,* a star-shaped fort, was begun in 1749. A third version, completed in 1828, now has an excellent military museum and a commanding view of the Nova Scotia capital. Open year-round. Other installations, built in the late 1700's, include the *Prince of Wales Martello Tower* and the *York Redoubt,* which was modified and used throughout the 19th century as part of the harbor defense. Open June 1 to September 30. Telephone: 426-5080. There are also ruins of other fortifications in Point Pleasant Park.

The *Naval Dockyard* on North Barrington St. was begun in 1757 and is still in operation.

Charles Dickens called *Province House* "a gem of Georgian architecture." The building is still used as the province's legislature and has an excellent library. It is the oldest existing legislative building in Canada.

A number of Halifax churches are historically significant. *St. Matthew's Church* on Barrington St. is very old and has a fine interior. One of the earliest ministers was the great-grandfather of U.S. president Grover Cleveland. *St. George's Round Church* on Brunswick St. was built in 1800 and is a rare example of circular ecclesiastical architecture. *St. Mary's Basilica* on Spring Garden Rd. is a fine granite structure, reputed to have the highest granite spire in the world. *St. Paul's Church* on Barrington St., built in 1749, is the oldest Protestant church in Canada. The *Old Dutch Church* on Brunswick St., built in 1756, was the first Lutheran Church in Canada.

Admission is free to all historic sites.

 MUSEUMS AND GALLERIES. Museums: The *Halifax Citadel National Historic Park* is a hilltop fortress built in 1828 on the site of earlier fortifications dating back to the city's founding in 1749. Dominating the city and offering excellent views, The Citadel houses the Army Museum, depicting the history of colonial warfare. Kilted soldiers drill and there is a unique gift shop. On the fortress grounds is the Old Town Clock, originally built in 1803, and now the unofficial symbol of the city. Parking outside the fortress is limited. Open 9 A.M. to 8 P.M., June to October; 10 A.M. to 5 P.M., the rest of the year.

The *Marine Museum of the Atlantic,* 1675 Lower Water St. The seagoing tradition, housed in a restored chandlery and dockside warehouse. It includes, docked outside, the hydrographic ship *Acadia,* which was used to chart the coasts of Labrador and the Arctic earlier in this century.

The *Maritime Command Museum,* Admiralty House, CFB Stadacona, on Gottigen at Almon St., has military artifacts; open year-round.

The *Nova Scotia Museum* on Summer Street in Halifax features both permanent exhibits on *Man and His Environment* and general and natural history exhibits of Nova Scotia. Many parts of the museum feature "touch and feel" sections and there are special areas for children's activities. Open daily; call 429-4610 for opening and closing times.

The *Dartmouth Heritage Museum and Art Gallery* on Wyse Rd. features displays on early life in Dartmouth and the surrounding area. The art gallery features permanent and traveling exhibits. Open daily; call 463-3183 for opening and closing times.

Other museums include *Province House,* the seat of the Nova Scotia government and the oldest legislative building in any Canadian province; *Prince of Wales Martello Tower; York Redoubt National Historic Park;* and the *Public Archives of Nova Scotia* at the corner of Robie St. and University Ave.

Galleries: The *Art Gallery of Nova Scotia,* on Coburg Rd., is the main non-commercial gallery. Others are located at the *Dartmouth Heritage Museum, Mount Saint Vincent University, Dalhousie University* and *St. Mary's University.*

Of the several commercial galleries in Halifax, the best are *Manuge Galleries* on Hollis St. near Sackville; *Zwicker's Gallery* on Doyle St. near Brunswick; *Gallery 1667* in the Promenade Block from the Potomac Bldg., Historic Properties; and *Atlantic Art Gallery* at Hollis and Duke Sts. *Three Oaks Corporation,* 3 Albert St. in Dartmouth is owned and operated by Tom Forrestall, a popular Canadian realist, and his works are featured in this pleasant gallery.

Admission to any of the private or public museums or galleries is free.

MUSIC AND THEATER. The *Rebecca Cohn Auditorium* (sometimes referred to as the *Dalhousie Arts Centre*) is one of Halifax's centers for live concerts and musical presentations featuring international artists, year round. Call 424-2298 for box-office information and bookings.

Major musical presentations in Halifax take place at the *Metro Centre,* a new sports and cultural complex located downtown. For up to date information on what's playing where, check with the Halifax Tourist Bureau.

Neptune Theatre is Nova Scotia's only professional live theater group. Most of their presentations are given at *Neptune Theatre* on Sackville St. Most of the plays are in repertory and offer comedy and drama, both modern and traditional. For box office and information call 429-7300.

A better-than-average amateur group known as the *Kipawo Showboat Company* performs at the new amateur playhouse at Historic Properties. Members perform mostly musicals. What they lack in professional polish they make up in enthusiasm, offering an evening of theater that is fun.

SHOPPING. There are several specialty shopping areas in Halifax. The Spring Garden Rd. area is the older one with more traditional goods, particularly British imports. The newer and more exquisite area is actually in the oldest part of Halifax—*Historic Properties* and the *Barrington Inn* complex —where you can find fine crafts in such stores as the Pewter House, Nova Pine, and The Eskimo Gallery, as well as top line manufactured goods. A block away, in the *Scotia Square* complex, is the city's main downtown mall for day-to-day shopping. The principal suburban shopping centers are *Micmac Mall* in Dartmouth and the *Halifax Shopping Center,* the *Maritime Mall,* and *Bayer's Road Shopping Center* in Halifax.

DINING OUT. Dining out in Halifax/Dartmouth is usually good to excellent in the better restaurants. The surroundings are usually excellent too. Many restaurants are set in refurbished historic homes or other restored quarters.

Service is generally good in the better restaurants, although it can be slow, especially if the place is busy. Your waiter or waitress can usually suggest the best items on the daily menu or the specials of the day.

Restaurants are categorized on the basis of full course dinner, with drinks, tax and tips excluded: *Expensive,* over $17; *Moderate,* $12–$17; *Inexpensive,* under $12. A 10% provincial tax will be added to all meals over $3.00.

Most places accept the following major credit cards: American Express, MasterCard and Visa; others may also be honored. Not all establishments accept credit cards, therefore we suggest you call for information.

HALIFAX. *Expensive:* **The Grand.** 5640 Spring Garden Rd. Food well prepared and service efficient. Menu ranges from steaks to seafood. Phone 421–1116. Major credit cards.

Clipper Cay. Historic Properties. Restaurant with the best location, overlooking Privateer's Wharf and Halifax Harbour. Ask for window table with a harbor view. The *Cay Side,* downstairs, has lunch outdoors on the wharf during summer months. Phone: (Clipper Cay) 423–6818, (Cay Side) 429–5639. All major credit cards (both restaurants).

Fat Frank's. 5411 Spring Garden Rd. Edwardian atmosphere, gourmet dining (Fat Frank's boasts it can prepare any known dish on demand). Lunch and dinner. Seats only 55, so reservations, especially in summer, are recommended. Phone 423-6618. Major credit cards.

The Henry House/Little Stone Jug. 1222 Barrington St. Dining room and pub-style restaurant in historic granite building. Food is excellent and the atmosphere classic Georgian. Call for reservations. Dress casual, but no dungarees. Phone 423–1309. All major credit cards. Specialty: Champlain's Feast (dinner Theatre).

Les Deux Amies. 1522 Birmingham St. An elegant restaurant in old Victorian townhouse with French gourmet cooking. Phone 425–5222. All major credit cards.

Moderate–Expensive: **Old Man Morias.** 1150 Barrington St. Open year-round. Hellenic cuisine (spitted lamb, moussaka, etc.) served in renovated townhouse. Licensed. Phone 422–7960. Major credit cards.

Moderate: **DA's.** Dresden Arms Motor Hotel, 5530 Artillery Pl. Good food in pleasant dining room. Try the Maid's Brunch at lunchtime. Call for reservations. Phone 422–1625. All major credit cards.

The Gondola Restaurant. 5175 South St. Known locally as "Pino's." Features authentic Italian cuisine in trattoria-style surroundings; terrace dining during summer. Start with appetizer of spaghetti and continue from there. Call for reservations. Phone 423–8719. Major credit cards.

The Hermitage. South Park St. at Inglis St. Swiss and French décor and cuisine. Phone 421–1731. Major credit cards.

The News Room. Carleton Hotel, Argyle and Sackville Sts. Old brick and glassed-in courtyard. Seafood and prime rib are specialties. Phone 423–0624. Major credit cards.

Pepe's. 5680 Spring Garden Rd. Superb surroundings and food to match. A bright and cheerful restaurant. Phone 429–7321. Major credit cards.

Sanford's. In *The Brewery,* Lower Water St. Sanford's offers natural foods, crêpes and quiche. Phone 423–4560. American Express and Visa only.

Other fine moderate restaurants are **Five Fishermen,** Argyle St.; **Thackery's,** Spring Garden Rd.; **Lawrence of Oregano's,** Argyle St.; **My Apartment,** Argyle St.; and an excellent little café called **Quelque Chose,** serving quiche, salads, light dinners and mouthwatering desserts, Hollis St.

Inexpensive: **The Boardroom.** Lower Mall, Scotia Square. Lunch spot for young executives from 11:30 to 2:30. Then it becomes a piano bar where the same types gather. Specials are chowder and thick sandwich with beer or wine. Phone 422–3553. All major credit cards.

Privateer's Warehouse. Historic Properties, Lower Deck and Middle Deck for lunch. 11:30 to 2:30. Sandwiches, chowder, sauerkraut, and sausage with beer are the specials. Informal atmosphere popular with young professionals, secretaries, and students. The Upper Deck dining room is in the *Inexpensive* category for lunch and the *Moderate* category for dinner, but the average quality of the food does not make up for the lack of atmosphere. Phone 422–1289. Major credit cards.

NIGHTCLUBS AND BARS. Night life in the area tends to be centered in downtown Halifax with a variety of clubs and bars offering entertainment, food, and congenial surroundings.

The most popular nightspot with the young professionals in Halifax is *Privateers Wharf* in Historic Properties. The Lower Deck on the ground floor is a tavern with beer only and accordion music. The Middle Deck on the second floor is a bar with light jazz music. Both Decks are usually packed on weekends so get there early. Cover charge on weekends.

The second most popular nightspot for young Halifax/Dartmouth people is the *Jury Room* in the Carleton Hotel on Argyle St. Although the hotel is somewhat down at the heels, new owners have revitalized the bar. Packed on weekends; full house during the week.

My Apartment on Argyle Street is an extremely popular watering hole.

The Palace, across from the Halifax Citadel, and the *Misty Moon,* 3700 Kempt Rd. in the city's north end, are the two largest nightclubs. They carry rock, blues, and other popular recording genres.

For a quiet drinking place, try the *Victory Lounge* in the Lord Nelson Hotel on South Park and Spring Garden Rd. The *Wyse Owl Tavern* on Wyse Rd. in Dartmouth is a workingman's tavern with a rough interior which offers the best blues and country blues music in the area.

The Split Crow, corner Duke and Granville, a decorous pub popular with young professionals.

PRACTICAL INFORMATION FOR CAPE BRETON

HOW TO GET THERE. By air: *Air Canada* has direct flights to Sydney from Halifax, Toronto, Montréal, and Québec City with connections to international flights. *Eastern Provincial Airways* has flights to Sydney from Montréal, Newfoundland, New Brunswick, and Prince Edward Island. Sydney is also the connecting airport for flights to the French islands of St. Pierre and Miquelon which lie off the south coast of Newfoundland. *Air St. Pierre* (with Eastern Provincial Airways) operates a year-round schedule of flights to France's last North American possessions.

By boat: Regular ferry service connects North Sydney with Port-aux-Basques, Newfoundland. A summer service is operated to Argentia, Newfoundland. For information and reservations, contact any *CN Marine* ticket office in Canada or your travel agent.

By bus: Daily bus service to Cape Breton from Halifax is operated by *Acadian Lines Limited* which connects with other bus lines throughout the country.

By car: The automobile (camper, motorcycle, or other recreational vehicle) must cross the Canso Causeway if approaching Cape Breton from mainland Nova Scotia. The toll is $1.50 per vehicle, payable only when entering Cape Breton.

By train: *Canadian National* operates train service to Sydney and intermediate points from Halifax and Truro. For information and reservations, contact any *Via Rail* ticket office.

ACCOMMODATIONS. Accommodations in Cape Breton are generally comfortable with at least one excellent seasonal hotel. Hotel/motel rates in Cape Breton, based on double-occupancy, are categorized as follows: *Expensive,* $39 or more; *Moderate,* $30 to $39; *Inexpensive,* under $30. Reservations for accommodations throughout Cape Breton and Nova Scotia can be made by dialing the toll-free numbers listed under "Tourist Information" in the "Exploring Halifax-Dartmouth" section.

The 10% provincial sales tax is added to all hotel/motel rates.

Most places accept the following major credit cards: American Express, MasterCard and Visa; others may also be honored. Not all establishments accept credit cards, therefore we suggest you call for information.

BADDECK. *Expensive:* **Inverary Inn.** One of the best places to stay in Cape Breton. Motel units, efficiency units, and cottages. Dining room is licensed. Private beach and children's playground. Open May 1 to November 1. Off-season rates before May 15 and after October 15. Phone 295-2674. Major credit cards.

Silver Dart Motel. Good view over Bras d'Or. Licensed dining room. Open mid-May to mid-October. Off-season rates before June 15. Efficiency units available; pets permitted. Phone 295-2340. Major credit cards.

Moderate: **Telegraph House.** Traditional place to stay. Dining room. Open year round. Phone 295-9988.

CHETICAMP. *Moderate:* **Acadian Motel.** Licensed lounge and dining room. Open year-round. Off-season rátes October 30 to May 15. Phone 224-2640. Major credit cards.

Laurie's Motel. Breakfast and dinner available to registered guests. Open year-round, except closed weekends from mid-October to mid-May. Off-season rates mid-October to mid-June. Pets permitted. Phone 224–2400. Major credit cards.

IONA. *Expensive:* **Highland Heights Inn.** Comfortable and friendly hosts. Licensed dining room with good food. Open May 1 to October 31. Off-season rates before July 1 and after September 15. Croquet, hiking, birdwatching. Phone 622-2360. Major credit cards.

MARGAREE HARBOUR. *Moderate:* **Duck Cove Inn.** Licensed dining room, canoe rentals, deep-sea fishing, horse shoes, giant checkers; river salmon and trout fishing, guides available. Open June 1 to October 31. Off-season rates are in effect before June 15 and after October 15. Phone 235-2658. Major credit cards.

Whale Cove Summer Village. Modern deluxe housekeeping and overnight cottages. Laundry facilities, store, playground, deep-sea and freshwater fishing nearby. Open mid-June to mid-October. Phone 235-2202. Major credit cards.

ST. PETER'S. *Inexpensive:* **Macdonald's Hotel.** Fifteen rooms in renovated house; pets permitted; open year-round. Licensed dining room. Phone 535-2997. Major credit cards.

SYDNEY. *Expensive:* **Cape Bretoner Motel.** King's Road. 51 units. Licensed dining room. Phone 539-8101. Major credit cards.

Isle Royal Motel. Dining room, lounge and gift shop. Do not confuse with Isle Royal Hotel downtown. The motel, in the suburbs, offers comfortable accommodations. Phone 564–4567. Major credit cards.

Keddy's Motor Inn. Licensed dining room. Part of a chain noted for inconsistent quality, particularly in food service. Off-season rates November 1 to April 30. Phone 539-1140. Major credit cards.

Wandlyn Motor Inn. Coffeeshop, licensed dining room, games room. Part of chain offering clean but usually plain accommodations. In converted nursing institution which is adequate for the purpose but its architecture is odd. Pets permitted with permission from manager. Phone 539-3700, 800–561–0000. Major credit cards.

Holiday Inn of Sydney. Typical Holiday Inn located a bit away from downtown area. Coffee bar and dining room are both of minimum quality and service; pool, cocktail lounge and bar, one with live entertainment; open year-round. Off season rates October 1 to May 31. Phone 539-6750. Major credit cards.

Moderate: **Vista Motel.** Comfortable, plain accommodations. Off-season rates October 15 to June 1. Phone 539-6550. Major credit cards.

Inexpensive: **Paul's Hotel.** On the corner of Pitt and Esplanade Sts., handy to shops. 24 rooms, 5 with bath; coffee bar. Cape Breton working people use Paul's in Sydney. Phone 562-5747.

HOSTELS. Canadian Hostelling Assoc. (Nova Scotia office, P.O. Box 3010, 5516 Spring Garden Rd., Halifax, N.S., B3J 3G6, 425–5450) has information on hostels in Halifax, Chester, Liverpool, Shelburne, Yarmouth, Annapolis-Royal, Wentworth, New Glasgow, Antigonish, Wolfville, Seal Island, and Cape Breton.

 BED-AND-BREAKFAST. More than 50 Cape Breton families participate in the bed-and-breakfast program. Rates for private bedroom in the family home are about $16 a night for one, $18 per night for two, including full breakfast the following morning. For visitors on a budget or wanting to meet some very hospitable people, this is an excellent program.

Participating families display a distinctive bed-and-breakfast sign. For reservations or listings of bed-and-breakfast locations, contact the Cape Breton Tourist Information Bureau, 20 Keltic Dr., Sydney River, Nova Scotia; the Cape Breton Development Corporation, P.O. Box 1750, Sydney, Nova Scotia, or the Nova Scotia Department of Tourism.

 HOW TO GET AROUND. From the airport: Transportation from Sydney airport is operated by *Briands Cabs.* A one-way trip is about $3.00 to downtown hotels. Briand's Cabs and *Bill's Yellow Cabs* operate scheduled tours of the Cabot Trail and to the Fortress of Louisbourg.

Car rental: Rent-a-car agencies are located at the airport and most also have downtown offices. Cars should be reserved in advance, particularly during the summer season.

By bus: Several small bus companies operate local service to communities in Cape Breton from Sydney. For up-to-date schedules, contact the Cape Breton Tourist Board.

By car: Using your own transportation is still the best way to get around Cape Breton. Most highways are paved and in good condition, although secondary roads may be winding and hilly. The local people know the roads and will drive faster than most visitors. Pull over and let them pass if they seem to be tailgating—it makes everyone happier and a lot safer.

By ferry: Two car ferries operate on route 223—one at Little Narrows and another at Grand Narrows. Both operate 24 hours a day on a 10- to 15-minute schedule. Fare for each passage is about 50¢ per vehicle.

 TOURIST INFORMATION. The Department of Tourism operates a tourist information center at Port Hastings (625–9991) at the entry point to Cape Breton by highway. The Cape Breton Tourist Board has bureaus at Baddeck, Louisbourg, Margaree Forks, Martinique, St. Peter's, and Sydney Mines. Otherwise, all Nova Scotia tourist bureaus have information on Cape Breton. Or write: Nova Scotia Department of Tourism, P.O. Box 130, Halifax, Nova Scotia B3J 2M7.

For information on seasonal events, camping parks and national parks, regional theater, and other bits of practical information for Cape Breton see the *Practical Information for Nova Scotia* section.

 TOURS. Tours by passenger car to Louisbourg, Miner's Museum, Bell Museum, and the Cabot Trail are operated by *Cape Breton Tours,* 263 Esplanade, Sydney; call 564-6200 or 564-6151. Operates from mid-May to September 20. *Yellow Cabs Ltd.* operates tours to the same Cape Breton destinations from May 15 to October 15. Address is 10 Pitt St., Sydney; call 564–4481 or 564–8161. Contact operators for rates, duration, and departure times.

Cape Breton is part of many coach tours operating from points in the United States and Canada. For information, contact a travel agent or the Nova Scotia Department of Tourism.

RESORTS. The Keltic Lodge at Ingonish Beach is one of the province's most elaborate resorts. It has 32 rooms in the main lodge, 40 motel rooms, and 24 cottages. It has convention space, sitting rooms with fireplaces, and there's evening entertainment in a licensed lounge. It operates year-round and features a wide array of indoor and outdoor activities—golf, skiing, fishing, tennis, swimming and so on. European Plan and Modified American Plan (dinner and breakfast included). Two-, three-, five- and seven-day packages available. Phone 285–2880. Major credit cards.

The **Dundee Golf Course and Cottages** at Dundee, overlooking the Bras D'Or lakes, is more modest. It has 39 fully equipped housekeeping cottages, swimming pool, marina, tennis, 9-hole golf course, pro-shop, licensed dining room and lounge. Phone 345–2649. Major credit cards.

 SPORTS. Several Cape Breton waters, ranging from quiet rivers to expert white water runs, are highly regarded by **canoeing** enthusiasts. The Cape Breton Tourist Association has several good publications and maps. For canoe route information, contact Canoe Nova Scotia, P.O. Box 3010 South, Halifax, N.S. (425–5450), or the Nova Scotia Bookstore, 1597 Hollis St., Halifax, N.S.

Golf courses come in various sizes and ratings from several good nine hole courses like the professionally designed lakeside course at Dundee (off Rte. 4) to the championship 18 hole Cape Breton Highlands in the National Park. **Tennis** is also a popular sport; a number of communities have outdoor courts open to the public.

Scuba divers find Louisbourg Harbour and waters off southern Cape Breton excellent for wreck hunting. Contact Jim Wilson at Dive Cape Breton Ltd., P.O. Box 130, Louisbourg, or call 733-2877 for information on underwater tours of 1–5 days.

Hikers will find a variety of trails in the national park. There's a booklet on hiking called *Walk Cape Breton* available at tourist bureaus. **Anglers** may seek Atlantic salmon and trout in streams and rivers. Angling regulations are available from the Nova Scotia Department of Tourism.

Yacht rentals for **sailing** the 450 square mile Bras d'Or Lakes are available from: Baddeck Marine & Sports (sloop daysailers & charters), 295-2434; Bras d'Or Charter (all types of sailboats), 295-2756; Anchors Aweigh (paddleboats, canoes, tours) in Baddeck, 295-2713 and on *The Balaema,* a 32-ft. diesel schooner out of Margaree Harbour, 235-2943. Cruises to Bird Islands ($6 a person) by Boularderie Cruises in Big Bras d'Or, 674-2384.

For those who bring their own boat, launching ramps are located at a number of sites along the Bras d'Or. Check with the tourist information bureau for the closest one.

The Nova Scotia Department of Recreation operates supervised **swimming** at Port Hood Beach, Inverness Beach, Dominion Beach, and East Bay Beach.

For **skiing** during the winter months, the Cape Smokey Ski Centre at Ingonish on the Cabot Trail operates three major runs of about one mile each. The biggest drop is about 1,000 feet. Snow from December to mid-April. Double chairlift and pony. Call 285–2880 for snow conditions.

For specific information, contact the Cape Breton Tourist Board or the Nova Scotia Department of Tourism.

 MUSEUMS AND HISTORIC SITES. Cape Breton has a number of local history museums and several very unique museum complexes which will appeal to visitors. Mining coal has long been a way of life in Cape Breton. The first recorded mining operation was by the French who, in 1720, dug into an exposed ccal seam at Port Morien. The site of this mine and other 19th-century operations is the first stop on the *Three Mine Tour* in the Glace Bay area. Two hundred million year old fossils can be seen in the coal face at the walk-in mine. Open from noon to 8 P.M. during July and Aug.

The second stop is at the *Miners Museum* in Glace Bay which displays a 200-year history of mining in the area. Visitors can walk into the Ocean Deeps

Colliery with a veteran miner accompanying each group. The Men of the Deeps, an internationally known miners' choral group, sing weekly in summer evening concerts. Check with museum for times. The mining area has a very low roof in places and, although quite safe, is definitely not for claustrophobics. Helmets and protective shawls are provided. The adjoining *Miner's Village* has a replica of the company store and company housing. The Miner's Village Restaurant is licensed and serves seafood prepared by local women—nice surroundings with coal oil lamps. The museum, located at Quarry Point in Glace Bay, is open daily, mid-June to mid-September, from 9 A.M. to 8:30 P.M., and the rest of the year on Wednesday from 9 A.M. to 9 P.M., and Thursdays to Sundays from 9 A.M. to 5 P.M. The restaurant is open 9 A.M. to 9 P.M. daily, year-round (Reservations: 849–9344). Tour costs about $1.75 for adults and 75¢ for children, $1.00 for students. Museum free.

The third mine is the *Princess Colliery* in *Sydney Mines* where visitors descend 682 feet to the pit bottom before being hoisted back to the surface in coal boxes on the mine railway. Protective clothing is provided. Quite safe but not for the claustrophobic or the faint of heart. Open during July and August from 11 A.M. to 7 P.M. Admission is about $2.00 for adults.

The *S&L Railway Museum* in Louisbourg is in a restored 1895 railway station. Open June 15 to Sept. 30, daily. Free. Special tours, by appointment.

The *Old Sydney Museum* in the St. Patrick's Church Building is open daily, June to mid-Oct. Free.

The Garrison Church, circa 1784, in Sydney, Charlotte at Nepean St., allegedly the oldest parish in Cape Breton, was built with stones from the wrecked buildings of Louisbourg.

In Sydney, *Cossitt House,* is the restored residence of Rev. Ranna Cossitt, the oldest house in Sydney, built around 1787. Open May 15 to October 15.

In Baddeck, the *Alexander Graham Bell Museum* has excellent displays of the works of the inventor of the telephone and the first airplane to fly in the British Empire. A replica of Bell's schooner-sized Hydrofoil, along with the dismembered original are on display. Free admission. Open May 20 to October 15 from 9 A.M. to 9 P.M. and October 15 to May 15 from 9 A.M. to 5 P.M., except holidays. Tel. 295–2069.

Victoria County Archives & Museum in Baddeck offers well-organized archives of local history. Free. Open summer months to the public.

Fortress Louisbourg, at Louisbourg, is the most ambitious restoration project ever undertaken in Canada. The original fortress, constructed by the French 1720–45, was the major French fortification in Acadia and a focal point of struggle between the French and English until its total destruction by the English in 1760. Restored homes are "inhabited," and the lifestyle is that of 1750, complete with town "characters." A new interpretive center was opened in 1976 and provides a long range view of the fortress, looking much as it did in 1750. If you are a history, architecture, or restoration buff, plan to spend at least a half day there. A park bus takes visitors from the interpretive center to the Fortress proper. 733–2280. Bus fare is included in the fee which is about $2.00 for adults and about 50¢ for children. A maximum family rate of about $4.00 gets everybody in.

The *Nova Scotia Highland Village* on Rte. 223 at Iona is a collection of refurbished and reconstructed buildings—a carding mill, forge, country store, school and cabin—recalling the early Scottish settlers to the area. Open June 15 to Sept. 15, 10 A.M. to 5 P.M. daily. Admission is about 50¢ for adults and 25¢ for children. The *Acadian Museum* in Cheticamp is more of a handcraft shop and village center. Local women demonstrate Acadian-style rug hooking, weaving, and spinning. Snack bar.

The *Margaree Salmon Museum* at North East Margaree has a collection of fishing paraphenalia used on the famous Margaree River in search of the fighting Atlantic salmon. Open 9 A.M. to 5 P.M. daily, mid-June to mid-October. Admission for adults is about 50¢, children 25¢.

In Margaree, the *Museum of Cape Breton Heritage* has a collection of Scottish, Acadian and Indian household items, and arts and crafts. Free. Closed Sundays.

The *Gaelic College of Celtic Folk Arts and Highland Crafts* at St. Ann's on the Cabot Trail welcomes visitors to the daily concerts and the grounds. Bagpipes and drums only. Small charge for the evening concerts; afternoon practice sessions are free. For information, call 295–2877.

St. Ann's has the *Giant MacAskill Highland Pioneers Museum.* Free. Open June 1–October 15 from 9 A.M. to 5 P.M.

South Cape Breton. In Arichat, the *Le Noir Forge* (off Rte. 4 on 320), a restored 18th-century stone blacksmith shop with working forge. Open June 15 to Sept. 15; Mon. to Sat., 9–12 A.M., 1–5 P.M.; Sun., 1–4 P.M. Free.

The Nicholas Denys Museum in St. Peter's (Rte. 4) has implements and artifacts from as far back as 1638. Adults 50¢, children 25¢. Open June 1 to September 30 from 9 A.M. to 5 P.M.

The *Marble Mountain Museum & Library* in Marble Mountain (off Rte. 105 or Rte. 4 at Cleveland) shows the history of limestone quarries and the business of Marble Mountain. Free. Open in summer months only.

MUSIC. Much of the music of Cape Breton takes a traditional form—bagpipes, fiddle, guitar, and piano with voices singing folk style songs in English, French, or Gaelic. Throughout the summer visitors will find Scottish concerts at places such as *Broad Cove* and traditional Scottish Ceilidh's (kay'lees) in various Cape Breton communities.

The *Gaelic College* at St. Ann's has daily concerts by students. Afternoon session, from about 2 to 3 P.M.; evening session, from about 7 to 8 P.M. most days during July and August. For exact times, contact the Cape Breton Tourist Association at 20 Keltic Dr., Sydney River, or the nearest local tourist bureau.

The *Gaelic Mod* at St. Ann's in early August and *Iona Highland Village Day,* usually the first weekend in August, are excellent showcases for Scottish and other Cape Breton talent in dance, piping, and traditional music.

Every second year in early July, the village of Glendale (in Inverness County just off Rte. 105) hosts a weekend festival of Cape Breton fiddling and stepdancing, with fiddlers returning to Cape Breton from all over the continent. *The* music event of the year in Cape Breton when it's held. Look for Scottish concerts in Frenchvale, Cheticamp, Mabou, St. Ann's and summer festivals in Marion Bridge, St. Joseph du Moine, Wycocomagh, Margaree, Petit de Grat, and Louisbourg—and for Cape North's *Blueberry Festival: Action Week & Highland Games* in Sydney; the *Community Bazaar* in Arichat; *Highland Dancing* festival in St. Peter's (Rte. 4); the *Richmond Exhibition* in Louisdale (off Rte. 4); and the *Festival of the Strait,* a week-long celebration in Port Hawkesbury. N.S. Department of Tourism's *Calendar of Events,* or local newspaper supplements, will give you exact dates and times.

The *Men of the Deeps* is a male choir made up of coalminers from the Cape Breton area. They have toured many North American centers and have also toured China. Tourist information bureaus have schedule.

DINING OUT. Dining out in Cape Breton can be something of an adventure in the specialty restaurants and a taste delight (French cuisine) in the island's best dining room.

Ask your waiter or waitress to suggest the best items on the daily menu or the specials of the day.

Most places accept the following major credit cards: American Express, MasterCard and Visa; others may also be honored. Not all establishments accept credit cards, therefore we suggest you call for information.

Restaurants are categorized on the basis of a full-course dinner, with drinks, tax, and tips excluded: *Expensive,* over $15; *Moderate,* $10–15; *Inexpensive,* under $10.

LOUISBOURG. *Expensive:* **Épée Royale.** 18th-century French dining with 18th-century animation. Open June to September from 11 A.M. to 8 P.M. daily. Licensed. Phone 733–2280. Major credit cards.

L'Hotel de la Marine. Part of the Fortress Louisbourg restoration, the dining room has been recreated to portray the lifestyle of Louisbourg of the 1740's.

Food is prepared from authentic 18th-century French recipes and served in that informal style. Atmosphere is excellent; food is wholesome and interesting. Open from about 11 A.M. to 8 P.M. from June to Sept. Phone 733–2280. Major credit cards.

Moderate: **Grubstake Restaurant.** Pleasant surroundings, good food. Phone 733–2308. Credit cards.

Inexpensive: **Lobster Kettle,** Seafood by the wharf. Phone 733–2877. Visa only.

INGONISH BEACH. *Expensive:* **Keltic Lodge Dining Room.** International cuisine and an excellent choice of menu—all for the one table d'hôte price. Good wine selection. Strict atmosphere of resort luxury: Jackets for men; women requested not to wear casual attire at dinner (e.g., no daytime pant suits, jeans, etc.). Open mid-June to mid-October. Reservations necessary. The Lodge's Coffee Shop, open 8 A.M. to 10 P.M., is moderately priced. Phone 285–2880. Major credit cards.

IONA. *Moderate:* **Highland Heights Inn.** Scottish home-style cooking, with fresh fish in season. Atmosphere of a Scottish inn with huge stone fireplace in dining room, overlooking the Bras d'Or at Grand Narrows. Licensed. Phone 622–2360. Major credit cards.

MARGAREE HARBOUR. *Moderate:* **Schooner Restaurant "Marian Elizabeth."** Aboard a former fishing schooner built in Nova Scotia in 1918; now permanently beached in Margaree Harbour. Licensed with seafood specialties. The chowder is usually excellent; the atmosphere is an experience. Open June 15 to mid-October. Call for reservations. Phone 235-2317.

CHETICAMP. *Moderate.* **Acadian Museum** serves delicious old Acadian food in tiny restaurant.

ST. PETER'S. *Moderate–Expensive:* **Macdonald's Hotel.** Home-style and French cuisine; children's plates half price; open year-round. Licensed. Good food, nice people. Attached to a 13-room inn in an old Richmond County Home on Rte. 4. Phone 535-2997. Major credit cards.

SYDNEY. *Expensive:* **Petit Jean.** Tries to be French; succeeds moderately well. Lunch on Monday to Friday only from noon–2 P.M.; dinner daily 6 P.M. to 10 P.M. Call for reservations. Phone 539-4671.

Moderate: **Jasper's.** Open 24 hours with plain, tasty food. Beer and wine license. Phone 564–6181.

Joe's Warehouse. Good food. Cabaret on lower floor called *Smooth Herman's.* A fun place. Phone 539–6686.

Inexpensive: **Venice Pizzeria.** On Welton St. Try their Mexican food. Phone 539-4973.

SYDNEY MINES. *Moderate:* **The Cauldron.** Located at the Princess Tourist Mine. Open daily May to September. Home-cooked-style food with daily specials. Phone 736-6823.

WHYCOCOMAGH. *Moderate:* **Village Inn.** Home-cooked meals in tiny country inn. Old-style friendly service and delicious food. Licensed. Make reservations, 756–2002. Major credit cards.

PRACTICAL INFORMATION FOR NOVA SCOTIA

 HOW TO GET THERE. By car: The Trans-Canada Hwy. eastbound will deliver you to Nova Scotia by the overland route through New Brunswick, entering the province at Amherst.

By ferry: Visitors may also reach Nova Scotia by one of the six-car ferry connections from Maine, New Brunswick, Prince Edward Island, and Newfoundland.

Passenger and vehicle ferry service is operated between Yarmouth, Nova Scotia, and Portland, Maine, by *CN Marine* and by *Prince of Fundy Cruises.* A one-way trip takes between 10 and 12 hours. Cabins, dining facilities, entertainment, and recreation are available on both ferries. Advance reservations must be made for both vessels, especially during the summer season. Contact Prince of Fundy Cruises at the International Terminal in Portland. Call (207) 775-5611. CN Marine may be booked through any CN ticket office in Canada or by calling toll-free in Maine (800) 432-7344 or toll-free (800) 341-7981 in mid-Northeastern United States. Or contact a travel agent for bookings. There is also a CN Marine passenger and vehicle ferry service between Yarmouth and Bar Harbour, Me. Crossing time: six hours. Same telephone information as for Portland ferry.

CN Marine also operates frequent vehicle and passenger service between Saint John, New Brunswick, and Digby, Nova Scotia. The 40-mile crossing takes about 2½ hours. Make reservations in advance, especially for summer months. Book through any CN ticket office in Canada or by calling toll-free in Maine (800) 432-7344 or toll free in mid-Northeastern United States or book through a travel agent.

The ferry service between North Sydney, Nova Scotia, and the Newfoundland ports of Argentia (summer service) and Port-aux-Basques (year-round service) is also operated by CN Marine. The crossing to Port-aux-Basques takes about 6 hours; to Argentia about 18 hours. Cabins, dining, entertainment, and recreation facilities are available on the vessels. Bookings may be made at the above CN Marine numbers or through a travel agent. Make reservations for Argentia, especially during the summer season, and on the Port-aux-Basques night service. Reservations are not accepted on the Port-aux-Basques day service.

Passenger and vehicle service between Wood Islands, Prince Edward Island, and Caribou [near Pictou], Nova Scotia, is operated from May to late December by *Northumberland Ferries Limited.* The 14-mile crossing takes about an hour. Lunch-counter facilities are available but there are no cabins. Reservations are not accepted and the line-ups may take several hours during the summer season. It is best to cross early [first ferry leaves at 6 A.M. in summer] or late in the evening. For information, contact Northumberland Ferries, P.O. Box 634, Charlottetown, P.E.I., or call (902) 894–3473. In Caribou, Nova Scotia (902) 485–9015.

By train: *Via Rail* provides train service to Nova Scotia from major centers across Canada. *Amtrak* from New York makes connections with CN in Montréal.

By bus: Service to most Nova Scotia areas is provided by *Acadian Lines* and other bus companies. Connections are made at Amherst, Nova Scotia, and with the ferries at Yarmouth, Digby, Caribou and North Sydney, Nova Scotia.

By air: *Eastern Provincial Airways* flies to Halifax and Sydney, Nova Scotia, from centers within Atlantic Canada and from Toronto. *Air Canada* also flies into Halifax, Yarmouth, and Sydney from Atlantic centers—Montréal, Québec, and Toronto. *CP Air* flies from Montréal. *CP Air* and *Air Canada* have extensive national and international connections.

ACCOMMODATIONS. Accommodations are generally good and friendly throughout the province. Reservations can be made by calling the toll-free numbers listed under "Tourist Information" in the "Practical Information for Halifax/Dartmouth" section. Rates based on double-occupancy. *Expensive,* over $39; *Moderate,* $30–39; *Inexpensive,* under $30.

A 10% provincial tax will be added to your bill.

Most places accept the following major credit cards: American Express, MasterCard and Visa; others may also be honored. Not all establishments accept credit cards, therefore we suggest you call for information.

AMHERST. *Expensive:* **Wandlyn Motor Inn.** 60 units outside of the town beside the highway. Clean, comfortable accommodations with large fields for children. Two miles from New Brunswick–Nova Scotia border. Coffeeshop, licensed dining and lounge, heated outdoor pool. Off-season rates October to June. Pets with permission. Phone 667–3331, 800–561–0000. Major credit cards.

ANNAPOLIS ROYAL. *Moderate:* **Royal Anne Motel.** 20 units with licensed restaurant, gardens, and open lawns. Pleasant surroundings near most historical sites in the area. Off-season rates mid-September to mid-June. Pets allowed with permission. Phone 532–2323. Credit card: Visa only.

AULD COVE. *Moderate:* **The Cove Motel.** Secluded, on peninsula; licensed dining room overlooking the Strait of Canso, near the Canso Causeway; 31 units including 12 chalets; pets permitted. Phone 747–2700. Major credit cards.

BRIDGETOWN. *Expensive:* **Bridgetown Motor Hotel.** 33 units, comfortable accommodation, licensed dining, and lounge with bar shaped like distillery barrel. Sauna, pool, table tennis. Off-season rates mid-September to June. Attended pets permitted. Phone 665–4491. Major credit cards.

BRIDGEWATER. *Expensive.* **Wandlyn Motor Inn.** Clean, comfortable accommodations. Coffeeshop, licensed dining and lounge, indoor pool, sauna. Gift shop. Off-season rates October to June. Pets with permission. Phone 543–7131, 800–561–0000. Major credit cards.

DIGBY. *Expensive.* **The Pines.** Elegant resort. Excellent golf. Tennis, pool, fine service and gracious dining. Phone 245–2511.

Moderate–Expensive. **Admiral Digby Inn.** 40 units, licensed dining room and lounge. Indoor pool. Phone 245–2531. Major credit cards.

Moderate. **Mountain Gap Inn.** Large motel. Some cottages with one to two bedrooms. Pool, tennis, beach, bar, dining room. Phone 245–2277.

KENTVILLE. *Expensive:* **Wandlyn Motor Inn.** 75 rooms, clean, comfortable accommodations. Coffeeshop, licensed dining and lounge, pool, playground, golf green, horseshoe pit, games room, pool table; pets with permission. Off-season rates October to June. Phone 678–8311, 800–561–0000. Major credit cards.

LUNENBURG. *Inexpensive:* **Bluenose Lodge.** 9 rooms with bath; licensed dining room; deepsea fishing excursions arranged; displays local crafts. Phone 634–8851. Major credit cards.

NEW GLASGOW. *Expensive:* **Heather Motor Inn.** 76 units, clean and comfortable, licensed dining room (good seafood) and lounge. Open year-round; pets permitted. Phone 752–8401. Major credit cards.

Moderate. **Peter Pan Motel.** 390 Marsh St. Good buy. Bar, dining room, pool. Phone 752–8327.

SHEET HARBOUR. *Moderate:* **Marquis of Dufferin Hotel.** 14 units overlooking the Atlantic. Adjacent restaurant; pets permitted. Off-season rates, October to May. Phone 654–2696. Major credit cards.

TRURO. *Moderate:* **Tidal Bore Inn.** 24 rooms. Clean and comfortable; in the viewing area for the tidal bore rapids. Licensed restaurant. Open mid-May to mid-October. Off-season rates before mid-June. Phone 895–9241. Major credit cards.

WESTERN SHORE–OAK ISLAND CHANNEL. *Expensive:* **Oak Island Inn.** 71 rooms, comfortable and well-appointed. Ocean view overlooks the marina and Oak Island treasure island. Licensed dining and lounge. Pool, marina, sailboat rentals, deep sea fishing charters. Open year-round. Phone 627–2600. Major credit cards.

WOLFVILLE. *Expensive:* **Old Orchard Inn.** 74 rooms and 30 chalets with 10 efficiency units; comfortable with a spectacular view over the Annapolis Valley from the main building. Licensed dining and lounge, with nightly entertainment; coffeeshop. Pool, sauna, tennis, nature trails, playground. Motel open year-round; chalets open May to October. Phone 542–5751. Major credit cards.

YARMOUTH. *Expensive:* **Rodd's Grand Hotel.** 138 rooms, clean and comfortable, near the ferries from Portland and Bar Harbor, Maine. Licensed dining and two lounges. Pets permitted. Phone 742–2446. Major credit cards.
Manor Inn. On Hwy. 1, Colonial mansion with rose garden, estate, and lakefront; 29 rooms, licensed dining and lounge with entertainment; pets permitted. Open mid-June to October. Phone 742–2487. Major credit cards.

 BED AND BREAKFAST. Nova Scotia also has a well-developed bed-and-breakfast program. Private homes that take overnight guests for as little as $15 to $22 a night. In the towns they go by the name of "guest homes." The provincial accommodations guide, available at tourist bureaus, lists them all.

TELEPHONE. The long-distance area code for the entire province (plus neighboring Prince Edward Island) is 902.

 HOW TO GET AROUND. By car: Major highways in Nova Scotia are good to excellent. The routes tend to follow the coastline and the three-digit routings [e.g. 104] are the faster, but less scenic, roads. Most of the 10 routes are paralleled by the older and more scenic highways. During the summer months, Nova Scotia's unpaved highways are usually in very good condition and, aside from raising some dust, make for quiet and scenic drives.

As in the rest of Canada, summer is "highway repair time" and motorists are cautioned to be alert for the flag-people with warnings of road works ahead.

Car-rental agencies are located at both the Halifax International and Sydney airports, all Nova Scotia entry points, and in the cities of Halifax and Sydney. Reservations are necessary during the summer months and may be made through local agency offices or a travel agency.

By train: *Via Rail* serves many major centers in Nova Scotia and Via Rail operates a daily service from Halifax to Digby. For the traveler, train service in Nova Scotia is inconvenient at best. The tracks usually run through the least interesting scenery and service is not frequent. Bookings may be made at any CN ticket office in Canada or through a travel agency.

By bus: *Acadian Lines Ltd., MacKenzie Bus Line Ltd.,* and *Zinck's Bus Company Ltd.* operate daily service to all parts of Nova Scotia. Information and bookings may be made through a travel agent or by contacting Acadian Lines

Limited, 6040 Almon Street, Halifax, Nova Scotia, (902) 454-9321, or an Acadian Lines office.

By air: Both *Air Canada* and *Eastern Provincial Airways* have flights between Sydney and Halifax several times daily. In Halifax, contact Air Canada at 429-7111 and EPA at 861-3860. In Sydney, call Air Canada at 539-6600 and EPA at 564-4545. Bookings may be made through any travel agency. The flight between the two cities takes about 40 minutes.

TIME ZONE. Nova Scotia is on Atlantic Time (1 hour in advance of Eastern Time).

 SEASONAL EVENTS. The winter season in Nova Scotia is a time of performances by Neptune Theatre and the Atlantic Symphony in *Halifax* and on tour. **Winter** carnivals are held at the major universities in *Halifax, Wolfville,* and at *Antigonish* as well as at larger centers with service club sponsorship.

During **March** and **April** (maple sugar weather) the *Glooscap* Maple Sugar Festival invites visitors to the sugar bush for pancake suppers and maple candy.

As **May** turns into **June**, the Apple Blossom Festival is celebrated in the Annapolis Valley towns of *Kentville, Wolfville,* and *New Minas.* In May and June the Blessing of the Fleet is held in many French villages—*Meteghan, Main-à-Dieu, Petit de Grat*—before the boats begin the inshore and offshore fishing season. Scottish Concert and Dance, with performers from around the Maritimes, is held annually in *Pictou.* Rhododendron Sunday in *Kentville* in mid-June brings out the flower lovers. The landing of explorer John Cabot in 1497 is remembered in late June at *Cape North* in an annual pageant.

Festivals and events ranging from week-long galas to community suppers are held throughout the summer months in all parts of Nova Scotia. The Department of Tourism can provide complete lists with dates. Many of the festivals have an ethnic background—Scottish or Acadian—or feature local fishery or agricultural fairs and exhibitions. Some events have special foods—such as lobster carnivals and steer barbecues—which provide excellent informal dining at minimal costs.

July 1, as well as being Dominion Day, is also the Gathering of the Clans in *Pugwash* and the beginning of the multi-cultural festival known as the Festival of the Strait in *Port Hawkesbury.* The first week sees the Annual Lobster Supper Weekend in *St. Peter's.* The *Sydney* Highland Games take place in early July, as do the Maritime Old Time Fiddling Contest in *Dartmouth,* the *Pictou* Lobster Carnival, the *Antigonish* Highland Games, and the Acadian Festival of *Clare* held at Meteghan River. In *Kingston,* two steers are barbecued in mid-July.

The *Margaree* Summer Festival is held in late July. The fictional clock salesman, Sam Slick, is remembered in the home town of his creator during Sam Slick Days and Regatta in *Windsor* at that time, and the Acadian Day Festival in *L'Ardoise* and the East Pictou Annual Fair in Thorburn are held in late July.

Once again in a Scottish vein, the Gaelic Mod is the attraction at the Gaelic College in *St. Ann's* early in **August** when the South Shore Exhibition in *Bridgewater* begins the series of agricultural fairs and exhibitions throughout the province. In *New Glasgow* early in August kilts swirl at the Festival of the Tartans and at Highland Village Day in *Iona.* The Piper's Picnic in *Earltown* is the scene for pipe bands, highland dancing and a gathering of the clans. In mid-August rockhounds from many parts of North America congregate in the *Parrsboro* area for the annual Rockhound Round-up. The *Canso* Regatta, the traditional *Johnstown* Milling Frolic, the Highland Summer Festival in *Inverness,* and Scallop Day in *Digby* are other local events in mid-August.

Throughout July and August there are Scottish concerts and many communities have a Ceilidh (kay-lee) with piping and fiddling and Gaelic folk singing.

During early **September** the blueberry is king in the *Amherst* area during the Blueberry Festival, while in *Lunenburg* the Nova Scotia Fisheries Exhibition celebrates the harvest from the sea.

TOURS. *Nova Tours Ltd.* operates several bus tours per season through Nova Scotia. For departure dates and rates, telephone 429–3702. Other operators offering bus tours through Nova Scotia and other Maritime Provinces are *Evangeline Tours,* Wolfville (542–9109); and *Atlantic Tours,* Saint John, New Brunswick (657–6386). Also *Bridges Tours,* Halifax (422-8462), and *Village Bus Tours,* P.O. Box 35, Cornwallis, Nova Scotia B05 1H0.

The Nova Scotia Department of Tourism can provide complete information on guided and self-guiding tours of the province.

SPECIAL INTEREST SIGHTSEEING. The Canada Department of Agriculture Research Station in Kentville conducts poultry and horticultural research on its 650-acre site. Open Monday to Friday from 8:30 A.M. to 5 P.M.

Wildlife parks with native animals and birds in natural open settings are operated by the province at Shubenacadie, about 48 kms. (30 miles) from Halifax on Rte. 102, at Upper Clements on Rte. 1 between Annapolis Royal and Digby, and near Marion Bridge, about 20 miles from Sydney. Open May 1 to end of October from 8:30 A.M. to 7:30 P.M. daily. Wear walking shoes and take a camera. A good way to entertain children.

NATIONAL PARKS. The two national parks in Nova Scotia offer you great contrasts. Cape Breton Highlands National Park is high and forested with sheer cliffs dropping off into the sea. Kejimkujik National Park is inland —a hilly forested area with many lakes.

Cape Breton Highlands is partially ringed by the spectacular Cabot Trail. The interior of the Park is wilderness and inaccessible by normal means. The 950 sq. kms. (367 square miles) area has numerous rivers which provide good fishing and the forest is home to many animals. Facilities in the park are available for fishing (provincial regulations apply), excellent hiking with nature trails starting at the highway, canoeing, and camping including a trailer park. There are also an interpretive center and a very good 18-hole championship golf course. Rates for golf are about $5 per day and about $25 weekly. A number of saltwater beaches on the eastern coast offer excellent swimming.

Cape Breton Highlands is both a summer and winter park, with extensive skiing facilities and other winter activities. For more information, contact the Superintendent, Cape Breton Highlands National Park, Ingonish Beach, Cape Breton, Nova Scotia B0C 1L0.

Kejimkujik (ke-jim-kú-gik) National Park is in the western part of the province and is reached by Hwy. 8 between Liverpool and Annapolis Royal. A former Micmac Indian reservation, the park was named for the largest lake.

The 381-sq.-km. (238-square mile) park has a relatively mild winter climate combined with many lakes inhabited by a wide range of reptiles and amphibians. Essentially a wilderness, Kejimkujik has well marked canoe routes into the interior with primitive campsites.

There are park facilities for camping, boating and boat rentals, hiking (nature trails), fishing (under provincial regulations), and freshwater swimming. There is also an interpretive center. Many animals live in the park and in the adjoining Tobeatic Game Sanctuary. Deer are often seen.

Kejimkujik has one minor problem—dog ticks, introduced into the area by the hunting dogs used by United States hunters earlier in the century. Although the ticks do not carry disease and are easily removed from the skin, tight-fitting clothing and a thorough examination after being in the woods are necessary. During midsummer, the pest declines in numbers and is virtually gone by autumn. Visitors with dogs and other domestic animals must be careful to avoid a tick infestation on the pet. Visitors who avoid the heavy woods are not likely to have any problem.

For additional information on Kejimkujik National Park, contact the Superintendent, P.O. Box 36, Maitland Bridge, Annapolis County, Nova Scotia B0T 1N0.

Both national parks have a user fee of about $1.00 per vehicle per day, $2.00 for a 4-day pass, and $10.00 for an annual pass valid for all Canadian national parks. There is no charge for vehicles passing through Cape Breton National Park on the Cabot Trail.

Camping fees in both parks range from about $4.50 to about $8.00 per day depending on the facilities.

 PROVINCIAL CAMPING PARKS. Provincial camp-grounds are located throughout the province. All have well-managed facilities and all except Beaver Mountain have picnic sites.

Battery. 114 acres, almost 2 kms. (one mile) north of St. Peter's on Rte. 4. Features hiking trails.

Beaver Mountain. 329 acres off Rte. 104 at Beaver Mountain Road between New Glasgow and Antigonish.

Blomidon. 1667 acres, 16 kms. (10 miles) north of Canning on Rte. 1. Has a spectacular lookout over the Bay of Fundy with the world's highest tides.

Boylston. 225 acres, 6½ kms. (4 miles) north of Guysborough on Rte. 16.

Caribou. 78 acres, 8 kms. (5 miles) north of Pictou on Rte. 106 near the ferry from Prince Edward Island. Has hiking and swimming area.

Ellenwood Lake. 281 acres, 19 kms. (12 miles) northeast of Yarmouth on Rte. 340. Has hiking trails and a boat-launch ramp. Lake swimming.

Five Islands. 1020 acres, 24 kms. (15 miles) east of Parrsboro on Rte. 2 along the Bay of Fundy coast. Has hiking trails and unique scenery.

Graves Island. 123 acres, 3 kms. (2 miles) east of Chester on Rte. 3.

Laurie. 71 acres, 40 kms. (25 miles) north of Halifax on Rte. 2. Has hiking trails and boat launch ramp.

Mira River. 216 acres, 24 kms. (15 miles) south east of Sydney on Rte. 22. Has boat launch ramp and hiking trails along the river.

Porter's Lake. 216 acres, 19 kms. (12 miles) east of Dartmouth on Rte. 7. Has hiking trails and boat launch ramp on the lake.

Risser's Beach. 18 acres, 27 kms. (16 miles) south of Bridgewater on Rte. 331. Has an interpretive center and one of the best beaches in Nova Scotia, but the water is cool at the best of times.

Salsman, 26 acres, 13 kms. (8 miles) south of Goshen off Rte. 316; *Saltsprings,* 76 acres, 24 kms. (15 miles) west of New Glasgow; and *Valleyview,* 134 acres, 5 kms. (3 miles) north of Bridgetown off Rte. 1, have no facilities except for camping and picnics, although *Valleyview* does have an excellent view over the lower Annapolis Valley farming country.

Smiley's. 100 acres, 13 kms. (8 miles) east of Windsor on Rte. 14; and *Wentworth,* 243 acres at Wentworth Centre on Rte. 104, have hiking trails.

The Islands. 62 acres, 5 kms. (3 miles) west of Shelburne, on Rte. 3; and *Whycocomagh,* 503 acres, east of the community of Whycocomagh on Rte. 105, have hiking trails and boat launch ramps.

These provincial recreation areas are open from mid-May to mid-October. Most have water, toilet facilities, fireplaces, and firewood or some of these; many have sewage disposal stations. Camping fees at most recreation areas begin at about $5 per day depending on the facilities.

A number of provincial camping parks and day-use parks (without camping areas) are spotted around the province overlooking scenic views or by the water.

 BEACHES. The Nova Scotia Department of Recreation operates supervised beaches in the following areas: on the Northumberland Strait coast at Heather Beach, Caribou Beach, Melmerby Beach; on the Nova Scotia Atlantic coast at Summerville Beach, Rissers Beach, Queensland Beach, Crystal Crescent Beach, Lawrencetown Beach, Martinique Beach, Clam Harbour Beach and Taylor Head Beach. There is a supervised swimming area in Kejim-kujik National Park with freshwater swimming. There is also supervised fresh-water swimming at Ellenwood Lake Beach and both fresh and saltwater beaches in the Cape Breton National Highland Park.

In addition, there are dozens of unsupervised beaches ranging from small strips to huge sandy beaches such as Mavililette Beach at Cape St. Mary about 24 kms. (15 miles) north of Yarmouth. On the Northumberland Strait coast, the summer water temperature is in the 18–21°C. (65–70°F.) range, quite pleasant for swimming. The Atlantic coast water temperatures range from distinctly cool to dangerously cold.

FARM AND COUNTRY VACATIONS. More than 40 Nova Scotia families are members of the farm and country vacation program. This includes farmers, fishermen, and rural people who have opened their homes to guests on a year-round or seasonal basis.

Country vacation guests live, eat, and become part of the host family for a few days or weeks. Guests may take part in the farm activities or go fishing with the host. Many country vacation homes have swimming, fishing, and hiking facilities on or near their property.

Guests are advised to take along old clothes and extra shoes and boots. Paying for the vacation is more easily done on arrival. Ask before bringing along the family pet.

Costs range from about $85 to $125 per person per week; children under twelve from about $50 to $60 per week. Includes three home-cooked, home-grown meals plus snacks each day. Reservations should be made early and directly with the country family chosen. Information and listings of families in the program may be obtained from the Nova Scotia Department of Tourism or at individual tourist bureaus.

RESORTS. *Expensive:* **Liscombe Lodge.** At Liscombe Mills, on Hwy. 7 (Marine Dr. 35 units, including cottages and chalets. Tennis, boat, and canoe rentals, lawn games, deep-sea and freshwater fishing, marina. Phone 779–2307 (in winter, 424–3258). Major credit cards.

The Pines Resort Hotel. At Digby. 90 bedrooms in main lodge, 60 more in deluxe cottages. Licensed dining room with dress regulations in effect. Live entertainment, outdoor swimming pool, floodlit tennis courts, 18-hole golf course, other activities. Modified American Plan optional (breakfast and dinner). Phone 245-2511. Major credit cards.

Moderate: **The Mountain Gap Inn.** At Smith's Cove near Digby. 100 motel units and 12 cottages. Licensed lounge and dining room. 25 acres of landscaped ground with tidal-beach frontage. Swimming pool, tennis courts, conference and convention facilities. Phone 245–2277. Major credit cards.

White Point Beach Lodge. At Hunt's Point, near Liverpool. 300-acre beach resort with ocean beach, freshwater lake, heated pool, golf course, tennis courts, boating facilities. 24 rooms in lodges and 40 cottages with one to three bedrooms. Phone 354-3177. Major credit cards.

CHILDREN'S ACTIVITIES. With many picnic and recreation areas, the main highways tend to follow the coast where children can safely explore beaches and rocks.

The wildlife parks at Shubenacadie, near Halifax/Dartmouth, in Upper Clements near Digby and at Marion Bridge, near Sydney, are good for a half day each. No admission fee.

Many of the provincial parks have special areas for kids, and many of the commercial camping parks have playgrounds. At Cabotland, Cape Breton, at the junction of Rte. 105 and the Cabot Trail, there is a children's farm with pettable animals, pony rides and other attractions.

Fishing can provide hours of enjoyment. Saltwater fishing requires no license and in most places youngsters can fish from the local wharf with some hope of a catch.

Bryce and Sylvia Milne, Grand Pré, Nova Scotia, have a large farm with riding horses and lots of pets. The Milnes are members of the farm and country vacation program, but they take only children—up to three at a time. Cost is about $125 per week per child, which includes everything. Address: P.O. Box 31, Grand Pré, N.S. 3OP 1M0; 542–3054.

SUMMER SPORTS. Boating: During the summer Nova Scotians take to the water. Nova Scotia's most famous ship, the *Bluenose II*—a reproduction of the original race champion fishing schooner, *Bluenose I*—sails daily except Mondays from the Privateer's Wharf in Halifax for 2-hour harbor cruises. Call 424-4247 for information. Halifax Water Tours offers tours of Halifax Harbour and environs, starting from Historic Properties. Phone 423-7783. Guided walking tours of the islands of Halifax Harbour take place May 15 to September 25. Boat leaves from near the Maritime Museum of the Atlantic. Call 422-9523. Along the *South Shore*, the Oak Island Inn Marina at Western Shore, Lunenburg County (627-2600) gives tours of the Mahone Bay area and charters large and small sailboats. In Dayspring, R.R. No. 3, Bridgewater, in Lunenburg County, Brian Stokes has a 34-foot ketch, two lasers, and 18-foot keel sloops available, with or without crew; he also gives sailing lessons. 543–3658. In Chester, Lunenburg County, you can take 2½-hour cruises on the *Buccaneer Lady*, a 50-foot cabin cruiser, sailing from the Buccaneer Lodge in Chester (275–5255). In Mahone Bay, Whitehouse Marine Ltd. (627-2641 in-season, 861-3418 off-season) charters a crewed boat, sailing out of Oak Island Marina. Marriotts Cove Charter (275-4886) has bare boat or skippered charters in the Mahone Bay–St. Margaret's Bay area aboard the 25-foot diesel auxiliary ketch *Ailsa III*. In Lunenburg, *Timberwind*, an authentic 35-foot gaff-rigged sailing schooner, sails daily, June to late September, from the Lunenburg Fisheries Museum four times a day. $8.50 per person. Charters also available. Phone 634–8966. Along the *Northumberland Shore*, contact the Tatamagouche Tourist Bureau in Tatamagouche, Nova Scotia, for information.

The Nova Scotia Dept. of Tourism's brochure *Nova Scotia Sports and Activities* has additional information on marinas, charters and rentals.

Canoe route information is available from the Nova Scotia Government Bookstore, 1597 Hollis St., Halifax. The publication, *Canoe Routes of Nova Scotia,* is available from Canoe Nova Scotia, P.O. Box 3010 South, Halifax, N.S. Phone 425–5450. Cost: $9.25.

Golf: Nova Scotia and Cape Breton have 38 golf courses as well as driving ranges and miniature golf courses, all described in *Nova Scotia Sports and Activities,* available, free, from the N.S. Dept. of Tourism.

Tennis is popular and many private clubs have excellent courts. For a list of public courts, contact the Nova Scotia Department of Tourism.

Bicycling: *Bicycle Tours in Nova Scotia* is available for $3.50 postpaid. Write to: Bicycle Nova Scotia, P.O. Box 3010 South, Halifax, N.S.

Other Sports: The Tourism Department will also supply complete information on other popular activities such as *hiking, flying, skiing, snowmobiling, scuba diving, fishing* in both fresh- and salt-water, and *hunting.*

CAMPING OUT. Nova Scotia has a large number of private and provincial (government) campgrounds throughout the province. The provincial recreation areas listed in the previous section all have camping facilities, as have the two national parks.

Private campgrounds are inspected by the provincial department of tourism and licensed if they pass inspection. The better campgrounds display the "Approved Campground" sign issued by the Department of Tourism. The awarding of the approval sign is based on an operation displaying a high degree of cleanliness, comfort, and hospitality over and above the necessary minimum for licensing.

Minimum charge at most private campgrounds is about $5.00; the maximum is dependent on the services provided. Provincial recreation area campground charges begin at about $4.00; and, in the national parks, at about $3.50. The national parks also have a user permit of about $1 per vehicle per day, $2 for a four day pass, and $10 for an annual pass valid at all Canadian national parks.

Camping in Nova Scotia is allowed only at designated camping areas. No camping is allowed in picnic areas, day use parks, or along public highways.

WINTER SPORTS. Skiing, particularly cross-country, is becoming more popular in Nova Scotia but the province does not have the heavy and consistent snowfall necessary to make it a great ski area. January, February, and March usually provide the best snow, but it is not unusual for snow to be wiped out by a warm rain early in the season.

Other sports: *Ice skating, ice boating,* and *snowshoeing* are also popular winter sports.

Contact the Nova Scotia Department of Tourism for information.

HISTORIC SITES. The first permanent European settlement north of the Gulf of Mexico was at Port Royal in what is now Nova Scotia. Here, in 1605, the French explorers Champlain and de Monts established their *Habitation,* or trading post, which stood until Virginian raiders scattered the French and leveled the buildings in 1613.

To reach the Habitation compound, now rebuilt, follow Rte. 1 toward Annapolis Royal and turn off to the right (if approaching Annapolis Royal from the east) just before crossing the Annapolis Causeway.

Fort Anne National Historic Park in Annapolis Royal documents part of the two-century French-English struggle for North America. Check open hours; call 532–5197.

Longfellow's poetic story of Evangeline and Gabriel, two Acadians driven apart by the French-English struggles, has its memorial at *Grand Pré National Historic Site* near Wolfville. The interpretive center has displays and artifacts. Call 542–3631.

Fort Edward, in the town of Windsor, has the oldest surviving blockhouse in Canada. Call 426–5080.

With the exception of Fortress Louisbourg (see *Practical Information for Cape Breton*) there is no admission charge to any National Historic Sites which are usually open from mid-May to mid-October, 9 A.M. to 8 P.M., though times may vary with the site. For material on any of the sites, write to Parks Canada— Atlantic Region, 5161 George Street, Halifax, Nova Scotia B3J 1M7, (902) 426–3405.

MUSEUMS AND SITES. Nova Scotia has a well developed series of museums, living museums, and historic homes and buildings. Most towns have a small local museum which depicts the history of the area.

The Nova Scotia Museum operates the following sites in the province:

Perkins House in **Liverpool** is a fine restored New England-style example of the Nova Scotia lifestyle prior to the American Revolution. In **Shelburne,** the *Ross-Thompson House* has been restored with trade items of the day.

Uniacke House, at **Mount Uniacke** near Halifax, presents one of the finest examples of the architecture and furnishings of the early 1800's to be found in North America. Thomas Chandler Haliburton, creator of the famous Sam Slick stories, completed his home in **Windsor** in 1836. *Haliburton House.* *"Clifton,"* is now open to the public. *Lawrence House* in **Maitland** was the home of the builder of Nova Scotia's largest wooden ship. The gracious Georgian brick house of Charles *Prescott* was completed about 1814 at **Starr's Point** near Wolfville. The early 19th-century home of *Thomas McCulloch* in **Pictou** has fine examples of carved interior woodwork.

The Museum also operates three historic mills in Nova Scotia. The *Wile Carding Mill* in **Bridgewater,** water-wheel driven, is unchanged since the days of the mid-1800's. The *Woolen Mill* in **Barrington** shows how the wool was woven into bolts of twills and flannels, blankets and suitings. The *Balmoral Grist Mill* at **Balmoral Mills** is one of the oldest operating mills in the province, dating from 1860. Visitors may purchase sample bags of stone ground flours and meals. A pleasant picnic ground overlooks the mill pond and falls.

The historic homes and mills are open from mid-May to mid-October, 9:30 A.M. to 5:30 P.M. daily. No admission charge.

Sherbrooke Village on Rte. 7 is a living village museum—a restoration of a 19th-century lumbering and gold-mining community. The inhabitants of the village still live in their homes within the "museum" and all of the buildings are staffed by costumed residents "working" at their trades. Wear walking shoes and try the excellent home-made soup or other fare at Bright House or What-Cheer-House. Open May 15 to October 15, 9:30 A.M. to 5:30 P.M. daily. Adult admission is $1.50; children enter free.

Ross Farm Museum, on Rte. 12 about 19 kms. (12 miles) north of Chester Basin, is a living museum which illustrates advances in farming from 1600 to 1925. Wear comfortable shoes or boots and old clothes. Adult admission is $1.50, children under 14 about 25¢. Family admissions are about $3.50. Open mid-May to mid-October, 9:30 to 5:30 daily. Open by appointment only the remainder of the year; 389–2210.

Museums on the Tourist Trails: On the **Evangeline Trail** (reached by Hwys. 1 and 101). In Yarmouth, the *County Historical Society Museum & Research Library* displays ship models and paintings, and the *Firefighters Museum* which illustrates the history of firefighting in the province; in Clementsport, the *Old St. Edwards Church Museum* (1797) is built like a ship of hand-hewn timbers; *North Hills Museum* at Granville Ferry has English furniture and bric-à-brac from the Georgian (1714–1830) period; in Annapolis Royal, the already-mentioned historical sites and the *O'Dell Inn & Tavern* and *The McNamara House* are restored buildings from the 19th and 18th centuries; in Middleton, the *Phinney Clock Collection* at the *Annapolis Valley MacDonald Museum,* an exhibit of 115 clocks and 52 watches, most of them brought to Nova Scotia by original settlers; in Wolfville, the *Historical Museum* features historical material from the New England Planters and Loyalists; in Hantsport, the *Churchill House and Maritime Museum* (1860) has a collection of shipbuilding tools, nautical instruments, old ships' logs and pictures.

Lighthouse Route (reached by Hwys. 3 and 103). The *Acadian Museum,* West Pubnico, tells of local history; *The Old Meeting House,* which is the oldest nonconformist church building in Canada (1766), and the *Cape Sable Historical Society Archives,* both in Barrington; in Lockeport, the *Little School Museum* is a restoration project housing a local history collection; in Bridgewater, the *Des Brisay Museum and Park,* which is the oldest municipally owned museum collection in Nova Scotia; the *Fort Point Museum* in La Have, a former lighthouse keeper's house; in Parkdale, the *Parkdale-Maplewood Museum* which emphasizes the German heritage of the area; in Blockhouse, the *Roaring 20's Museum* houses Nathern Joudrey's private collection of antique cars; in Lunenburg the *Lunenburg Fisheries Museum* and the *Aquarium* which is aboard two former fishing vessels and a one-time rumrunner; and via Rte. 332 from Lunenburg is the site of an old-time goldrush with monuments, caverns and a museum at the *Riverport-Ovens Natural Park.*

Glooscap Trail (reached by Hwys. 2 and 215). In Minudie, the *Amos Seaman School Museum,* which is housed in a restored one-room schoolhouse; the *Geological Museum* in Parrsboro has minerals and semiprecious stones from the region; in Springhill, visitors can go down into an actual mine and dig coal from the face at the *Miners' Museum;* in Truro, the *Colchester Historical Society Museum;* in Walton, the *Walton Museum* of local history; and on Rte. 14 the *South Rawdon Museum* has a small collection reflecting the former local temperance movement in a one-time Sons of Temperance Hall.

Sunrise Trail (reached by Hwy. 6). The *Sunrise Trail Museum* in Tatamagouche features memorabilia of the local-born giantess Anna Swann; in Pictou, the *Micmac Museum* is located next to a 17th-century Micmac burial ground and is the largest archeological discovery of its kind in Eastern Canada; in New Glasgow, the *Pictou County Historical Museum* which features "Samson", the first steam locomotive used in Canada; and in nearby Stellarton, the *Mining*

Museum & Library; in MacPherson Mills, *MacPherson's Mill & Farmstead* has a water-powered grist mill and restored farm buildings.

Marine Drive Trail (reached by Hwys. 7, 316, 16 and 344). In Musquodoboit Harbour, the *Railway Museum* is housed in a 1917 CNR station and features two restored railway cars; in Jeddore Oyster Pond, the *Fisherman's House & Museum* illustrates the life of the inshore fisherman from 1890–1920; in Sheet Harbour the *Marine Gallery Museum* has local history collected; and in Sherbrooke, the whole center of the village has been restored as a living museum; in Guysborough town, the *Old Court House* (1843) and in Canso town, the *Canso Museum* features a special marine exhibit and a widow's-walk.

 MUSIC. With the vast Scottish heritage, bagpipe music and Gaelic songs are an important part of Nova Scotia culture. Although Gaelic is spoken only by a small minority, the skirl of the pipes has been adopted by Nova Scotians of every background. Scottish concerts are held throughout the summer months in a number of communities. If you find an announcement for a ceilidh (pronounced kay-lee), that means a Scottish concert. Check *"Seasonal Events"* section earlier in this chapter, the newspaper events supplements, and Nova Scotia Tourism's *Calendar of Events.*

 REGIONAL THEATER. Live amateur theater is alive and well in Nova Scotia. The *Kipawo Show Boat Company* in Wolfville (542–3500 or 3542) is the best-known, but the *Mulgrave Road Co-op Company* in Mulgrave, *Mermaid Theatre* in Wolfville, *Theatre Antigonish* in Antigonish, the *Deaf-Gypsy Mime Company* in Centreville, *Savoy Theatre* in Glace Bay, and *Mermaid Theatre* in Dartmouth also are making themselves known. Some of these companies tour the province, putting on two or three productions a year. Also the puppet theater, *Canadian Puppet Festivals* in Chester (275–3171 or 3430), has drawn critical acclaim. The department of tourism or the department of culture can tell you more.

 SHOPPING. Nova Scotia's shopping centers tend to be uninspiring, not much different from anything you might find anywhere else in North America. The exciting shopping and fascinating browsing is found in the shops of craftspeople all over the province—where you'll find everything from blacksmiths in East Dover, silversmiths in Waverley, to leaded glass hanging ornaments in Purcells Cove, to wooden toys in Middleton, pewter in Wolfville, pottery in Arichat, apple dolls in Halifax. Beware the junky lobster ashtrays on the tourist trails. The N.S. Dept. of Culture, Recreation and Fitness (P.O. Box 864, Halifax, N.S. B3J 2V2, 424-4061) or the Dept. of Tourism will send you the Handcraft Directory, an excellent guide to the craftspeople of Nova Scotia.

Antique stores proliferate all over Nova Scotia and Cape Breton. One of the better—and most genuine—ones is *Dana Sweeny Antiques* in Mahone Bay.

Another source of unique shopping and browsing experiences (and, likely, good stories from the shopkeepers) are the hundreds of tiny, rural general stores in villages all over the province. In these you might find anything from yard-goods to harnesses, sou'westers to weird ointments—well worth poking around in these stores.

The largest shopping center in the province is MicMac Mall in Dartmouth off the A. Murray Mackay Bridge. It is also the largest east of Montréal. Next is Scotia Square in Halifax, which has dozens of chain stores as well as dozens of specialty shops; the next largest is the Woolco shopping center in Sydney, on the highway as you go in on Rte. 4. Here, you'll be able to get recordings of local but well-known musicians like Lee Cremo or the Men of the Deeps, The Steel City Players, "Rise & Follies of Cape Breton" or the Glendale Concert albums.

DRINKING LAWS. The legal drinking age in Nova Scotia is 19 years. Bottled alcoholic beverages are sold only in Nova Scotia Liquor Commission (NSLC) retail stores, located in most major communities. NSLC hours vary from place to place, but they are usually open from 10 A.M. to 5 P.M. weekdays and Saturdays, and to 9 P.M. on Friday evenings, and all are closed on Sundays.

Beer and alcoholic beverages by the glass are sold in licensed restaurants (food must also be ordered) and in licensed lounges (cocktail lounge, a bar with entertainment, only the name is changed). Beer by the bottle and draught beer by the glass are sold in taverns and beverage rooms, which often offer surprisingly good snacks and light meals. Open hours average from 10 A.M. to midnight. Licensed lounges average from 11 A.M. to 2 A.M.

There are no restrictions on women entering taverns in Nova Scotia, although the atmosphere in many taverns tends to be a bit rough.

A few "dry" areas still remain in Nova Scotia, but barriers are falling rapidly and the "wets" are prevailing. For a list of dry districts, contact the Nova Scotia Department of Tourism.

DINING OUT. The food in most Nova Scotia restaurants in well prepared—especially the seafood. In the past few years the standard of cuisine and its presentation have improved greatly.

Service is generally good in the better restaurants although it can be slow, especially if the place is busy.

Restaurants are categorized on the basis of a full-course dinner, with drinks, tips and tax excluded. *Expensive,* over $15; *Moderate,* $10 to $15; *Inexpensive,* under $10.

A 10% provincial tax will be added to all meals over $3.

Most places accept the following major credit cards: American Express, MasterCard and Visa; others may also be honored. Not all establishments accept credit cards, therefore we suggest you call for information.

ANTIGONISH. *Moderate–Expensive:* **Lobster Treat Restaurant.** On the Trans Canada Hwy. Undistinguished-looking on the outside, a pleasant surprise inside. Seafood specialties. Licensed. Phone: 863–5465.

BRIDGETOWN. *Moderate:* **Continental Kitchen.** Spotlessly clean, excellent food prepared in a country style, huge portions. Licensed. Be sure to make reservations early in the day. Phone 665–2287.

CHESTER. *Expensive:* **Rope Loft.** One of the best views in the province. Food usually excellent. Licensed. Bring a camera. Open summer season only. Open noon to 10 P.M. Reservations recommended. Seafood specialty. Phone 275–3430. Major credit cards.

The Captain's House. Restored to its early 1800's elegance. Specializes in fine Maritime recipes. An experience. Phone 275–3501. Major credit cards.

DIGBY. *Expensive:* **The Pines Resort Hotel Dining Room.** Usually good food served in large dining room of older resort hotel. Pleasant grounds overlooking Digby harbor. Specialty is Digby scallops. Call for reservations. Dancing. Phone 245–2511. Major credit cards.

LISCOMBE MILLS. *Expensive:* **Liscombe Lodge Dining Room.** A good dining room in this resort overlooking the Liscombe River. Licensed with stone fireplace, often lit for dinner. Specialty is fresh salmon caught in river nearby. Call for meal hours and reservations. Open May to mid-Oct. Phone 779–2307. Major credit cards.

NEW GLASGOW. *Expensive:* **Heather Motel Dining Room.** Clean, comfortable place, licensed, with friendly service and usually good food. Call for reservations. Phone 752–8401. Major credit cards.

SHERBROOKE VILLAGE. *Moderate:* **The Bright House.** A licensed dining room on Main Street serving lunch and dinner, specializing in roast beef. Phone 522–2691. Open May to Oct. Visa and MasterCard accepted.

Inexpensive: **What Cheer House.** In historic Sherbrooke Village living museum. Turn of the century village inn with hearty seafood chowder, beef stew, home-baked beans & bread. Not licensed. Lunch & tea only.

TRURO. *Expensive:* **The Palliser Restaurant.** Excellent family restaurant overlooking tidal bore river. Open 8 A.M. to 8:30 P.M. mid-May to mid-Oct. Call for reservations. Phone 893–3895. Major credit cards.

Glengarry Motel Dining Room. 138 Willow St. Features home cooking in large dining room. Phone 895–5388. Major credit cards.

YARMOUTH. *Expensive:* **Harris' Seafood Restaurant.** (Restaurant on the right side of the highway is run by the same people but is a short order place.) Possibly the best seafood in Nova Scotia. Lobster is a specialty. Call for reservations.

Manor Inn. Good food in pleasant surroundings. Beer garden, dining room in manor with folk singers. Licensed. Steak and lobster especially good. Call for reservations.

Moderate: **Grand Hotel Dining Room.** Ordinary hotel dining room except for Hot Lobster Sandwich—big chunks of creamed lobster served on toast. Live entertainment & dancing except on Sundays. Phone 742–2446. Major credit cards.

NEWFOUNDLAND AND LABRADOR

An Early European Beachhead

by
ALAN FREEMAN, RALPH SURETTE
and
COLLEEN THOMPSON

Perhaps the legendary Leif Ericson was among the Viking crew and passengers of the Norse longship that came ashore, sometime about A.D. 1000, on a point of land that is now thought to be Newfoundland. Perhaps not. At least we know that the half-barbarian, half-literate adventurers were the first discoverers of Newfoundland—and possibly the first Europeans who landed on North American shores. While the Norsemen made several voyages to this area during the next 100 years, it was not until 1497 that John Cabot, sailing from Bristol on the west coast of England, found the almost invisible niche in the rock leading into a protected harbor. Legend has it that he arrived on St. John's Day, and thus named the port St. John's.

Nearly a hundred years passed and the "new found land" remained unknown in Europe except to a handful of Bristol merchants and the fishermen employed by them. For a century, these westcountry men carried back the rich harvest from the Newfoundland fishing banks, even establishing seasonal colonies from which to support the fishery. Yet little is known of this early period of exploration. For years, the West of England fishermen sought to conceal their profitable voyages from the scrutiny of a tyrannical Crown in order to avoid payment of oppressive taxes. But the trade became too large and too prosperous to be hidden for long; in 1583 Sir Humphrey Gilbert claimed the land for Elizabeth I. To reinforce his claim, he set up a trading stall on what is now the St. John's waterfront, and opened it up for business. Sir Humphrey also distinguished himself by bringing from England the first professional dancers and musicians to play in the New World; these were the "hobby horses and Morris dancers and many like conceits" who performed on shore at St. John's on August 5, 1583.

Hard Times for Settlers

Gilbert's claim for Britain ended the laissez-faire days of international fishing off the coast of Newfoundland by 30,000 fishermen from half a dozen nations who operated in relative peace and security. It began the infamous era of the Fishing Admiral which was to last for another century. The Fishing Admiral was the first captain to sail into any Newfoundland harbor each year. This distinction allowed the fortunate skipper to set himself up as a total despot for the season, thereby creating unceasing turmoil between permanent settlers and English adventurers.

It was also the time of bitter dispute between the merchant overlords in Devon and the English west country and the would-be colonists. Settlement in Newfoundland was against the law and anyone who tried colonization was laying his life on the line. The colonists could see the rich future in settlement and pursuit of the rich inshore fishery. The merchants could see the colonists rapidly wresting control of the rich trade in salt fish away from the motherland.

In 1711, the colony was placed under the rule of Naval Governors and the Fishing Admirals' empire was dissolved. Although harsh legislation had been enacted, settlement had continued during the reign of the admirals. Around the bays and inlets were tiny settlements and individual families. Most could be reached only by boat and signs of habitation were usually well hidden from outsiders. Sometimes known as "the lost men," these tiny communities were enlarged by further groups of settlers, some successful, some doomed.

Though harsh anti-colonization laws were passed and repealed from time to time at the whim of the British monarchy, Newfoundland settlements became a fact. Some credit for their survival may go to the New England colonies who aided and abetted a settlement policy for many years.

Dominion to Colony to Province

In 1811 the British government legalized permanently the granting of land and the building of houses in the colony. By 1855, Newfoundland had become a self-governing Dominion within the British Commonwealth.

By 1934, having weathered the growing pains of a new country, a world war, and the first years of the Great Depression, Newfoundland was bankrupt. There was no alternative but to become a British colony once again with a commission government to administer its affairs. With the advent of World War II, however, Newfoundland found itself in the middle of supply lines from North America to Europe, and the Allies poured money and men into Newfoundland to spur on the effort of building bases where only wilderness had existed before. The problem was no longer to find money, but to find men to do the work.

Prosperous throughout the war and the post war period, Newfoundland again considered its future. To join the nation of Canada, with Newfoundland on its front doorstep, seemed the logical choice to many Newfoundlanders. Finally, after a bitter and stormy campaign and referendum, Newfoundland joined Confederation on March 31, 1949, becoming Canada's tenth province. Since that time, it has developed its natural resources and, in some part, rearranged the once isolated outport society which made up most of Newfoundland.

Settlement in the larger communities, university and trades education, and modernization of the fishing, forestry, and mining industries characterize the contemporary directions of the province. Yet, despite the encroachments of 20th-century living, Newfoundland and Newfoundlanders have managed to retain their special personality and their culture, a combination that makes Canada's newest province a most unique acquisition.

The Newfoundland flag—a new one proclaimed in 1980—has two triangles (representing Labrador and the Island of Newfoundland) and stylized ornamentations representing the Christian, and Beothuk and Naskapi Indian backgrounds of the province. The colors are blue (the sea) and red (human endeavor) on a background of white (snow). It replaces the Union Jack which had served as the provincial flag before. The provincial coat of arms—developed in 1637, lost, rediscovered, then finally adopted officially in 1928—is a red shield quartered by the white cross of Saint George. The quarters contain the white unicorns of England and gold lions of Scotland.

A Craggy Isle

Newfoundland, an island off the coast of northeast North America and situated between the Gulf of St. Lawrence and the Atlantic Ocean, is separated from the mainland by the Strait of Belle Isle on the North and Cabot Strait on the southwest. Labrador, the northeast corner of the continent, is the province's mainland section. To neglect to mention the massive land area of this province is to leave the unsuspecting traveler unprepared for his journey. In terms of the United States, only Alaska, Texas, and California are greater in size.

Largest of the four Canadian Atlantic provinces, Newfoundland has a total area of 404,520 sq. kms. (156,185 square miles). Most of the province's population of 582,900 is concentrated on the island—in the cities of St. John's, the capital, and Corner Brook, and in the towns of Gander and Grand Falls. The Labrador towns of Goose Bay/Happy Valley, Wabush, and Labrador City are also on the upswing.

Visitors flying overhead have commented that the province seems to be made up of bodies of water surrounded by bits of land. Indeed, about 10 percent of the province is lakes and streams—thousands of them!

Labrador is mountainous, dotted with lakes, and cut by rivers. The mountains are ancient, ground blunt by the passage of glaciers eons ago. Most of the slopes are forest covered up to the tree line with a

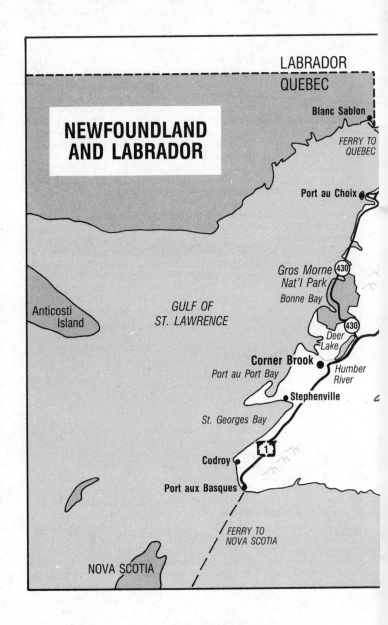

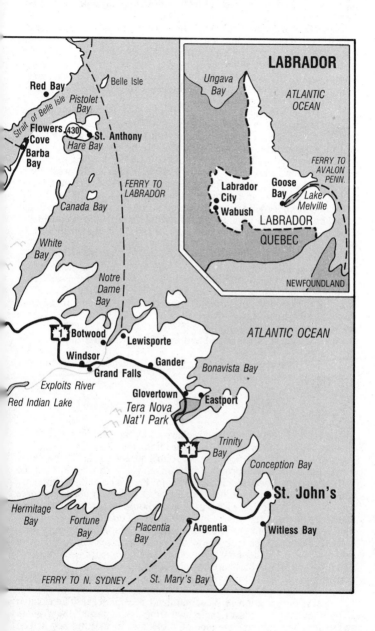

Red Bay

Belle Isle

Pistolet Bay

Flowers Cove

Strait of Belle Isle

430

St. Anthony

Barba Bay

Hare Bay

FERRY TO LABRADOR

Canada Bay

White Bay

Notre Dame Bay

1 Botwood

Lewisporte

Windsor

Gander

Grand Falls

Bonavista Bay

Exploits River

Red Indian Lake

Glovertown

Eastport

Tera Nova Nat'l Park

1

Trinity Bay

Conception Bay

Hermitage Bay

Fortune Bay

Placentia Bay

Argentia

Witless Bay

St. John's

FERRY TO N. SYDNEY

St. Mary's Bay

ATLANTIC OCEAN

LABRADOR

Ungava Bay

ATLANTIC OCEAN

FERRY TO AVALON PENN.

Labrador City

Goose Bay

Lake Melville

Wabush

LABRADOR

QUEBEC

NEWFOUNDLAND

hardy, slow-growing spruce, suited to endure severely cold winters and short summers.

The island of Newfoundland is also mountainous and lake-strewn. On the west coast, the flat, forested mountains form an escarpment some 2,000 feet high which plunges sharply into the sea at the coast. In the central region, the mountains give way to low land and boggy forests and more ranges of hills and mountains. Along the east coast, the mountains again drop off into the sea, although the cliffs are not as steep as on the opposite coast.

It was this forbidding landscape which made the fishery the chief economic mainstay of Newfoundland for 450 years. With the riches of the Grand Banks there for the taking and an inshore fishery which yielded vast quantities of cod and other fish, there was no need to look inland. Even today, agriculture tends to be concentrated in smaller operations and in areas such as the Codroy Valley in the west coast.

The inland riches of Newfoundland now lie in the forests and under the barren rock and in the tumbling water. Forestry, mining and the production of hydroelectricity are major industries. Newfoundland has generally the highest unemployment rate of Canada and is considered its poorest province. But the discovery of huge oilfields on the Continental Shelf may change all that.

Newfoundland is in a unique time zone, one-half hour later than Atlantic Canada. The weather varies widely as the province extends more than 1200 kms. (750 miles) north to south. In St. John's, average summer temperatures range from 21°C (70°F) to roughly 13°C (55°F) at night. In the north, the summer temperatures follow about the same range, although the season is shorter. Winter temperatures in St. John's are about 0°C (32°F) by day, dipping to about −7°C (20°F) at night. On the west coast of the island and in Labrador, winter temperatures can fall to −45°C (−50°F).

Another unique geographical fact is that the island part of the province has no skunks, snakes, or ragweed pollen.

Words . . .

The visitor to Newfoundland is charmed by the unique speech of the outport people, the originality of their idiom, and the dialects that one hears only in this province. The St. John's accent has an Irish quality (the name of the city is pronounced "sin jahns," with the accent at the end); accents in places like Harbour Main, Ferryland and Placentia are similar. In the north, one listens to a Dorset or Devon dialect of three centuries ago complete with words and idioms long forgotten in England. Then there are the traditional figures of speech that have been retained through four centuries of settlement. Words like "ballycater" —ice formed on the shore by spray or little cakes of sea ice; "cuddy"—a covered space in the bow of a boat, and "kingcorn"—a person's Adam's apple. "Sparbles" are bits of grit or gravel, and a "yaffle" is an armful of dried fish—the word used as a unit of measure—a yaffle of fish.

In 1811, immigration to Newfoundland became legal. The isolated settlers kept the words of their own times, and passed them on to succeeding generations. Absence of books and formal literacy helped preserve the old words. Terms relating to the sea and the fishery were kept to the forefront and if a suitable word did not exist, one was made up "right off the bat."

. . . and Music

Newfoundland seems to have more folk songs than any other part of Canada, most of them with an Irish flavor. Many old folk songs were brought from Britain with the settlers through 300 years of illegal and legal settlement. Another group of songs originated in Newfoundland —songs of the sea, of love affairs, the eternal triangle, and the loss of a lovelorn man or maiden.

One of the most prolific of later-day Newfoundland folk song writers was Johnny Burke whose home was a gathering place for many of the finest singers in Newfoundland. Born in 1851, he lived here with his sister until his death in 1930. Burke's most popular piece was *The Kelligrew's Soiree,* the story of an all-out party in the community of Kelligrews, just outside St. John's.

Dancing is part of Newfoundland musical heritage. Local square dances are full of movement, rhythm, and grace. When no one is available to play on a fiddle or jew's-harp, somebody has to furnish "chin-music."

A Modern City

But Newfoundland is not all mountains and folk music. St. John's, its capital, is a flourishing, contemporary city, symbolizing new directions of the province (and the country). It is a pleasure to visit.

EXPLORING ST. JOHN'S

A Strategic Location

St. John's is situated on the eastern coast of the Avalon Peninsula, an "H"-shaped promontory jutting out by a spindly isthmus from the southeast corner of the Island of Newfoundland. Because of its strategic location almost halfway between Montreal and Europe, St. John's has long been connected with shipping across the North Atlantic. Lying almost on top of one of the world's richest fishing banks, the old city has been a second home to European fishermen for more than four centuries. A walk along St. John's waterfront, even today, reveals a polyglot culture that adds great vitality to the life of the city.

John Cabot, as noted earlier, arrived in 1497, naming the harbor St. John's and the whole island New Founde Isle before sailing off to the Canadian mainland.

Six years later, the British Bristol Company tried, without success, to plant a colony on Cabot's new found harbor in the New World. But more hardy people were to follow. In 1583, Sir Humphry Gilbert proclaimed the land for Elizabeth I, announcing that anyone daring to disobey the rule of Her Majesty would have his ears cut off. By this time St. John's was a prosperous town—the rocky walls of the harbor sheltering the fishing fleets of many nations. Well-established merchants did a thriving business and the town was ruled by the law of the Fishing Admiral.

Despite the harsh winters and a forbidding landscape, St. John's was coveted by several European nations over the centuries including the

Dutch, Portuguese, Spanish, French and British. Thus, the city was periodically besieged by contending nations as well as attacked several times by freelancing pirates. The final shots of the Seven Years' War between the French and English were fired in St. John's in 1762.

Under strong British rule, St. John's settled into a comparatively quiet and stable way of life. The merchants traded and prospered. The fishermen struggled and barely made a living. The cosmopolitan character of the city broadened and international history continued to be played out around the old port. The "townee" of St. John's (as distinguished from the "bayman" who lived outside the town) cast a curious eye at these events, but refused to become overly excited. So he took it in stride when Guglielmo Marconi received the first wireless signal from across the ocean at his receiver atop Signal Hill in St. John's in 1901; and few well-wishers cheered Alcock and Brown when they took off from Lester's Field to complete the first trans-Atlantic flight in 1919. And it seemed only natural to the "townee" that Roosevelt and Churchill should choose to meet on the quiet waters of nearby Placentia Bay to draft the terms of the Atlantic Charter.

Two world wars brought successive waves of uniformed "mainlanders" from Canada as well as seafaring men of a dozen nations to walk the steep cobblestone streets along the waterfront, waiting to board convoy ships for Europe. Many young men and women joined the much-decorated Newfoundland fighting units and merchant marine, and died in defense of the countries which had given life to their city centuries before.

St. John's was probably closer to the wars than most North American cities. During World War II, German U-boats constantly cruised the waters off Newfoundland in search of allied shipping and convoys, torpedoing ships only a few miles outside St. John's harbor.

After the signing of the Lend-Lease agreements, St. John's became familiar with the uniform and accents of United States military personnel as Britain exchanged leases on territory in return for American shipping and hardware with which to continue the war. The complex by the shores of Quidi Vidi (pronounced *Kiddy-Viddy*) Lake was built by the United States and known as Pepperell Air Force Base. It has since been returned to the city, and renamed Pleasantville, and is now office space for various government agencies, a hospital, and other institutions.

Following the last war, a new era began for Newfoundland and for St. John's, which was named capital of North America's oldest territory and Canada's youngest province. This change (which some Newfoundlanders still regard, with good humor, as the time when Canada joined Newfoundland) was to have a dramatic effect on the new province and especially on St. John's.

Old City, New Life

The old city—one of the oldest in the New World—rapidly became the showplace of the province. As it took its place as Newfoundland's leading retail, wholesale, and service center, a major ocean port, and a focus of transportation, its citizens benefited economically. With expansion of its shipbuilding, fish processing, and manufacturing industries, a new and more contemporary lifestyle began to emerge.

The townie took the changes, both good and bad, with a philosophical attitude. Mainlanders arrived by the boatload and "tried to teach us their way." But the city simply sighed, and made room for them, and proceeded to turn them into Newfoundlanders.

The sprawling campus of Memorial University is a far cry from the tiny college-school of only a few years ago. New housing and high-rise buildings have changed the skyline. The discovery of oil offshore has changed the economic base; but attitudes have remained traditional in many ways and the citizenry retains its unique character. Though friendly and hospitable to all visitors, the people are hardy to the point of stubbornness. How else to account for their unbounded resilience in the face of extreme hardship and a succession of tragedies over the years? The original settlers were mostly fishermen from the villages of Devon, Cork, Dorset, Somerset, and Waterford. Their descendants survived England's harsh policy toward permanent settlement only to watch their city captured and plundered four times and finally leveled by fire in 1817. Indeed, St. John's was the first North American city to have been totally destroyed by fire. Fire struck again in 1846 and, for the third time, in 1892 when 13,000 people were left homeless. Yet today, St. John's is alive and well, as cosmopolitan as London or Montréal and as English as Victoria.

Tea is still the favorite nonalcoholic drink, with rum in first place for those who like something a bit stronger. English biscuits are still preferred over mainland cookies and many offices still close for lunch between 12:30 and 1:30. Living is still leisurely and everyone celebrates all the provincial and federal holidays with a few extra of their own, such as St. Patrick's Day and Orangemen's Day. One special nonholiday event is Bonfire Night—Guy Fawkes Night—on November 5th. Gambling is a Newfoundland passion—bingo, wheels of fortune, and raffles for live turkeys and pigs at Christmas are well attended. Every townie is expected to go trouting, or angling, and he enjoys his leisure, extending hospitality to any who will enjoy it with him.

Water Street, running quite naturally along the waterfront, is probably the oldest street in North America. In the shops and stores one can purchase everything from an anchor to a needle. Secretaries in the latest fashions mingle with fishermen in rubber boots and school children in English-style uniforms. Even if you do not buy, it is interesting to walk the length of the street. Stop at the Speakeasy in newly-restored, historic Murray Premises and enjoy your tea with the locals.

A number of walking and self-drive tours have been developed for St. John's and the surrounding area. The best way to see St. John's is on foot even though the hilly streets, as the natives say, go in only two directions—up and down. A heritage foundation has restored many of the quaint clapboard houses in the downtown core.

A publication entitled *Everyman's Complete St. John's Guide* costs about $3.00 and offers several detailed walking and self-drive tours. And remember—when you journey outside the city, take your camera or your sketch book! (For further information, see *"Special Interest Tours"* under Practical Information for St. John's.)

No matter what time of year you visit St. John's and whatever historic sites you choose to see, your most enduring memory will be of the people. St. John's has an accent all its own—mainly Irish and a bit English, with unusual idioms spicing the conversation. The accent is soft and expressive, tumbling off the tongue; most visitors will come to adopt it during their stay, even in spite of themselves.

Find any excuse to start a conversation with a total stranger. Your new friend will accompany you, just to keep you on track, pointing out all the sights along the way. And if you ask a few questions about the old city, you may have found a friend for your entire visit to St. John's.

PRACTICAL INFORMATION FOR ST. JOHN'S

HOW TO GET THERE. By air: *Eastern Provincial Airways* and *Air Canada* operate regularly scheduled flights to St. John's from points throughout Canada, the U.S., and within Newfoundland.

By car: St. John's is the eastern terminus of the Trans-Canada Hwy. (Hwy. 1) from Port-aux-Basques and the car ferry from North Sydney, Nova Scotia. Visitors taking the other ferry from North Sydney to Argentia, Newfoundland, follow highway 100 to the intersection of the Trans-Canada Hwy. (TCH). Turn east toward St. John's.

By train/bus: Passenger train service in Newfoundland has been discontinued. Motorcoaches operated by *Terra Transport* (737–5912) carry passengers from the ferry terminals to St. John's. For tickets and information, contact any *Via Rail* ticket office (agents for *Terra Transport*) in Canada; see also the "How to Get There" section in Practical Information for Newfoundland and Labrador.

ACCOMMODATIONS. St. John's is changing rapidly since oil was discovered off the shores of Newfoundland. Accommodations can be hard to come by at times. Make reservations. Most St. John's hotels are on the expensive side. There are some "Hospitality Homes," however, that provide inexpensive accommodation. Double-occupancy rates are as follows: *Expensive,* $46 or more; *Moderate,* $35–45; *Inexpensive,* under $35.

A 12% provincial tax will be added to your bill.

Most places accept the following major credit cards: American Express, MasterCard and Visa; others may also be honored. Not all establishments accept credit cards, therefore we suggest you call for information.

Airport Inn. *Expensive.* Plain, comfortable accommodations near airport. Dining room and cocktail lounge. Phone 753–3500. Major credit cards.

The Battery Inn. *Expensive.* Top place to stay in St. John's. Located about half way up Signal Hill with harbor rooms offering a great view of the city. Dining room and coffeeshop (good food), cocktail lounge, sauna, and pool. Phone 726–0040. Major credit cards.

Château Park. *Expensive.* Mt. Pearl St. Excellent dining and lounge facilities. Phone 364–7725. Major credit cards.

Holiday Inn. *Expensive.* Portugal Cove Rd. Typical Holiday Inn; dining room and coffeeshop; cocktail lounge and outdoor pool. Phone 722–0506. Major credit cards.

Hotel Newfoundland. *Expensive.* Cavendish Sq. downtown location. Newly built. Pool, sauna, squash courts, restaurant and lounges; babysitting can be arranged. Phone 726–4980. Major credit cards.

Kenmount Motel. *Expensive.* Elizabeth Ave. Comfortable; dining room and cocktail lounge. Phone 726–0092. Major credit cards.

Lester Hotel. *Expensive.* Blackmarsh Rd. Dining room, cocktail lounge. Phone 579–2141. Major credit cards.

Hotel St. John's. *Expensive.* Dining room, cocktail lounge. Phone 722–9330. Major credit cards.

Skyline Motel. *Moderate.* Plain, comfortable accommodations. Restaurant, cocktail lounge. Phone 722–5400. Major credit cards.

Sea Flow Tourist Home. *Inexpensive.* 5 rooms, kitchen facilities. Phone 753–2425.

Bonaventure House. *Inexpensive.* 4 units with room service and a nice little dining room. Phone 753–3359.

TELEPHONE. The area code for St. John's and all Newfoundland, including Labrador, is the same: 709.

HOW TO GET AROUND. From the airport: *Gulliver's Taxi* operates a taxi/limo service from the St. John's Airport to downtown hotels. Cost is about $3.50 per person **Car rental:** Major car rental agencies have desks at the St. John's airport and in some hotel lobbies. Advance booking recommended through a travel agent or the local office of the rental agency. Most agencies will deliver cars to St. John's hotels.

By bus: The *Metrobus* system operates throughout St. John's and into the outlying areas. Routes start operating between 6:45 and 8:00 A.M. and stop running between 6:00 P.M. and 12:30 A.M. depending on the route. For information, call 722–9400. Single adult fares are 60¢. Persons using the Metrobus must have exact fare as drivers do not carry change. Fares outside the city limits are higher. Fare to Mount Pearl is about 80¢. A number of small bus operators run services to other regions of the Avalon Peninsula. Contact the nearest tourist information office for routes and timetables or call the St. John's tourism office.

By taxi: Taxis do not generally "cruise" in St. John's. It is usually necessary to call one of the stands and have the cab meet you. The meter starts at about $1.50 and runs up to about $2.40 for the first mile and about 90¢ per mile thereafter, depending on traffic.

TOURIST INFORMATION SERVICES. St. John's Tourist Chalet, Trans-Canada Hwy. Call 368–5900. St. John's Tourist Commission, City Hall, New Gower St. Call 722–7080. Tourist Information Desk, Colonial Building, Military Rd. at Bannerman Rd. Call 753–9380. Tourist Information Desk, Confederation Building, Confederation Parkway. Call 576–3630. Tourist Information Desk, Newfoundland Museum, Duckworth St. Call 576–2461. Provincial Department of Development, Tourism Branch, Atlantic Place, Water St. Call 576–2830. Hospitality Newfoundland. Call 722–2000, or 1–800–563–NFLD.

RECOMMENDED READING. The indispensable book for tourists in Newfoundland is Harold Horwood's *Newfoundland,* a superb account of the people, traditions, resources, and places of the province. Horwood is the greatest Newfoundland writer, a novelist *(Tomorrow Will Be Sunday, White Eskimo)* and biographer *(Bartlett: The Great Canadian Explorer)* and natural historian *(The Foxes of Beachy Cove,* a minor masterpiece). Ray Guy is a brilliant humorist, whose mordant wit is collected in *You May Know Them As Sea Urchins, Ma'am,* and the award-winning *That Far Greater Bay.* Guy has been known to shake Newfoundland governments. Other contemporary novels are Percy Janes' *House of Hate* and Gordon Pinsent's *The Rowdyman.*

Poet Al Pittman's *Down by Jim Long's Stage* and the plays of Michael Cook are published by Newfoundland's own Breakwater Books, a venture which has achieved remarkable national stature despite its youth and distance from major markets. Former premier Joey Smallwood compiled *The Book of Newfoundland,* and his memoirs *I Chose Canada* include a lively account of the campaign which brought Newfoundland into Confederation in 1949. Cassie Brown specializes in marine disasters; her *Death on the Ice,* about a catastrophe at the famous (or infamous) seal hunt in 1914, was an international success. Paul O'Neill's *The Oldest City* is a detailed history of St. John's.

TIME ZONE. St. John's is on Newfoundland Time, as is the rest of the island—that is, ½ hour in advance of Atlantic Time and 1½ hours ahead of Eastern Time.

SEASONAL EVENTS. In **February** and **March** there are winter carnivals in many Newfoundland towns and villages. In **February,** the Kiwanis Music Festival; in **April,** the Provincial Drama Festival. In **May,** the Newfoundland Kennel Club All-Breed Championships, and the Lion's Trade Fair.

May to **October,** sailing races around St. John's, including the annual Regatta, said to be the oldest continuous sporting event in North America. **June,** the St. John's Day civic celebrations. In **August,** there is the Newfoundland and Labrador Folk Arts Festival, of international repute. From mid-July to the end of August, the Newfoundland Militia perform a colorful military tatoo on Signal Hill on Tuesdays, Thursdays, Saturdays and Sundays at 3 and 7 P.M., weather permitting. Musket and cannon fire, military drill, and the red uniforms of the militiamen make this an exciting performance. In **September,** the Newfoundland Amateur Golf Championship.

TOURS. *Overland Tours* (576–4412), the *St. John's Transportation Commission* (722–9400), *Newfoundland Historic Trust* (754–1742), *Newfoundland Nature Tours* (754–2052), *Fleetline Tours* (722–2608) and *Chalet Tours* (368–6027) have bus tours of the city and environs. *Harbour Charters* (754–1672) and *Lucky Strike Boat Charters* (753–3940) take passengers sightseeing and fishing in the harbor and beyond.

SPECIAL INTEREST TOURS. A number of **walking/ driving tours** of St. John's are available at the tourist information desks or by mail from the St. John's Tourist Commission, City Hall, New Gower St., St. John's. **Self-guided driving tours** to outlying areas of the city and environs include tours to Marine Drive/Pouch Cove, Portugal Cove/St. Phillips, and Petty Harbour/ Maddox Cove. All these drives offer dramatic seacoast scenery and take you to fishing villages and inland forested regions.

A well-marked **nature trail** starts at King George V Park and leads walkers for some distance along the river and ponds to an area outside the city. Inquire at the travel information desk for the best place to begin the trail.

For bicyclers, a **cycle path** begins at Kent's Pond, just west of the junction of Portugal Cove Rd. and Confederation Pkwy., leading through the woods and coming out on Higgin's Line.

Eight-day **nature excursions** to make "human contact" with the whales, porpoises and dolphins that abound off eastern Newfoundland are offered by *Ocean Contact Ltd.* Reservations needed well in advance. Write Box 10, Trinity, Trinity Bay, Newfoundland AOC 2S0.

Newfoundland has three important **seabird sanctuaries**—one on Gull Island in Witless Bay, 30 km. (19 mi.) south of St. John's on Rte. 10; one at Cape St. Mary's, approximately 193 km. (120 mi.) southeast of St. John's; and one on the Funk Island, 50 mi. off the northeast coast of Newfoundland.

The best time to go to Gull Island is June 15–July 15 and the best way to reach the island three miles offshore is by making arrangements with local fishermen. Special permission is needed to land. The best time for Cape St. Mary's is June 15–August 15. A rough 16 km. (10-mile) road branches off Rte. 100 about 3.2 km (2 mi.) past St. Bride's and leads to Cape St. Mary's. The bird colonies at Cape St. Mary's are viewed from a spectacular clifftop lookout. A trip to Funk Island is a major expedition. Further information from the Department of Development and Tourism.

PARKS. *C. A. Pippy Park*—4,000 acres on the city's northern boundary—is St. John's favorite open-air recreation spot, and a marvelous place to take children. There are extensive woodlands with nature trails, picnic areas, campgrounds, golf course, a small botanical and wildlife reserve, playground, children's farm, and others. The Memorial University campus, the Confederation Building, and several other noteworthy buildings are within the park's confines.

Another favorite relaxation spot for residents and visitors is *Bowring Park,* in the west end. It has a year-round playground with wooded areas, open fields, swimming pools in summer and skating rink in winter. *Bannerman Park* on Bannerman Rd. behind the Colonial Building has an outdoor pool and playground. *Quidi Vidi Picnic Ground* on the north shore of Quidi Vidi Lake has tables and fireplaces for picnics. *Cochrane Pond* and *Butterpot Provincial Parks* are within easy driving distance of St. John's on the Trans-Canada Hwy. With the exception of the provincial parks, there is no entrance fee to any St. John's park.

CHILDREN'S ACTIVITIES. St. John's is an outdoor city with lots of open space and walking areas along the waterfront and seacoast. See the sections on "Parks," "Special Interest Tours," and "Sports" for activities for younger people.

PARTICIPANT SPORTS. For **golf,** the *Bally Hally Golf and Country Club* is a private club but visitors can play. Call 753–6090. Also in St. John's is the *Halliday Farms Golf Club* in C. A. Pippy Park; 753–7110. Stephenville, Gander, Corner Brook and Grand Falls also have courses, as does *Terra Nova National Park.*

Ice skating during the winter and **roller skating** during the summer at the half-dozen arenas and rinks in town. **Bicycling** is becoming popular. The *St. John's Club* has tours Wednesdays and Sundays. All invited.

For **swimmers,** there are outdoor summer pools at *Bowring Park,* Waterford Bridge Rd., call 364–3880; *Bannerman Park,* Bannerman Rd., call 753–4655, *Victoria Park,* Water St., call 726–8181. Indoor year-round pools are located at the *Torbay Recreation Centre* at St. John's Airport, call 737–2792; *Downtown Boys and Girls Club,* Water St., call 753–7080; *Mount Pearl Swimming Pool,* Park Ave., call 368–0128, and *Wedgewood Park Pool,* 45 Gleneyre, call 753–0570. Also the new *Aquarena,* call 754–1977.

SPECTATOR SPORTS. *Regatta Day* on Quidi Vidi Lake is St. John's big holiday of the year. Called for the first Wednesday in August, or the first fine day following, it is the oldest (1826) sporting event in North America still being held. It is probably the only civic holiday that is decided at 7 A.M. on the morning of the holiday. Townies listen to their radios for the magic phrase "The races are on!" which signals the holiday. Thousands crowd the lakeshore to watch the events as teams of oarsmen and oarswomen in racing shells compete up and down the lake, and to gamble on the games of chance at the booths set up throughout the area.

The *Avalon Raceway* at Gould's, 16 km. from St. John's, has **harness horse racing** Wednesdays, Sundays and holidays, spring to fall, on a variable schedule. Usually at 7:45 P.M., but better check for times.

HISTORIC SITES AND SIGHTS. *Signal Hill National Historic Park* is probably the focal point in St. John's. At the top, the *Cabot Tower,* near where (the precise spot is marked by a plaque) Marconi received the first overseas wireless message, has become a symbol of the city. The bleak and rocky headland was the site of early forts as well as the last battle of the Seven Years' War in North America. Here you will have a breathtaking view of St. John's and the harbor as well as the last landfall before Europe. In spring, large white and turquoise Arctic icebergs, known as "growlers," can sometimes be sighted. *Gibbet Hill* near Deadman's Pond was the site of the old gallows. The *Interpretive Centre* halfway up Signal Hill offers another great view of the city and the harbor; it also has a number of interesting displays and artifacts that document the city's history. There are interpretive walks and lookouts in the park. Obtain information from the Interpretive Centre—open 9 A.M. to late evening in summer.

The *Sir Humphrey Gilbert Memorial* is a plaque set below the National War Memorial on Water St., and marks the spot where Sir Humphrey planted the Royal Standard of Elizabeth I in 1583 and claimed Newfoundland for England;

the *National War Memorial,* whose figures represent freedom, was unveiled on July 1st, 1924. The *Queen's Battery,* overlooking the harbor entrance just below the crest of Signal Hill, dates back to the 18th Century when France and England were still struggling for possession of Newfoundland, to the time of the last battle on Signal Hill in 1762 when the English took St. John's. *Chain Rock Battery* was located at the narrowest part of the harbor entrance, and in the late 1700's a large chain was put between Chain and Pancake Rocks so that two capstans were used to raise it to obstruct enemy vessels, and during World War I a chain boom was used to protect ships in the harbor, then in World War II the place was used for an anti-submarine net.

The Anglican *Cathedral of St. John The Baptist,* a fine example of North American church Gothic architecture, was started in 1816, destroyed by fire in 1842 and again in 1892, then the present building was restored in 1905. The clergy is pleased to provide information. The *Basilica of St. John The Baptist,* started in 1841 and finished in 1850, is made of limestone and Irish granite, built in the shape of a cross, with 138-foot towers, and holds 2,000 people.

 MUSEUMS. *Newfoundland Museum* on Duckworth St. opposite Cathedral St. has a number of artifacts from shipwrecked vessels, displays of early settlements in Newfoundland, as well as the only known relics of the Beothuk Indians, a vanished race that once roamed the island. Open days seven days a week plus Thursday evenings until 9 P.M. Admission free.

The Newfoundland Museum at the Murray Premises, a downtown branch of the main museum, has displays of the province's sea-going history, plus a collection of military firearms, equipment, uniforms and other exhibits. The hours are the same as those of the main branch.

Presentation Sisters Museum at their convent on Cathedral Square has artifacts and photos about this third oldest English speaking order of nuns in North America. Appointment is required. The *Anglican Cathedral* (with a small museum) on the corner of Gower St. and Church Hill, is rated one of the finest examples of ecclesiastical architecture in North America. Its museum is located behind the small organ screen to right of altar. Usually open when cathedral is open.

Commissariat House, a provincial historic site, is a former military residence and rectory restored to the style of the 1830's. The small restoration of Quidi Vidi Battery on Quidi Vidi Rd. has a small museum of military objects. Open June 1–Sept. 15.

 ART GALLERIES: The *Memorial University Art Gallery* at the Arts and Culture Centre has lectures, films, and other presentations, in addition to art exhibits. The Gallery, 284 Duckworth St., deals in Canadian paintings, prints and sculpture. Other galleries featuring local artists are: *Rostotski,* 296 LeMarchant; *Spurrell Gallery,* 87 Longs Hill; *Finishing Touch,* 127 Queens Rd.

 THEATER AND MUSIC. Live theater in St. John's is not necessarily abundant, but it is lively. *CODCO* is one group that has caught national attention. *The Resource Centre for the Arts* is a center for original theater and dance. More formal theater, including Shakespearean presentations, are staged at the auditorium of the *Arts and Culture Centre* at Memorial University, and also at the *Little Theatre* at the university. *The Arts and Culture Centre* is the city's main stage and also hosts symphony orchestras, jazz concerts, and the like. Phone 737-3900 for information.

SHOPPING. Newfoundland handcrafts have an international reputation. It is the home of such exotica as Grenfell parkas, Labradorite jewelry, and so on. St. John's abounds in craftshops—most of them being concentrated in the commercial area along Duckworth St. Restored Murray Premises has excellent quality shops. The Newfoundland and Labrador Crafts Development Association, 265 Duckworth St., has a complete list of craft shops, products, and information on prices. The Department of Development and Tourism, Atlantic Place, Water St., also has booklets listing crafts and outlets. The *Avalon Mall* is the main shopping mall. Malls are mostly open Monday–Saturday, 10 A.M.–9 P.M. Other shopping areas open Monday–Saturday, 9 A.M.–5 P.M., except Friday night when they stay open to 9 P.M. Most stores are closed Victoria Day (late May), Memorial Day (late June), Labor Day, and Thanksgiving. Some stores may be closed St. George's Day (late April), Discovery Day in mid-June, Orangemen's Day in early July, and Remembrance Day (November 11).

 DINING OUT. Restaurants are categorized on the basis of full-course dinners; drinks, tax and tips excluded: *Expensive,* over $16; *Moderate,* $10–$16; *Inexpensive,* less than $10.

A 12% provincial sales tax will be added to your bill.

Most places accept the following major credit cards: American Express, MasterCard and Visa; others may also be honored. Not all establishments accept credit cards, therefore we suggest you call for information.

Dining out in St. John's can be a pleasant experience if one samples the various Newfoundland dishes and chooses wisely from the menu. Seafoods tend to be the best choice. Expect them to be prepared in a fairly traditional manner —wholesome but not too exciting. Most of the better restaurants can provide small side orders of traditional food such as cod tongues, scrunchions (bits of fat pork, crisply fried), fish and brewis, or seal flipper.

Service is generally good in the better restaurants although it can be slow, especially if the place is busy. Strike up a conversation with your waiter who can often provide you with an enjoyable meal and friendly humor.

The ACT III Restaurant. *Moderate-Expensive.* At the Arts and Culture Centre. Quality dining in a relaxed atmosphere. Phone 754–0790. Major credit cards.

The Fishing Admiral. *Moderate-Expensive.* Live lobster, seafood, Newfoundland dishes. Phone 753–6203. Major credit cards.

Battery Motel Dining Room. *Moderate.* On Signal Hill. One of the best places in St. John's. Ask for a window table overlooking St. John's at night. North American menu with Newfoundland specialties. Organ music most nights during dining. Phone 726–0040. Major credit cards.

Cabot Club. *Expensive.* Elegant dining in the new Hotel Newfoundland. Phone 726–4980. Major credit cards.

Colonial Inn. *Moderate.* In community of Topsail on Hwy. 3 just outside St. John's. Good but limited menu; décor should be seen only in dim light. Fireplace, nice, little bar, cozy. Reservations. Phone 722–6933. Major credit cards.

Starboard Quarter. *Moderate.* Royal Trust Building on Water St. Has good view of waterfront and ships. Service sometimes slow but friendly. Nice atmosphere for lunch or dinner. Reservations. Phone 753–9510. Major credit cards.

Captain's Cabin. *Inexpensive.* Cafeteria in Bowring's Department Store on Water St. has nice view of harbor and waterfront. Specialties—Newfoundland dishes and Irish coffee. Phone 726–3280.

 NIGHTCLUBS AND BARS. A St. John's pub crawl is a cultural experience in itself. It's a city that expresses itself, rather in an Irish way, in its multitudes of ebullient lounges, taverns, and bars. The minimum legal drinking age in Newfoundland is 19.

Club Max, 130 Water St., a lively disco club with psychedelic interior.

The *Brand E Saloon,* 379 Duckworth St., has soft pop and western music (live) and a small but cozy dance floor.

The Speakeasy, Murray Premises. Basically a wine bar, but everything available. Nice spot for a drink in restored historic premises.

The *Ship Inn,* 265 Duckworth St. Tinkling piano entertainment, roomy bar, good pub snacks. A very popular spot with the locals.

Christian's, 23 George St., specializes in coffees and wines.

The *Captain's Quarters* at the Holiday Inn is heavy on the distinquished nautical atmosphere.

The *Cock 'n' Bull,* 223 Duckworth St., and *Upstairs-Downstairs* are English-style pubs.

Other interesting spots include *Rob Roy's Pub,* with Scottish setting, *Bridgett's,* a popular neighborhood pub at 29 Cookstown Rd., The *Station Lounge,* the *Silver Knight Lounge,* and *Schoeder's Piano Bar.*

EXPLORING NEWFOUNDLAND'S WEST COAST

The west coast begins at the ferry terminal and fishing town of Port-aux-Basques, a name that reveals the Basque past of this part of Newfoundland.

On Table Mountain, just a few miles north of Port-aux-Basques on the Trans-Canada Highway (Highway 1), is a big yellow and black wind-warning sign: "Notice. Dangerous winds up to 120 miles per hour known to occur next 10 miles." The sign explains that if drivers have difficulty handling their cars they should wait or turn back "as high winds [are] known to blow trains from rails, and overturn motor vehicles." In characteristic Newfoundland style, no punches are pulled in wording the sign. The wind, funneled by the Long Range Mountains on one side and the open sea on the other, can blow a terrific gale across the plateau. The ground-hugging bushes and stunted, twisted trees quietly attest to the might of the wind.

Safely across Table Mountain, the mountains rise forested and quiet, one after another toward the horizon. Cottages nestle beside the lakes here and there. Privacy is the rule—there are enough lakes to go around.

The town of Stephenville was one of those created by World War II. Under the lend-lease agreement between Britain and the United States, land for an air base was turned over to the U.S. military. The complex was named Harmon Field and thousands of American military people at one time or another set foot in Newfoundland. The field and buildings were eventually turned back to the Newfoundland government and are used today as a commercial airport. A liner board mill was opened here during the 1960's, went bankrupt in the 1970's, but now has opened again as a paper mill. Forestry is the town's main industry.

Corner Brook, the "western capital," is the center of Newfoundland's west coast. At the mouth of the Humber River, the city is a major pulp and paper producer and retail distribution center for half of Newfoundland. Corner Brook is on the Humber River, which teems with salmon during the season. Journeying north past Deer Lake, one must stop to enjoy the grandeur of Bonne Bay and Gros Morne National Park. The *Practical Information* section on national parks toward the end of this chapter gives more detailed information.

To reach the park, one must turn off the Trans-Canada to Highway 430. Highways in the park region are maintained by the Parks Department and although some of the routes are gravel surfaced, they are usually in excellent condition.

North from Gros Morne Park, Highway 430 follows the coast for nearly 640 kms. (400 miles) to St. Anthony. Although the highway is well maintained, this is not a journey for the faint-hearted in the winter. During the summer it is a trip to be long remembered. The road passes through tiny villages at the foot of forested mountains beside the sea. The country is wild and if the interior looks uninhabited, that is because it is the domain of moose, bear, and other animals. If the drive gets tiring, a night at Cow Head or Hawke's Bay, is a good idea.

At Port au Choix, the National Historic Park is dedicated to the ancestors of Indians and Inuit who lived here 4,000 years ago. The Viking ruins at L'Anse-aux-Meadows National Historic Park, recently placed on the World Heritage list by UNESCO, have been preserved and housed for viewing. Standing on the barren headland, one can imagine the high-prowed longship bringing the Norsemen across the sea from Greenland as they sought the legendary Vinland.

At St. Barbe, a small ferry takes cars across the Strait of Belle Isle to the coast of Labrador at Blanc Sablon. A 48-km. (30-mile) drive brings one to the Pinware River Provincial Park for fishing and a view of one of the world's last frontiers. Check with a Newfoundland tourist center for ferry times and fishing regulations.

In general, the west coast has rather different weather from the central and east. Temperatures on the west coast tend to drop lower in winter and rise higher in summer, and areas such as the Marble Mountain Ski area may have more than 150 inches of snow on the ground at the end of the season.

EXPLORING CENTRAL AND EASTERN
NEWFOUNDLAND

Looking at a map of Newfoundland, one sees that the interior of the province is marked by an absence of roads and that communities along several hundred miles of the south coast have no roads, in or out. With Newfoundland entering confederation as late as 1949, it might be said that highway development had some catching up to do. The highway across the island, now known as Highway 1 (the Trans-Canada Highway), was for many years gravel surfaced and paved only in sections. To cross the province was something of an adventure. By the mid-1960's, the paving was completed and work has been directed at improving the remainder of the trunk roads. Most communities are now serviced by paved roads.

The paving of the TCH linked the east and west coasts and has assisted in opening up the central portion of the island. West from Deer Lake, the highway runs through what seems to be deserted country—forests of spruce, occasional bogs, and mountains in the background. Most of the exits turn to the seacoast. Pick an exit, find yourself a tiny community with a name like Sop's Arm or Harry's Harbour, and stop a while.

The twin towns of Windsor and Grand Falls straddle the TCH halfway across the province. Both are paper towns and retail centers for the surrounding area. The Mary March Museum in Grand Falls has displays of logging and natural history of the region. Mary March was the Christian name given to Shanawdithit, a young Beothuk Indian woman captured by John Peyton, Jr., near Grand Falls. Shanawdithit died in 1829 at the age of twenty-two, the last survivor of a tribe that may have numbered more than 50,000.

The town of Botwood at the mouth of the Exploits River might have become a world aviation capital. Prior to World War II, the aviation industry was undecided as to the merits of flying boats versus land-based aircraft. With the outbreak of war, the superiority of the wheeled airplane became evident and Botwood, which had been scheduled to become a major flying boat base, became the victim of technology. The town of Gander, only 91 kms. (57 miles) away and at the time just a small air station, was expanded as the airbase for the trans-Atlantic air ferry service and the first North American landfall when passenger crossings were being made by propeller-driven aircraft. A small museum in the Gander airport portrays the long history of trans-Atlantic aviation in Newfoundland and displays models of many of the early aircraft.

One of the best drives on Newfoundland's east coast is along the Eastport Peninsula. Take Highway 310 at Glovertown, follow the partly graveled road to the community of Salvage, and stop at the tiny local history museum. The museum was created by purchasing a house and all of the furnishings, fixtures and fittings from a retired fisherman and his wife. The couple was given a new completely furnished home nearby. Beaches, a shipyard, and even a community called Happy Adventure are there for the tourist's pleasure.

EXPLORING LABRADOR

Labrador, one of the last North American frontiers, has been called "the land that God gave Cain." Icy and desolate in winter, it has an austere charm in summer. It has few people but is rich in minerals, water, wildlife, and forests. Still relatively unexplored, Labrador is a land of mystery and power. Its land mass constitutes the larger part of the province of Newfoundland.

Goose Bay and the adjacent community of Happy Valley were once bustling and busy. Goose Bay was built as a ferry station for aircraft during World War II. The United States obtained the base under the lend-lease arrangement and the British and Canadian forces also owned portions of the base. Recently, the U.S. has cut back on the use of the base so that the future of the communities is now uncertain. The commercial airport uses part of the base facility and the community is a service center for the various outposts up and down the Labrador coast. "Goose" is also the jumping off point for anglers and hunters taking bush planes into private lakes and rivers. Visitors can reach Goose Bay only by plane or by CN Marine coastal boat.

Wabush and Labrador City are twin mining towns on the Labrador–Québec border which produce about 50% of Canada's iron ore. They are pleasant company towns with relatively few facilities for tourists except the Smokey Mountain Ski Club which attracts the hardier cross-country skiers. The area boasts one of the world's best cross-country ski ranges, at which international competitions are held occasionally.

Labrador's main appeal for tourists is fishing and a limited amount of hunting. Salmon, Arctic char, trout, and northern pike are fished. See *Practical Information* section on "Fishing" and other related sections at end of this chapter for further details.

PRACTICAL INFORMATION FOR
NEWFOUNDLAND AND LABRADOR

HOW TO GET THERE. By air: *Eastern Provincial Airways* operates scheduled jet services to a number of Newfoundland centers including St. John's, Gander, Corner Brook, Goose Bay, Churchill Falls, and Wabush, from Toronto, Montréal and other eastern Canadian points. *Air Canada* operates scheduled jet flights from Toronto, Montréal and eastern Canadian points to St. John's and Stephenville. *Quebecair* operates scheduled jet flights from Montréal to Wabush.

By car: With the exception of some 50 miles of highway from Blanc Sablon to Red Bay and local roads in Goose Bay and Wabush/Labrador City, Labrador has no roads. The island of Newfoundland has about 9,654 km. (6,000 miles) of highway, including the 906-km. (565-mile) Trans-Canada Hwy. from Port-aux-Basques to St. John's. Most main roads, including the Trans-Canada, are paved; however, the secondary highways are usually gravel surfaced.

From North Sydney, Nova Scotia, to Port-aux-Basques, Newfoundland, there is a daily year-round car/ferry service (with up to five crossings per day in summer). A crossing takes about six hours. During the summer season, it is best to travel early in the day and early in the week. Cabins, restaurants, bars, cinema and a tourist bureau are available during the summer. Reservations are required on all crossings and must be picked up at the ferry terminal 1½ hours before sailing.

CN Marine also operates a summer service from North Sydney, Nova Scotia, to Argentia, Newfoundland—an 18-hour mini-cruise for visitors with some room for cars. The service runs from mid-June to mid-September, three days per week. Cabins, a restaurant and bar, cinema, and tourist bureau are available. Reservations are required and must be picked up 1½ hours before sailing at the ferry terminal. For information and reservations, contact CN Marine, Reservations Bureau, P.O. Box 250, North Sydney, Nova Scotia B2A 3M3.

By train: Train service to Newfoundland is operated by *Via Rail* through the ferry crossings from North Sydney, Nova Scotia, to Port-aux-Basques, Newfoundland. Connections may be made to Via Rail by *Amtrak* from New York. Since Newfoundland had operated under the British rail system, all trains in the province ran on narrow-gauge tracks. The alternative to replacement of all track and antiquated rolling stock was to discontinue passenger service by rail during the 1960's and institute an efficient service by motor coaches (known in Newfoundland as "road cruisers"). Road cruisers reach most major communities in Newfoundland adjacent to the Trans-Canada Hwy.

CN Marine provides a toll-free telephone service from eastern Canada and the northeast U.S. From the latter (except Maine) call 1–800–341–7981; from Maine, 800–432–7344. From Nova Scotia, P.E.I. and New Brunswick call 1–800–565–9470; from Québec and Ontario, 1–800–565–9411. Via Rail offices in eastern Canada also have information. Or see your travel agent.

By bus: Most major bus lines throughout North America connect with *Acadian Lines* in Nova Scotia to take visitors to the ferry in North Sydney, Nova Scotia. For information, see your local bus line agent or your travel agent.

ACCOMMODATIONS. Visitors to Newfoundland will find traditional, comfortable accommodation throughout the province. In the larger centers, the motels may appear more modern, but they cannot exceed the hospitality of the smaller properties. Most lodgings are small and have a dining room and/or bar as part of the business. Some of the older properties may not have private bathrooms in all units; you must specify if you wish a private bath. Usually, the owners live on the property and welcome guests personally.

Double occupancy rates in Newfoundland are categorized as follows: *Expensive,* $40 or more; *Moderate,* $30–40; *Inexpensive,* under $30.

The 12% provincial sales tax will be applied to all accommodation rates.

Most places accept the following major credit cards: American Express, MasterCard and Visa; others may also be honored. Not all establishments accept credit cards, therefore we suggest you call for information.

BURGEO. *Moderate–Expensive:* **Sou'Wester Inn.** Accommodations by the sea. Lots of atmosphere. Adequate dining room. Phone 886–3309.

CLARENVILLE. *Expensive:* **Holiday Inn.** Typical Holiday Inn. Coffeeshop, dining room, cocktail lounge. Outdoor pool. Phone 466–7911. Major credit cards.

CORNER BROOK. *Expensive.* **Glymill Inn.** Lots of atmosphere; main dining room is baronial. Phone 634–5381. Major credit cards.

Holiday Inn. No surprises. Typical of the chain. Adequate dining room. Phone 634–5381. Major credit cards.

Mamateek Motor Inn. Good accommodations. Restaurant and coffeeshop. Phone 639–8901. Major credit cards.

DEER LAKE. *Expensive:* **Deer Lake Motel.** Basic accommodations. Coffeeshop and licensed dining room. Phone 635–2108. Major credit cards.

DUNVILLE. *Moderate:* **Northeast Arm Motel.** 8 rooms in a quiet setting. Restaurant and dining room. Phone 227–3560. Major credit cards.

EASTPORT. *Moderate:* **Eastport Motel.** Motel units and housekeeping cabins. Beach, restaurant and cocktail lounge. Saturday-night dancing. Phone 667–2458.

White Sails Inn and Cabins. Housekeeping units. Beach, playground. Open May 24 to October 15. Phone 677–3400.

FORTUNE. *Moderate:* **Sea View Motel.** Basic accommodation with restaurant and cocktail lounge. Phone 832–1411.

GANDER. *Expensive:* **Albatross Motel.** Excellent seafood dining room. Cocktail lounge, beauty salon. Phone 256–3956. Major credit cards.

Holiday Inn. Typical Holiday Inn. Nice, cozy cocktail lounge. Coffeeshop and dining room. Outdoor pool. Phone 256–3981. Major credit cards.

GLOVERTOWN. *Inexpensive:* **Ackerman's Hospitality Home.** Friendly hosts. Phone 533–2811.

GRAND BANK. *Moderate:* **Granny Motor Inn.** 10 rooms, lounge and dining room. Intimate little place. Phone 832–2180. Major credit cards.

GRAND FALLS. *Expensive:* **Mount Peyton Motel.** Good place to stay; dining room is excellent. Cocktail lounge. Children under 12 free, if in room with parents. Open year round. Phone 489–2251, 800–563–4894. Major credit cards.

Moderate: **Highliner Inn.** All housekeeping units; pleasant and comfortable. Cocktail lounge. Phone 489–5639. Major credit cards.

Inexpensive: **Town and Country Inn.** Lounge, functional dining room, Continental breakfast. Phone 489–9602.

HARBOUR GRACE. *Inexpensive–Moderate:* **Pike's Motel & Hotel.** 14 motel and 7 hotel rooms; adequate restaurant, separate dining room plus cocktail lounge. Phone 596–5072.

HAWKE'S BAY. *Moderate–Expensive:* **Maynard's.** Motel and housekeeping units. Specify if you wish motel unit with private bath. Dining room and cocktail lounge. Phone 248–3131. Major credit cards.

LEWISPORTE. *Moderate–Expensive:* **Brittany Inn.** Hospitable staff; good service. Dining room and cocktail lounge. Phone 535–2533. Major credit cards.

PLACENTIA. *Inexpensive–Moderate:* **Harold Hotel.** Basic accommodations in older hotel. Specify if you wish room with private bath. Restaurant and cocktail lounge. Phone 227–2107. Major credit cards.

PORT-AUX-BASQUES. *Expensive:* **Hotel Port-aux-Basques.** Basic accommodations in old-style ferry landing hotel. Major credit cards. Phone 695–2171.

PORT UNION. *Moderate:* **Seaport Inn.** Hotel and motel. Good food in dining room; licensed. Phone 469–2257.

ST. ANTHONY. *Expensive:* **Vinland Motel.** Basic motel accommodations. Dining room, coffeeshop and cocktail lounge. Phone 454–8843. Major credit cards.

Moderate: **St. Anthony Motel.** Basic motel accommodations. Dining room and cocktail lounge. Phone 454–3200. Major credit cards.

STEPHENVILLE. *Expensive:* **Island Inn.** 75 West St. Comfortable; breakfast only. Phone 643–5616. Major credit cards.

TRAYTOWN. *Inexpensive:* **Ledrew's Housekeeping Cabins.** Lovely spot, especially for families. Phone 533–2553.

Traytown Tourist Cabins. All housekeeping cabins. Clean and comfortable. Grassy fields for children; boats available. Open May to mid-October. Phone 533–2246.

TRINITY. *Inexpensive:* **Trinity Cabins.** All housekeeping cabins. $2 for each child under 12. Groceries, gift shop, beverage room, swimming pool. Drive-in and travel-trailer park. Open May to September 30. Phone 464–3657.

WOODY POINT. *Moderate:* **Stornoway Lodge.** Small clean motel with dining room and tea room. Phone 453–2282.

 HOW TO GET AROUND. By car: With the exception of a few miles of highway from Blanc Sablon to Red Bay and local roads in Goose Bay and Wabush/Labrador City, the Labrador area of Newfoundland has no roads suitable for normal vehicles. The island has about 9,654 km. (6,000 miles) of highway, including the 906-km. (565-mile). Trans-Canada Hwy. (signposted throughout Newfoundland as "TCH") from Port-aux-Basques to St. John's.

Secondary roads are generally paved; some gravel-surfaced roads remain, but they are usually in good condition in summer.

By train: Since Newfoundland operated under the British rail system, the trains in the province ran on narrow-gauge track. Passenger service by rail was discontinued during the 1960's and a bus service is operated by *Terra Transport.* Known as "roadcruisers," the buses reach most major communities in New-foundland adjacent to the Trans-Canada Hwy. For information, contact *Via Rail* (see information for trains in "How to Get There" section), call Terra Transport (737–5916) in St. John's or a travel agent.

By air: *Eastern Provincial Airways* operates jet passenger flights connecting St. John's, Gander, Corner Brook (via Deer Lake and Stephenville airports), Goose Bay, Churchill Falls, and Wabush/Labrador City. Charters: *Labrador Airways,* Box 12385, Station A, St John's, A1B 48B. Phone 753–9370. *Gander Aviation,* Box 250, Gander. Phone 256–3421. *Newfoundland and Labrador Air Transport,* Box 3, Corner Brook. Phone 686–2521. *Gracefield Aviation,* Box 55, Stephenville. Phone 643–2014.

By boat: One of the most interesting ways to see Newfoundland and Labra-dor is by one of the *CN Marine* coastal boats. The south coast service has sailings from Argentia to Port-aux-Basques, calling in at a number of tiny ports along the way. Many of these ports are not connected to the highway system and the boat brings in the mail, freight and passengers. Operates year-round.

The North Coast and Labrador CN boats service many tiny isolated com-munities on the Labrador coast from St. John's and Lewisport as starting points. Sailings from spring thaw (mid-May to mid-June) until mid-November.

A round trip on one of the Labrador boats can take up to a week, covering some 1,600 nautical miles and calling at up to 40 communities.

The coastal steamer service operated by CN Marine provides passenger and freight connections to the many settlements in Newfoundland and Labrador not reached by road or railway. Trips on these boats offer extremely interesting vacation travel, passing through numerous picturesque coastal villages. Reser-vations on this service can only be made from within the Province of Newfound-land by contacting CN Marine Reservations Bureau, P.O. Box 520, Port-aux-Basques, Newfoundland AOM 1C0. Phone 1–800–563–7381.

TOURIST INFORMATION. Travel information on Newfoundland may be obtained from Department of Development and Tourism, P.O. Box 2016, St. John's, Newfoundland A1C 5R8. For information while in St. John's, call 576–2830.

Tourist Information Chalets are conveniently located along the Trans-Cana-da Hwy. (Hwy. 1). They are: Port-aux-Basques, 695–2262; Corner Brook, 639–9792; Deer Lake, 639–2202; Springdale, 673–3110; Grand Falls, 489–6332; Clarenville, 466–3100; Marystown, 279–3830; Dunville, 227–5602; Notre Dame Junction, 535–8547; Twillingate, 629–7207; Whitbourne Junction, 759–2170; Stephenville, 647–9208.

Tourist desks are also located on the ferries sailing from North Sydney, Nova Scotia, to Port-aux-Basques and Argentia and at the ferry terminal at North Sydney.

TELEPHONE. The telephone area code for all Newfoundland is 709.

TIME ZONE. Newfoundland has its own unique time zone—Newfoundland Time. It's ½ hour in advance of Atlantic Time and 1½ hours ahead of Eastern Time. Some parts of Labrador, however, are on Atlantic Time and some are on Eastern.

SEASONAL EVENTS. January to March, is winter carnival time in many Newfoundland towns and vil-lages. The biggest carnivals are held in Corner Brook and Labrador City. Parades, snow sculpture, skiing, and other outdoor events and lots of parties are featured. **Mid-April,** Newfoundland and Labrador Drama Festival.

From spring to fall there are weekly harness horse racing cards at Goulds near St. John's. Also at Meadows Raceway near Corner Brook.

In the 1920's the late Johnny Burke wrote a song about the Kelligrews Soiree, a party to end all parties. In **July,** the village of Kelligrews on Conception Bay relives the soiree and the town of Placentia holds an annual regatta for the surrounding area.

On **July** 1 there are Canada Day celebrations in Corner Brook, Grand Falls, Paquet, and other communities. In mid-**July** Stephenville holds the Stephenville Theatre Festival.

August features a number of civic festival days in various Newfoundland towns including a festival of traditional French culture, music and dance at Cape St. George.

During **September** and **October,** regional agricultural exhibitions and fairs are held throughout Newfoundland.

All-Breed Dog Championship Shows are held at St. John's in **May,** at Corner Brook in **July,** and in Harbour Grace on the Labor Day weekend.

TOURS. Newfoundland's tourist industry is greatly geared to the traveler—especially the adventurous one —who wishes to fly in and experience the coast or the interior. There are boat tours and charters available in a half dozen places; there are organized canoe tours and "safaris" to the province's gripping interior; there's a "Trap Line Tour" by dogsled in Labrador; and there's wilderness sightseeing by air available. There's also whale-watching and bird-watching tours. And, of course, there are a half dozen companies offering bus tours to various parts of the province.

The Department of Development and Tourism, will supply brochures on request, or you may pick them up at tourist bureaus. The major agency handling tours of various kinds is *Newfoundland Nature Tours,* Box 1734, St. John's, Newfoundland A1C 5PS. Phone 754–2052.

NATIONAL PARKS. Newfoundland is a wild, rugged, and beautiful land of mountains, lakes, forests, and wild-life—a description that is also appropriate for the province's two provincial parks.

Gros Morne National Park covers 1942 sq. kms. (750 sq. miles) of seacoast and mountain about 120 kms. (75 miles) north of Corner Brook. The mountains of the area drop sharply into the sea; the escarpment is sometimes 610 meters (2,000 feet) high. A tiny ferry carries cars across Bonne Bay from Woody Point to Norris Point at the foot of flat, gray, bald Gros Morne which rises 806 meters (2,644 feet) above the village.

Gros Morne National Park was the home region for a number of peoples including Archaic Indians (4,500 years ago), Eskimos about 1,000 years ago and, more recently, the Beothuk Indians until the time of their extinction in 1829.

The park will be in process of development until some time in the 1980's with some upgrading of facilities each year. Now the park has 159 unserviced camping sites, heated washrooms and showers, kitchen facilities, picnic areas, swimming, hiking, boat facilities, fishing and wilderness backpacking as well as a sewage disposal station. The maximum stay permitted in a campground is two weeks.

The Park Information Centre near Rocky Harbour has a large facilities and activities map for easy reference, with staff to answer questions. During the summer, a free interpretive program is offered by the park naturalist staff which includes conducted hikes and illustrated talks.

Activities in the park include hiking in the summer and snow shoeing and cross-country skiing in the winter. The well-marked hiking trail to the top of Gros Morne offers a commanding view of Bonne Bay and the Long Range Mountains. Fishing for salmon and brook trout are popular in the lakes and streams while mackerel and cod may be taken in the salt water. Fishing regulations are available from park officials and local merchants in the villages.

For swimmers, a large sandy beach at Shallow Bay offers saltwater bathing in water which can reach 21°C (70°F) during July and August. The mouth of Western Brook is also suitable for swimming and has a small sand beach.

Camping fees are $8 for semi-serviced sites and $5 for unserviced sites. For additional information, write The Superintendent, Gros Morne National Park, Rocky Harbour, Newfoundland.

Terra Nova National Park is Canada's most easterly national park, covering 396 sq. kms. (153 square miles) of forested hills and lakes on Bonavista Bay. The park is about 232 kms. (145 miles) northwest of St. John's and 79 kms. (48 miles) southwest of Gander, on the Trans-Canada Hwy.

The surface of Terra Nova Park was scoured and gouged by the glaciers of the Ice Age; from convenient lookouts visitors can see six or more lakes; all at different altitudes, on the sides of the surrounding hills. In the park's bogs are a variety of wild flowers including the province's official flower, the pitcher plant. This unique plant is a carnivore that traps, drowns, and digests insects. Arctic char can be caught by patient anglers and brook trout are common in the streams. Whales and seals frequent the ocean shore. The park is home to numerous sea and land birds as well as animals of all sizes from moose to mink.

Park naturalists have developed an extensive interpretive program which includes guided hikes, boat tours and illustrated talks. During the summer, swimming, canoeing, boating, hiking, and fishing are popular. Winter activities include cross-country skiing, winter camping, and snowshoeing.

Serviced campsites are available at Newman Sound and Malady Head on a "first come" basis. Open year-round. Motel and restaurant facilities are available at Charlottetown and Newman Sound, at villages within the Park, or at various villages just outside the Park boundaries during the summer months.

Except for through highway traffic, an entrance fee to Terra Nova Park will be charged. Daily entry fee is $3. Newman Sound fee is $8 per night. Malady Head is $7.50 per night. The overnight boat docking fee is from $3 to $9 depending on the length of boat.

Staff at the Park Information Centre, located at the headquarters area just off the Trans-Canada Hwy., can direct visitors to facilities and special events. For additional information, write The Superintendent, Terra Nova National Park, Glovertown, Newfoundland A0G 2L0.

 PROVINCIAL PARKS. One good way to enjoy the great outdoors in Newfoundland is to use the network of provincial parks—43 camping parks, 15 day-use parks and 19 "Natural Scenic Attractions" parks. All 77 parks have picnic areas; most have swimming facilities and well marked trails for hiking or strolling.

From mid-July to mid-August, the fresh water lakes and salt water ponds on the shore are at their best for swimming, usually between 16–20°C (60–70°F). Open salt water can be uncomfortably cold.

Three types of parks have been designated in Newfoundland: (1) Camping parks, which have both camping and day use facilities. The maximum stay is 24 consecutive days and requires a camping permit costing $5 per day; plus you will have to buy a $10 vehicle-entry permit, which is valid for all provincial parks throughout the season. The vehicle permit fee for one day is $2. No reservations for camping are accepted. (2) Day-use parks have no camping facilities. (3) Natural Scenic Attractions are parks with special scenic qualities or natural significance. They have ample parking and walking trails, and some have interpretation centers. Anyone 65 years or over is admitted free to all provincial parks upon proof of age. Angling is permitted in all parks and is subject to the provincial regulations. For licensing information, see park staff. No hunting is allowed in the parks.

Although the parks offer outdoor living at its best, there are some drawbacks such as black flies, mosquitos, and various other pests. The underbrush has been cleared as much as possible, however, to allow freer circulation of air. When picking a picnic site, try for one with a good breeze. A commercial insect repellent is often helpful.

The following provincial parks offer a good sample of Newfoundland outdoors:

Aspen Brook. Day-use only with small pool for swimming. Highway 1 at Aspen Brook, 11 kms. (7 miles) west of Windsor.

Backside Pond. Near Whiteway on Hwy. 80; 51 campsites, picnic area, swimming, hiking trail, trout and saltwater fishing. The Atlantic Cable Museum at nearby Heart's Content tells the story of trans-Atlantic communication.

Barachois Pond. On Hwy. 1 about 64 kms. (40 miles) south of Corner Brook, there is one of the largest parks in the system. Swimming, boating, angling for salmon and trout, and water skiing on lake. Guided walks and evening programs by park naturalist; 158 campsites with dumping station. Hiking on Erin Mountain Hiking Trail for spectacular views.

Bellevue Beach. Hwy. 201 at Bellevue on Isthmus of Avalon. Picnic area, swimming, and boating in a protected barachois pond. Angling for trout and saltwater fish; 77 campsites.

Beothuk. Rte. 1 at Rushy Pond, just west of Windsor; 64 campsites, picnic and swimming, boating and trout fishing on Rushy Pond. Reconstructed logging camp open June 1 to September 6, 10 A.M. to 8 P.M. Admission included in permit fee.

Blow Me Down. At Lark Harbour on Hwy. 450, about 48 kms. (30 miles) west of Corner Brook; 27 campsites, picnic areas. Hiking trail to lookout over Bay of Islands. Saltwater angling.

Blue Ponds. Hwy. 1 about 32 kms. (19 miles) west of Corner Brook. Twin limestone lakes for swimming, hiking, picnic area; 37 campsites and trout streams.

Butter Pot. Probably Newfoundland's most popular park, on Hwy 1, about 32 kms. (20 miles) from St. John's. Freshwater beach, hiking trails to two spectacular lookouts, guided nature walks, interpretive center, picnic areas, 122 campsites, dumping station, and trout fishing.

Catamaran. Hwy. 1, about 48 kms. (30 miles) west of Windsor, on Joe's Lake; 55 campsites, picnic area, swimming, and boat launch. Trout fishing.

Chance Cove. On Hwy. 10 near Cape Race. Camping park with picnic area, 25 campsites, swimming, trout and saltwater fishing. Bay seals live along the shallows during certain seasons.

Cheeseman. Hwy. 1 just north of Port-aux-Basques and the CN ferry to Nova Scotia; 103 campsites, picnic area, swimming, trout and saltwater angling. Try beachcombing on the Cape Ray Sands.

Cochrane Pond. Hwy. 1 about 16 kms. (10 miles) south of St. John's. Day-use park with picnic areas, swimming, and trout angling in pond.

Crabbes River. Hwy. 1 near intersection of Hwy. 405; 32 campsites, picnic area. Good salmon and trout fishing.

Dildo Run. Highway 340 on New World Island. Take highway from Trans-Canada toward Lewisporte and continue toward Twillingate; 31 campsites, picnic sites, swimming, and saltwater fishing.

Duley Lake. Labrador City, Labrador; 100 campsites, sandy beach on lake with swimming, boating, and trout fishing.

Father Duffy's Well. Hwy. 90 about 24 kms. (15 miles) south of Holyrood. Day use only. Shrine dedicated to 19th century Irish priest.

Fitzgerald's Pond. Hwy. 100, about 32 kms. (20 miles) east of Argentia. Near CN ferry to Nova Scotia and Castle Hill National Historic Park; 24 campsites, picnic, swimming, and hiking. Angling for salmon and trout.

Flatwater Pond. Hwy. 410 to Baie Verte, about 40 kms. (25 miles) north from the Trans-Canada Hwy.; 25 campsites, picnic area, freshwater swimming, boat launching, trout angling.

Frenchman's Cove. Near Garnish on Hwy. 213. Burin Peninsula. Salt- and freshwater swimming, picnic sites, 81 campsites, trout and saltwater fishing, bird-watching.

Freshwater Pond. Hwy. 220 near Burin. Sandy beaches and freshwater swimming, 30 campsites, picnic areas, boat launch, salmon and trout fishing.

Glenwood. A day-use park on Hwy. 1, just west of Gander. Picnics, trout fishing, and fresh water swimming.

Grand Codroy. Hwy. 406, off Hwy. 1, about 40 kms. (25 miles) north of Port-aux-Basques; 25 campsites, picnic area, and freshwater swimming. Canoeing, salmon and trout angling.

Gushues Pond. Hwy. 1 about 48 kms. (30 miles) from St. John's. Two ponds for swimming; trout fishing and boating; 117 campsites.

Holyrood Pond. Hwy. 90 on St. Mary's Bay, more than 96 kms. (60 miles) south of the village of Holyrood. Long, narrow saltwater pond for warm salt water bathing, boating, trout and saltwater fishing; 15 campsites and picnic area.

Indian River. Hwy. 1 near Springdale. Canoeing on river, swimming, hiking, salmon and trout fishing, picnic area; 49 campsites.

Jack's Pond. Hwy. 1 near Arnold's Cove on Avalon Isthmus. Freshwater boating, swimming, trout fishing, picnic area; 74 campsites.

Jonathan's Pond. Hwy. 330 about 16 kms. (10 miles) north of Gander. Birch forest, boating, swimming, 96 campsites and picnic area.

LaManche Valley. Hwy. 10, about 48 kms. (30 miles) south of St. John's; 51 campsites, picnic area, hiking, swimming, trout and saltwater fishing. Waterfall and bird-watching.

Lockston Path. Hwy. 236 on the Bonavista Peninsula; 20 sheltered campsites, fresh water beach, picnic area, swimming, boat launch.

Mary March. On Hwy. 370 to Buchans. Named after Mary March, the last known Beothuk Indian, who was captured nearby. Red Indian Lake provides good swimming, trout fishing and swimming. Picnic sites and boating; 26 campsites.

Mummichog. Hwy. 1, about 24 kms. (15 miles) north of Port-aux-Basques. Named after a small fish found in the brackish waters of the lagoon; 38 campsites, picnic area, swimming, boat launch, and hiking trails. Salmon and trout fishing in stream.

Northern Bay Sands. Hwy. 70, about 24 kms. (15 miles) north of Carbonear. Fresh and saltwater swimming; 42 campsites, picnic area, and saltwater fishing.

Notre Dame. Hwy. 1, about 32 kms. (20 miles) east of Bishops Falls. Swimming, picnic area, and 100 campsites with dumping station.

Otter Bay. Hwy. 1, about 24 kms. (15 miles) east of Port-aux-Basques; 5 campsites, picnic area, swimming, trout and saltwater fishing.

Piccadilly Head. Hwy. 463 on the Port au Port Peninsula; 50 campsites, picnic area, hiking, swimming on a long sandy beach, and saltwater fishing.

Pinware River. Take the ferry from Flowers Cove on Hwy. 430 to the Labrador coast and follow Hwy. 510 toward Red Bay for about 48 kms. (30 miles). Camping park at the mouth of a good salmon river. 15 campsites. Trout and saltwater fishing, too.

Pipers Hole River. Camping park on Hwy. 210 near Swift Current. 30 campsites. Picnic area, scheduled salmon river, hiking trail. No swimming.

Pistolet Bay. Hwy. 437 near St. Anthony. Canoeing country with 27 campsites, picnic area, swimming, salmon and trout fishing; near L'Anse au Meadows Viking settlement and historic park.

River of Ponds. Hwy. 430 near the village River of Ponds; 40 campsites, picnic area, swimming, boat launch, salmon and trout angling; exhibit of whale bones.

Sandbanks. At the community of Burgeo. Accessible by boat or by hiking a half mile. 8 campsites, picnic area, and swimming at sandy beaches; trout and saltwater fishing.

Smallwood. Hwy. 320 north of Gambo; 27 campsites, picnic area, fine salmon angling; working model of a watermill.

Squires Memorial. Hwy. 422 near Deer Lake. One of the larger provincial parks; 159 campsites, picnic area, good salmon fishing, boat rental facility. Reserve the night before. Cost about $6 per day.

Square Pond. Hwy. 1 near Gambo; 93 campsites, picnic area, swimming, boat launch, hiking, salmon, trout and Arctic char angling.

Sop's Arm. Hwy. 420 near the village of Sop's Arm on White Bay; 25 campsites, picnic area, salmon, trout and saltwater fishing.

Windmill Bight. Hwy. 330 near Cape Freels on Bonavista Bay; 29 campsites, picnic area, fresh- and saltwater swimming, salmon, trout and saltwater fishing. Good place to watch for icebergs.

Natural Scenic Attraction parks, a Newfoundland specialty, are especially worthwhile. There are 19. Here are a few:

The Arches. North of Gros Morne National Park on Rte. 430. Natural rock archway created by tidal action.

Cataracts. Hwy. 91, 100 kms. (60 mi.) southwest of St. John's. A deep river gorge with two waterfalls. Stairs and walkways.

Deadman's Bay. Hwy. 330. Grand coastline; spot to watch for in early summer.

Dungeon. Rte. 238 near Bonavista. Features a sea cave with a natural archway carved by tidal action. A restored 19th-century lighthouse nearby.

Eastport North Beach. Hwy. 310. Excellent beach and scenery on Eastport Bay. Terra Nova National Park and craft shops nearby.

French Islands. Hwy. 220 south from Grand Bank. Excellent view of St. Pierre and Miquelon islands, owned by France.

Maberly. Rte. 238 near Bonavista. A sea bird colony nesting on an off-shore island is visible from the jagged shore.

Northeast Arm. Hwy. 310 off Glovertown. Spectacular ocean view overlooking Terra Nova National Park from across the water.

Point La Haye. Hwy. 90 about 150 kms. (90 mi.) southwest of St. John's. Historic beach utilized by Basque fishermen in centuries past for drying their catch.

CHILDREN'S ACTIVITIES. Keeping children occupied in Newfoundland should present little problem, but do not look for amusement parks or fully equipped playgrounds except in the larger centers. Concentrate on the network of provincial and national parks.

Obtain a fishing license for the family and pack a couple of rods and reels for hours of entertainment. Sturdy footwear and clothing make hiking and walking easier in the parks.

A trip to a fishing village in mid- to late afternoon should put visitors at the wharf in time to see local fishermen cleaning their catch and carting away the fish. Nature walks and lectures at the parks will hold the attention of older children and a camera may keep a child involved for the entire trip.

SUMMER SPORTS. Sports in Newfoundland tend to be the outdoors variety. **Water sports** such as water skiing, canoeing, power boating, and sailing are popular activities. There are **harness horse racing** cards at the Avalon Raceway in Goulds, near St. John's, from spring to fall every Sunday and Wednesday evening and at other unscheduled times. There is also great interest in **golf, tennis, bowling, roller skating,** and **rowing** in centers where facilities are available.

Golf courses include the Grand Falls Golf and Country Club and the Blomidon Golf and Country Club in Corner Brook. Nine hole courses are located at Stephenville and Labrador City. Check with local tourist information centers for rules on visitors at each course.

Newfoundland is a **canoeists'** paradise. The tourism department offers a list of about twenty routes, ranging in length from 12 to 336 kms., and they should be consulted about current restrictions on forest travel in the fire season. Canoe tours to the deep interior are arranged by some outfitters. Canoes can be rented at numerous places. Check with the tourist bureaus.

See sections on "Fishing" and "Hunting" for information on these sports.

FISHING. Newfoundland is one of the best fishing areas in North America. Brook trout can be found in most streams and salmon populate many of the larger rivers.

In saltwater, codfish can be jigged and sea trout, flounder, tuna, mackerel and caplin can be caught. Deep-sea tuna fishing is also available.

Nonresidents must have a valid fishing license. For salmon fishing they must be accompanied by a licensed guide. Inland fishing licenses are available from most service stations, sporting goods stores, hardware stores, and department stores. Nonresident salmon fishng licenses cost about $40 for the season. Family salmon licenses are about $60 for the season. Salmon may be taken by artificial fly only during the season from June 20 to August 31 on the Island of Newfoundland and from June 20 to Sept. 15 in Labrador.

Nonresident trout licenses cost $10 for individuals for the season and $15 for a family. The license covers all rivers except those indicated as scheduled rivers. These are usually well marked. Salmon licenses are required for these waters. Special licenses from park officials are required for fishing in Terra Nova National Park. The open season for rainbow trout is June 1 to September 15. The season for all other trout is January 15 to September 15.

Licensed guides are required for all fishing in Labrador where the fishing waters are usually located far from habitation and are reached by bush plane. The season for Arctic char, northern pike, and trout other than rainbow trout is January 15 to September 15 in unscheduled rivers in Labrador.

The bag limit for trout in Newfoundland and Labrador is 24 per day per license, or the number of trout totaling 10 pounds in weight plus one trout, whichever is the lesser. The limit for lake trout is four per day; northern pike, 24 per day; Arctic char, 4 per day.

Several dozen outfitters in both Newfoundland and Labrador operate special fishing cabins for the more serious sportsmen. They are listed in the *Hunting and Fishing Guide,* obtainable from any tourist bureau or by writing Department of Development and Tourism, Province of Newfoundland, P.O. Box 2016, St. John's, Newfoundland. This kind of fishing is expensive; expect to pay $1,000 a week or more.

HUNTING. The *Hunting and Fishing Guide* describes hunting opportunities (see "Fishing" section). Basically, Newfoundland is famous for its moose hunting. This, however, is for the serious hunter. You will need a licensed guide who also functions as an outfitter.

CAMPING OUT. Complete information on camping in Newfoundland Provincial Parks may be found in the "Provincial Parks" section.

Sixteen private campgrounds-trailer parks are in operation in Newfoundland.

Complete information on camping in Newfoundland's two national parks is in the *National Parks* section.

WINTER SPORTS. The west coast of Newfoundland averages 152 inches of snow per year with average temperatures in the −12 to −4°C. range (10 to 25°F). **Ski** runs over a mile long with drops of at least 213 meters (700 feet) make Marble Mountain Ski Resort one of the best ski areas in eastern Canada. The resort is about 24 kms. (15 miles) from Corner Brook on Hwy. 1.

The Smokey Mountain Ski Club in Labrador City can be reached only by air to Wabush/Labrador City. The hill has 5 trails and one open slope. The longest run is 299 meters (4,500 ft.) with a 1,372-meter (980 foot) vertical drop. Three of the trails are lit for night skiing.

Although many Newfoundland communities have indoor arenas or outdoor rinks for **ice skating,** ponds and lakes are excellent for outdoor skating in most areas.

Curling is a growing sport in Newfoundland and local and regional bonspiels are held throughout the winter months. Major curling clubs are located in St. John's, Gander, Grand Falls, Corner Brook, Labrador City and Stephenville. Snowmobiling is also a popular sport in winter. In Labrador, snowmobiles have been used as a prime source of winter transportation for some years now, replacing the traditional dog teams in the remote sections of the province.

HISTORIC SITES. *Cape Spear* is the closest North American point to Europe and the site of one of Canada's oldest surviving lighthouses, built in 1836. During World War II, a coastal battery was constructed here. Crashing waves and the sight of so much open sea make this 16-km. (10-mile) drive south from St. John's worthwhile. Open year round, with a guide service from June to Sept.

The remains of both French and British fortifications may still be seen at the *Castle Hill National Historic Park* at Placentia. Originally built by the French to protect their colony, the fortifications were taken over by the British in 1713. An interpretive center contains displays and artifacts. Guided tours are available from June to September.

Prior to the 1960's, scholars had long sought tangible evidence of *Viking settlements* in North America. Helge and Anne Stine Ingstad, over a seven-year period, excavated the area near L'Anse aux Meadows on the tip of Newfoundland's Great Northern Peninsula where they thought the Vikings had landed. Their patience was rewarded with positive evidence of Viking settlement at least 1,000 years ago. The dig site can be viewed by visitors. A reception center and museum are at the site.

The *Port au Choix National Historic Park* is located on an important Maritime Archaic Indian (and later Dorset Eskimo) burial ground. The interpretive center portrays the lifestyle of the people who lived here 4,000 years ago. Port au Choix is on Hwy. 430, about 8 kms. (5 miles) north of the community of Port Saunders.

Quidi Vidi Battery just outside St. John's is a small restoration of the original fortification which formed part of the St. John's harbor defenses. Inside the palisade is a small military museum. Open June 1 to mid-September.

MUSEUMS. There are many—for history buffs and fishermen: *Ferryland Museum.* General history museum in one of the oldest settlements in province. Open during summer months in courthouse. *Hibb's Cove Fishermen's Museum.* Fishing artifacts in typical Newfoundland fishing village combined with arts and music center. Open summer months. *Heart's Content.* History of the trans-Atlantic communications cable which first came ashore here. Open summer months. *Trinity Museum and Archives.* Local artifacts and papers. Open summer months. *Bonavista Museum.* Local history. Open summer; winters by appointment. *Salvage Museum.* Local history in fisherman's house. *Greenspond Museum.* Local history displayed in courthouse. Open summer months. *Durrell Museum.* Local history; open summer months. *Twillingate Museum.* Local history in old Anglican Rectory. Open summer months. *Cow Head Museum.* Local history; open year round. *Grand Falls, Mary March Regional Museum.* Local history of the logging industry and natural history. Named after Shadawdithit (named Mary March by her captors), the last known Beothuk Indian who was captured in the region. Open year-round. *Grand Bank. Southern Newfoundland Seamen's Museum.* Displays relating to the fishery on the south coast. Open year-round. *Gander Airport Aviation Exhibit.* Displays and history of pioneer aviation, trans-Atlantic and domestic, located in airport terminal building. Open year-round. The *Conception Bay Museum National Exhibition Centre* at Harbour Grace which is located in the old Court House displays traveling exhibits along with its own permanent collection, and it is open year-round. In Wesleyville, you can explore local history in the *Wesleyville Museum,* and the *Durrell Museum* in Durrel has local history and also artifacts from World War I. The *Fishermen's Museum* in Musgrave Harbour is also a local history museum, as is the *Placentia Area Museum* in Placentia.

MUSIC. Newfoundland has its own indigenous rhythms, mostly of Scottish and Irish derivation, and you'll find them everywhere—in local festivals, in night-clubs, bars and taverns, and at local concerts.

SHOPPING. For the most part, goods and services tend to be slightly more expensive in Newfoundland than elsewhere in Canada. The same general range of merchandise is available as on the mainland.

Newfoundland handcrafts, such as knitted goods, woven items, and clothing are usually good purchases because of the quality of the product.

Other unique Newfoundland items include: Labradorite jewelry (Labradorite is a quartz-like rock which takes a high polish), earrings of codfish ear bones (quite attractive), seal skin products, and Eskimo and Indian carvings.

Store hours are roughly the same as for St. John's, except that some stores outside St. John's may be closed on Mondays. Holidays closings are roughly the same, except for local civic holidays. See the "Shopping" section in *Practical Information for St. John's*.

DRINKING LAWS. The legal drinking age is 19.

DINING OUT. In general, the best places to dine in Newfoundland (outside of St. John's) are the hotels and motels which usually combine accommodation, a cock-tail lounge, and dining room or restaurant.

At best, dining out in Newfoundland is something of an adventure. Visitors should sample home-cooked food and specialties of the area and the season. Fish and salt meat dishes are the best bets everywhere—expect it to be wholesome and hearty, rather than delicate and gourmet-style. Restaurants are categorized on the basis of full-course dinners, drinks, tips and tax excluded: *Expensive,* over $13; *Moderate,* $8–$13; *Inexpensive,* less than $8.

The 12% provincial sales tax will be added to your bill.

Most places accept the following major credit cards: American Express, MasterCard and Visa; others may also be honored. Not all establishments accept credit cards, therefore we suggest you call for information.

CORNER BROOK. *Expensive:* **The Carriage Room.** In the Glynmill Inn. Newfoundland dishes and all types of fish. Licensed.
The Wine Cellar. On Cobb Lane. Steaks and Italian food. Licensed.

GANDER. *Moderate:* **Albatross Motel.** Seafood platters. Licensed.
Sinbad's. Canadian food. Licensed.

GRAND FALLS. *Expensive:* **Mount Peyton Hotel.** Canadian food. Licensed.

MAP
OF
CANADA

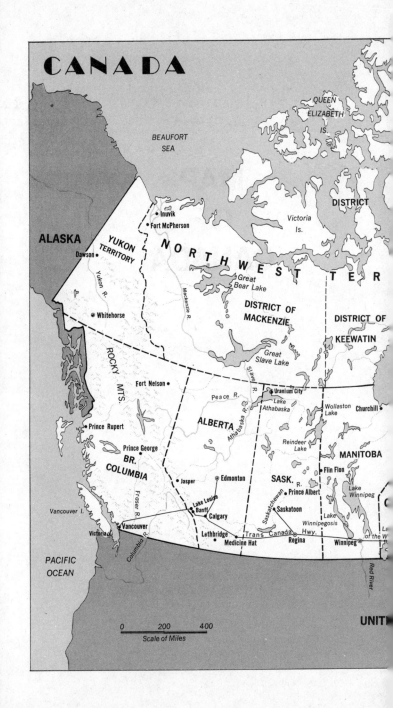

CANADA

QUEEN
ELIZABETH
IS.

BEAUFORT
SEA

DISTRICT

ALASKA

YUKON
TERRITORY

Dawson •

• Inuvik
• Fort McPherson

Victoria
Is.

N O R T H W E S T   T E R

Great
Bear Lake

• Whitehorse

DISTRICT OF
MACKENZIE

DISTRICT OF
KEEWATIN

Mackenzie R.

ROCKY

Great
Slave Lake

Yukon R.

MTS.

Slave R.

• Fort Nelson

Peace R.

• Uranium City

Churchill

Lake
Athabaska

Wollaston
Lake

• Prince Rupert

ALBERTA

Athabaska R.

Reindeer
Lake

MANITOBA

• Prince George

BR.
COLUMBIA

• Flin Flon

• Jasper

Fraser R.

Vancouver I.

Victoria ◉

Lake Louise
Banff

⊙ Edmonton

Calgary

• Lethbridge

SASK.   R.

• Prince Albert

• Saskatoon

Lake
Winnipeg

Saskatchewan R.

Lake
Winnipegosis

Columbia R.

Vancouver

Trans Canada

Medicine Hat

Regina

Hwy.

Lake
of the W

Winnipeg

PACIFIC
OCEAN

Red River

UNIT

0   200   400

Scale of Miles

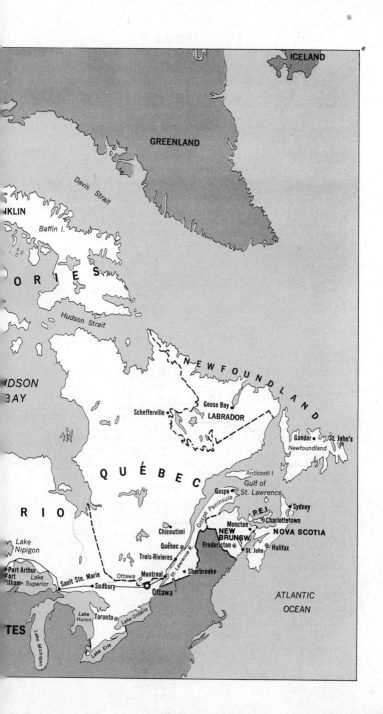

Index